SIR PHILIP SIDNEY AND THE ENGLISH RENAISSANCE

SIR PHILIP SIDNEY
Engraving by I. de Courbes
From J. Baudoin's translation,
L'Arcadie de la Comtesse de Pembrok, 1624

SIR PHILIP SIDNEY
AND THE ENGLISH
RENAISSANCE

BY

JOHN BUXTON

FELLOW OF NEW COLLEGE, OXFORD

LONDON
MACMILLAN & CO LTD
NEW YORK · ST MARTIN'S PRESS
1954

MACMILLAN AND COMPANY LIMITED
London Bombay Calcutta Madras Melbourne

THE MACMILLAN COMPANY OF CANADA LIMITED
Toronto

ST MARTIN'S PRESS INC
New York

PRINTED IN GREAT BRITAIN

PREFACE

In recent years much has been said about patronage of the arts in modern society. Very seldom, and then only for exceptional reasons, has the writing of poetry brought the poet an adequate income; and there is no reason to suppose that it ever will. But this question of cash is the least important part of the problem: poets have contrived to live in spite of the lack of sale for their product, and have written in poverty, ill-health, in prison, or when starving. The true problem of patronage is that of the relation between the poet and his audience, which has been complicated latterly, not so much by penal taxation as by the Romantic theory of poetry as self-expression. The poet has been inclined to say 'Give me my bread and butter and I will reveal my soul' — and has been a little pained at the unenthusiastic response. Patrons have been too ready, none the less, to accept this doctrine, and have either given prizes for work already written, or have made gifts to young writers to enable them to work on their own for a period. Now I certainly do not wish to be thought ungrateful if I criticize a system by which I myself have benefited; but patronage once implied something of much more value. It implied the commissioning of poets to produce works of a particular kind. It implied lively and stimulating criticism of the poet by the patron. Above all, it gave the assurance to the poet that the work he had been asked to write was something the patron wished to have. In other words, patronage meant that the poet was producing something to meet a known taste.

During the war (as everyone knows) many more people read poetry than in the years before or since. Why?

Because the poets, or some of us, were making articulate a shared experience. The Norwegian poet, Arnulf Øverland, in the preface to a collection of poems of his which had been circulated secretly during the occupation, tells how they reached a far wider audience than his earlier poems had ever attained with all the paraphernalia of printing-press, publisher, bookshops, advertisements, and reviews. 'These poems', he says, 'have done their job', for he 'wished to be a servant and an interpreter for those who could not perhaps find words themselves'.

The problem therefore is how to discover a coherent, imaginable audience in this twentieth century. We are merely being evasive if we make an excuse of our 'disintegrated society'. When, except under the pressure of a common danger or a common ambition, has human society been anything else? Such periods are, happily, brief and intermittent.

When I began thinking about this problem, I realized that a study of literary patronage in another age might be relevant. It seemed to me that the Romantic ambition to write for mankind had proved illusory, but that if I considered the Elizabethan poets I could see how they met a challenge not unlike ours; for the Elizabethans were very conscious in the first half of the Queen's reign that the art of poetry was spurned and neglected in England. From a study of literary patronage generally in the time of the Renaissance I soon discovered that I could most usefully treat the subject by concentrating on the patrons to whom the poets and writers of the time acknowledged their principal debt, Philip and Mary Sidney. At the same time I must state my views on the nature of Renaissance poetry, which we, unlike the Romantics, have tended to misunderstand and to neglect. Necessarily I have drawn certain comparisons with the Romantics, not always to their advantage. This is not because I wish to disparage Wordsworth, Coleridge, or Keats, but because I wish to revalue Daniel, Drayton, and Browne as they valued them.

This book is the outcome of studies that have taken me to many libraries in several countries, to whose staffs, and to the many others who have so generously helped me, it is now my pleasant duty to make acknowledgment.

In 1951 the Leverhulme Trustees gave me a grant, and my College gave me leave of absence, so that I could spend several months in Italy where I worked especially in the Venetian Archives, and also in the following libraries : Marciana, Querini-Stampalia, Civico Museo Correr in Venice ; the Library of the University of Padua ; the Ambrosiana in Milan. In 1953 I was able to visit the University Library and the Bibliotheca Thysiana in Leiden. Here in England I have worked in the Bodleian Library, the Library of the British Museum, the University Library at Cambridge, and the Libraries of the Taylor Institution and the Warburg Institute. I have borrowed many books from the London Library. The Henry Huntington Library in California kindly sent me a photostat of their unique copy of Scipio Gentili's *Nereus*. In Venice Dott. Tursi very generously put at my disposal his fine collection of books relating to English visitors to Venice. I am most grateful to Lord De L'Isle and Dudley who not only allowed me to look at books and MSS. of his at Penshurst and in the Public Record Office (where Mr. R. L. Atkinson gave me much help), but also gave me permission to reproduce part of a page from the Davies of Hereford transcript of the Psalms (no. 13).

For the other illustrations I am indebted for photographs and permission to the Trustees of the British Museum (nos. 4, 8, and 14), to Bodley's Librarian (nos. 5 and 11), the Keeper of the Ashmolean Museum (nos. 2, 3, 7, 9, and 15), the Master and Fellows of Pembroke College, Cambridge (no. 6), the

Syndics of the Fitzwilliam Museum (no. 12). The photograph of no. 12 was supplied by the Victoria and Albert Museum, and is Crown copyright.

Many friends have helped me in various ways. Dott. Gaetano Cozzi made my visits to the Venetian Archives far more valuable than they could otherwise have been, and introduced me to other Italian scholars in Padua and Milan. Since then he has, with true Italian courtesy, helped me constantly, by answering my questions, obtaining photographs for me, and sending me information that he came across in his own researches. William Thomas, writing four centuries ago, observed that 'a stranger cannot be better entertained, nor more honourably entreated than amongst the Italians', and I gladly agree. In Holland Prof. Dr. Th. J. G. Locher helped me to see all that I wished to see in the shortest possible time. In Cambridge Mr. A. N. L. Munby has helped me on several occasions. In Oxford Mr. D. M. Sutherland has spared no effort to obtain obscure French and German books for me ; Mr. D. G. Neill, once my pupil but now often my instructor, has for some years sent me a steady stream of references ; Dr. B. E. Juel-Jensen has found or lent me many books. Others, too numerous for me to name, have given me notes of books, have answered my questions, or helped me to find illustrations. In Norway Hr. Finn Seyersted invited me into the seclusion of the mountains where I could write undisturbed and so conclude what at times had seemed an interminable task.

Mr. A. L. Rowse read my typescript with a vigour of attention that was at times unnerving, and for which I am truly grateful. To my wife I owe my gratitude both for her help in typing, indexing, and so forth, and for her gentle tolerance of the claims this book has made upon time and temper.

J. B.

CONTENTS

LIST OF ILLUSTRATIONS

CHAPTER I

The Tradition of Patronage

PATRONAGE of poets, as of other makers of beautiful things, was part of the tradition of the antique world. When therefore in the fifteenth and sixteenth centuries men's minds turned again to seek among the ruins of the past the foundations of a new civilization, the princes and nobles accepted the obligations of patronage, just as the new poets sought to imitate their ancient models. The immense prestige of Virgil and the critical influence of Horace combined to make men recognize in their patron the princely ideal that they should follow, so that no more acceptable compliment could be paid to Lorenzo de' Medici in Florence, to Francis I in France, or to Philip Sidney in England, than to liken each in turn to Maecenas. Famous patrons are rare, not (as is vulgarly supposed) because only a few can afford the luxuries of fine poetry or painting, but because only a few have the wit to demand them. If patronage were merely a matter of signing cheques, patrons would far outnumber artists, whereas artists have always been much commoner than patrons. Philip Sidney, whose lively intelligence and sure taste stimulated and guided the poets of the English Renaissance, was not a wealthy man, and his gifts to the poets were neither frequent nor bountiful. Richard Robinson, whose piety must have commended him (for his poetry could not), records a gift of four angels from Sidney in 1579 for the dedication of a book of prayers translated from Melanchthon and others. This

I

sum seems to have been quite generous. Long afterwards Matthew Prior, complaining of the stinginess of eighteenth-century patrons, compared them with the Elizabethans, to their disadvantage :

> For now no Sidneys will three hundred give,
> That needy *Spenser* and his Fame may live.

Where Prior discovered his information he does not divulge : most probably he invented it, for Spenser was not needy at any time during his acquaintance with Sidney. The poets who acclaimed Sidney, with Spenser chief among them, were not soft-bodied parasites clinging to him for a living : his critical encouragement, his example, his knowledge of the Renaissance in Europe, above all his taste and judgment, were the things that they valued. They enjoyed his hospitality and his sister's at Leicester House, at Penshurst, and at Wilton, where they could write poetry, talk poetry, argue poetry together. So, sixty years after Sidney's death, in the midst of civil war, Richard Crashaw recalled the memory of these times, of

> *Sydnaean* showers
> Of sweet discourse, whose powers
> Can crowne old Winter's head with flowers.

For the patronage of Philip Sidney and of his sister Mary, Countess of Pembroke, remained in men's minds long afterwards, until, at the Romantic Revolution, a new conception of poetry and its purpose dispelled this, and the famous brother and sister were remembered less for what they did than for what they were.

In the early years of the nineteenth century the very meaning of the word patronage began to be debased until, in our own day, a man may call himself a patron of the arts if he buys a picture painted three hundred years ago and presents it to a museum. He may be a man of exquisite discrimination and unparalleled benevolence ; or he may merely be eager to suggest that a rapid acquisition of money has not prevented a similar acquisition of taste. He may possibly be doing something well worth doing, but he is not, except by courtesy of twentieth-century jargon, a patron of anything, or of anyone. The task of a patron is much less expensive, and much more difficult. He is concerned with living, unknown artists. He must have the good taste to demand fine poetry or painting or music — or silver, pottery, furniture — and he must have the perspicacity to discover the artist who can supply him. He must not ask a song-writer to compose an epic, nor request a tragedy of a poet whose view of mankind is frivolous and gay : he must be as ready to suggest a theme for a poem of ten thousand lines, as to commission an epitaph in two. He needs all the insight and flair of a good critic, but, in addition, the faculty for seeing where a young and untried artist may make the most of his gifts : he needs the tolerance and tact to ensure that he will do so. No wonder that great patrons should be so rare, or that poets should have so often recognized the primacy of patronage. Martial gave it as his opinion that if you have your Maecenases you will get your Virgils :

Sint Maecenates, non deerunt, Flacce, Marones.

The Elizabethan poets never doubted that but for Philip and Mary Sidney their work would have been negligible.

If we doubt this we do so because to us the achievement of these poets seems so assured and confident, and because we have forgotten the long and learned discourses that so often preceded the writing of the poetry. Besides, we are beguiled by Wordsworth and his successors into a belief that poetry must be 'the spontaneous overflow of powerful feelings', and we conclude that what was alleged after the

French Revolution was true in the time of the Renaissance.
The Elizabethans were ready enough to quote the old tag
about a poet being born, not made, but they did so with no
blind Romantic approbation. For the men of the Renaissance
inhabited an intelligible world constructed by a rational mind,
a world in which it was therefore possible to know the final
truth about the motions of the stars or the correct method of
writing an epic. The English Renaissance insisted on the
moral nature of man, where the Italian had been more concerned with his intellectual nature, but none the less the
Elizabethans were never tempted to 'deduce moral thunder
from buttercups'. Thus they never praised a poem as sincere,
but on the contrary thought that the epithet 'artificial' might
properly commend what, after all, was made by art. They'
believed that the initial divine gift of poetry was necessary,
but they did not think it sufficient : a poet must study and
think, not merely surrender to sensations, for the evidence of
divine interest in the world lay in its order and measure, in its
essential reasonableness, and in man's liberty of choice.

Mary, they that delight in Poesie it selfe should seeke to knowe
what they doe, and how they doe ; and, especially, looke themselves in an unflattering Glasse of reason, if they bee inclinable unto
it. For Poesie must not be drawne by the eares ; it must bee gently
led, or rather it must lead. . . . A Poet no industrie can make, if
his owne *Genius* bee not carried unto it : and therefore is it an old
Proverbe, *Orator fit, Poeta nascitur.* Yet confesse I alwayes that as
the firtilest ground must bee manured, so must the highest flying
wit have a *Dedalus* to guide him. That *Dedalus*, they say, both in
this and in other, hath three winges to beare it selfe up into the ayre
of due commendation : that is, Arte, Imitation, and Exercise.

So does Sidney sum up the matter, and none of his contemporaries would have disputed with him. Elsewhere in his
Apologie for Poetrie Sidney describes the poet as a combination
of *vates*, divinely inspired seer, and poet, or maker — and he

4

rejoiced (as did others) to find that 'maker' was an exact translation of the Greek word 'poet'. Since divine inspiration was inexplicable, criticism must be concerned with the poet rather than with the seer ; so Sidney, even while he is describing David in his Psalms as the very pattern of a seer, characteristically calls attention to 'his notable Prosopopeias, when he maketh you, as it were, see God comming in his Maiestie'.

Similarly E. K. in his glosses to Spenser's *Shepheardes Calender*, praises this first achievement of the New Poetry in notes such as these :

A patheticall parenthesis, to encrease a carefull Hyperbaton.
A pretty Epanorthosis in these two verses, and withall a Paronomasia or playing with the word.
An Epiphonema.
A figure called Fictio.

These are not the sort of terms that readily spring to mind nowadays when we would express appreciation of poetry, but they are the terms that Elizabethan critics used. Neither is this pedantry : far from it, for the poets deliberately used these rhetorical figures, as they used every metrical and linguistic device that they could learn from their wide reading. They did not seek originality, and they would not have understood the meaning of 'self-expression' — or if they had they would have rejected it as easy, vulgar, and therefore disgusting. A poem was to be discussed objectively as a work of art, as an object made by human skill. 'An elegant Epanorthosis.' 'At this point Hutton produced a flashing off-drive which left extra cover standing' : the critical attitude of the journalist in the Press-Box at Lord's or of an Elizabethan commenting on a poem is much the same, and we should not too easily discover something derogatory in the comparison. We may think the gift that enabled Sidney to win the prize in a tournament before Queen Elizabeth and the Duke of Anjou less desirable than the gift that enabled him to celebrate it the same evening in a sonnet — though it is at least doubtful whether Sidney himself would have thought so — but we must not deny the possibility of applauding both achievements on similar grounds as exhibitions of human skill. 'The verse runs off smoothly and gallantly', says Charles Lamb. 'It might have been tuned to the trumpet; or tempered (as himself expresses it) to "trampling horses' feet".' Certainly; but for an Elizabethan there were other things to be noted about a sonnet: the arrangement of the rhymes, the poise between octave and sestet, the felicitous borrowing from Petrarch — 'that sweet enemy, France' (which Lamb too picked out) — the rhetorical figures. The Elizabethan critics talk about the poetry, not about themselves.

They enjoyed talking about the poetry, at the 'Mermaid', in the Apollo room at the 'Devil and St. Dunstan' tavern, in country inns where Sir Aston Cokayne wrote verses for the innkeepers; but years before that they had talked of poetry in the Universities and the Inns of Court, and in the country houses such as Penshurst and Wilton. And here we may note that peculiarly English preference for country life to town life which contrasts so strongly with the preferences of Latin peoples. In the Mediterranean lands culture and civilization have always been the product of cities, but in England poetry, painting, and music have been cherished and made in the country seats of nobility and gentry. Penshurst Place and Wilton House; the Castles of Kenilworth, Warwick, and Ludlow; Wivenhoe, Althorpe, and Hardwick; Holdenby, Longleat, and Knole, all hospitably welcomed the scholars and artists of these times. Many similar instances will come to the mind of anyone who knows the history of his own county, for even in the smaller houses the tradition has been the same. Michael Drayton was brought up as a page in the cultivated

6

household of Sir Henry Goodere at Polesworth; Sir John Harington built his house at Kelston to the designs of Vignola, and made an elaborate fountain there from a description of Ariosto's; Wilbye wrote his madrigals in the musical household of the Kytsons at Hengrave in Suffolk, where he lived for many years. In Italy we think of Florence and Venice, Naples and Rome, of Mantua, Urbino, Ferrara, and many another city where painters, poets, and musicians flourished. In England we think not of cities but of houses where they worked, and houses, almost always, deep in the country. The contrast is reflected in the work of the poets of the two countries, as if we compare the *Orlando Furioso* with the *Faerie Queene*, *Il Pastor Fido* with *As You Like It*, Petrarch's Sonnets and Sidney's. It would be superficial to conclude that these differences arise from different conditions of patronage; rather both the poetry and the patronage reflect differences (whencesoever derived) between Englishmen and Italians.

Whatever the circumstances in which men preferred to talk and write poetry, they were, in these early years of Queen Elizabeth's reign, ambitious to make English poetry rival the poetry of Italy — even to emulate the poetry of Greece and Rome. They went about the task with the same practical thoroughness that characterized them in all they did, planning, thinking, ordering with the greatest diligence, and leaving as little as possible to chance. We ought not to think of Spenser's poems or Shakespeare's plays as the outpourings of uninhibited genius, nor of Drake's attack on the mule-train as the product of mere gallantry and good luck. Drake's successes were due to long and patient staff-work, the careful and secret setting forth of expeditions, the reconnaissance of safe and defensible harbours, concern for the friendliness of the Cimaroons and for the health of his own men. When all these things had been achieved, and only then, might courage win its reward. The Elizabethans did not believe in improvisation alone either in the field of action or in the writing of poetry, and the qualities of care and patience to which Drake owed his success were never neglected by the poets, least of all by Spenser in preparation for writing the *Faerie Queene*. 'To overgo Ariosto' was not a task to be lightly undertaken, or committed to the uncertain workings of *furor poeticus*. Only the ignoramuses praised Shakespeare because he never blotted a line. 'My answer', Ben Jonson said, 'hath beene, Would he had blotted a thousand. . . . I had not told posterity this, but for their ignorance, who choose that circumstance to commend their friend by, wherein he most faulted.' So much for spontaneity of overflowing. Doubtless Jonson numbered Shakespeare among the best writers, of whom he says, 'They impos'd upon themselves care and industry. They did nothing rashly. They obtain'd first to write well, and then custome made it easie, and a habit.'

We find it difficult, with Romantic conceptions of poetry still dominant, to imagine the problems that faced the Elizabethans nearly four hundred years ago. They had no long and continuing tradition of poetry, no vast body of poems of every kind to assure them that English was one of the outstanding literatures of the world. There had been one great poet, Chaucer, whom they read and admired, but whose vocabulary was obsolete, and whose lines they could not scan. They were conscious, as Lucretius had been, of that *patrii sermonis egestas*, the inadequacy of their current language. And if Chaucer's language had become obsolete in a century and a half, why should not theirs? They looked with envy to the writers of Greece and Rome, as Pope was to do long after them.

The ancients [says Pope] writ in languages that became universal and everlasting, while ours are extremely limited both in extent and

in duration. A mighty foundation for our pride! when the utmost
we can hope, is but to be read in one Island, and to be thrown aside
at the end of one Age.

So pessimistic a view was not often expressed by Elizabethan
writers, but they too recognized the problem, and some
thought that Latin should be the medium for the literature
of Englishmen. 'These modern languages will play the
bank-route with bookes', said Francis Bacon ; and he had
his more serious works translated into Latin. The same
view had been held in Italy, most notably by Petrarch who
valued his Latin epic *Africa* far above the Italian poems to
Laura ; but, while his epic is forgotten, they set a fashion for
all Europe and long ago secured him a place among the most
influential poets of the European tradition. Even Lorenzo
de' Medici found it necessary to justify the use of the vernacular
in his poems. Here in England when in 1635 Sir Francis
Kynaston published his translation of *Troilus and Criseyde*
into Latin, he did so in order to give Chaucer the everlasting
strength of Roman eloquence, and to make him for all time
stable and unshifting. So towards the end of the English
Renaissance the magnificent aberration of Milton's style
was due to his wish to contrive for English the static and
durable perfection of Latin. He believed that after ages
would not willingly let his poetry die, but by his choice
of language he meant to make their task easier. He wrote
poems in Greek, Latin, and Italian not as academic exercises
but because these were the unchallengeable languages of
literature. As Waller wrote about the same time :

> Poets that lasting marble seek,
> Must carve in Latin, or in Greek ;
> We write in sand, our language grows,
> And, like the tide, our work o'erflows.

However surprising these views may be to us, who survey

9

the English Renaissance in the perspective of three centuries, there is no doubt that they were sincerely held. The Elizabethans were less diffident than their successors, not because they were unaware of such views but because, after careful examination, they had rejected them. As Richard Mulcaster put it :

> If this opinion had bene all waie maintained, we had allwaie worn Adam's pelts, we must still have eaten, the poets akecorns, & never have sought corn, we must cleve to the eldest and not to the best. But why not all in English, a tung of it self both depe in conceit, & frank in deliverie ? I do not think that any language, be it whatsoever, is better able to utter all arguments, either with more pith, or greater planesse than our English tung is, if the English utterer be as skilfull in the matter, which he is to utter : as the foren utterer is.

Mulcaster's most distinguished pupil, Edmund Spenser, agreed with him.

When this fundamental question, what language to use ? had been settled, there remained many others to be considered. Was poetry to be scanned by quantity, or by accent ? Latin poets had taken over their metre from the Greeks : were English poets to do so too ? How was the vocabulary to be enlarged and dignified ? Were the poets to use classical or native sources ; obsolete words or words from various dialects ? Granted that they were to write in English, what did 'English' mean ? How was this living, changing language, that was spoken so many different ways, even at court, to be made into a fit medium for the poetry they wished to write ? What sort of poems were they to write ? And what was the best method of writing the greatest kind of poetry, heroic ? Who provided the best pattern : Homer or Virgil, Lucan or Ariosto, Tasso or Camoens ? And what was the most suitable metrical form in which to write your heroic poem ?

Michael Drayton wrote his *Mortimeriados* in the seven-line stanza, but rewrote it, as *The Barons Warres*, in *ottava rima*. He did so, he says, because in the seven-line stanza

the often harmony softened the verse more than the majesty of the subject would permit, unless they had all been . . . complete. Therefore . . . I chose Ariosto's stanza, of all other the most complete and best proportioned. . . . This . . . holds the tune clean through to the base of the column (which is the couplet, the foot, or bottom) and closeth not but with a full satisfaction to the ear for so long detention. Briefly this sort of stanza hath in it majesty, perfection, and solidity.

Again, were your lines to be of eleven syllables, as in Italian, or of ten, or perhaps of twelve? Samuel Daniel, on the advice of Hugh Sanford, went through his long historical poem, *The Civill Warres*, to remove all the lines of eleven syllables, so that

there are not above two couplettes in that kinde in all my Poem of the Civill warres : and I would willingly if I coulde have altered it in all the rest, holding feminine Rymes to be fittest for Ditties, and either to be set for certaine, or els by themselves.

Such were the considerations that Elizabethan poets had in mind when they were revising their poems. These matters could be much more profitably discussed by a group of friends than could the personal feelings of the Romantics.

With problems of these kinds Elizabethan poets and critics were concerned. They wished to create a national literature, as the Italians had done, as the French were trying to do : like the Italians and the French they had not only to write the poetry but first of all to fashion the medium in which to write it. For them learning and experiment were essential, and they delighted in discussing problems and precedents together, in writing poems to each other, in friendly rivalry and parody. Here the offices of a patron were most needed, to gather into his house gifted poets and learned scholars who might talk of these matters and write poems, two of them perhaps sitting together at the same table and writing on the same theme, as Sidney and Fulke Greville must have done, as John Donne and Sir Henry Goodere were to do. The patron could not create the talents of a Spenser, nor even of an Abraham Fraunce; but he could encourage these men by his interest, by his knowledge, and by his taste. In this sense for Spenser Sidney had been 'the Patron of my young Muses'; in this sense for Daniel Lord Pembroke was 'the fosterer of me and my Muse'; in this sense, finally, Sidney was 'accompted . . . a generall *Maecenas* of Learning' and, as such, won a European reputation unrivalled by any Englishman of his time. This was important, for these English poets were by no means insular. Their patriotic ambition made them seek a European fame for English poetry,

> Planting our roses on the Apenines;

and Nashe dared to 'preferre divine master Spencer, the miracle of wit, to bandie line for line in the honor of England, gainst Spaine, France, Italie, and all the worlde'.

At the accession of Queen Elizabeth, there had been little cause for confidence in the future of English poetry. A year before, in 1557, Tottel published his miscellany *Songes and Sonettes*, in which he had gathered three hundred and ten short poems by the Earl of Surrey, Sir Thomas Wyatt, and other courtiers of Henry VIII. Two years later was published *The Mirrour for Magistrates*, a collection of cautionary tales in verse which set the fashion for much later narrative poetry. These, and the earlier anthology *The Courte of Venus*, of which but two fragmentary copies survive, provided almost all the recent poetry available in print. There were, no doubt, manuscript commonplace books and collections, such as those made by the elder John Harington which were continued by his son, the translator of Ariosto ; and there would certainly be private poems written for circulation among a group of friends. Few of these survive, though the elder Harington's '*Sonnet made on Isabella Markham, when I firste thought her fayer as she stood at the Princess's Windowe in goodlye Attyre, and talkede to dyvers in the Courte-Yard*', shows the quality of what we have lost. For this poem must have been written not later than 1554, when John Harington and Isabella Markham married ; yet it has a grace and movement we too readily deny to the poetry of that time.

> Whence comes my love, O hearte, disclose,
> 'Twas from cheeks that shamed the rose ;
> From lips that spoyle the rubies prayse ;
> From eyes that mock the diamond's blaze.
> Whence comes my woe, as freely owne,
> Ah me! 'twas from a hearte lyke stone.

Side by side with these poems of the courtiers there was also the oral, popular poetry so much derided by Shakespeare, but which Sidney was not too sophisticated to enjoy ; and here and there in farmhouses about the country Thomas Tusser's proverbial doggerel was being thumbed over, and committed to memory.

The dissensions and uncertainties of the Marian interlude had, none the less, ended the development of a national literature that had been begun by the courtiers of Henry VIII, and in the 1560s it must have seemed likely that the sixteenth century would be as barren of poetry as the fifteenth had been. Then, the gracious and cultivated society of the court of Richard II, for which the Wilton diptych was painted and in which Chaucer found an audience, had been destroyed in the turmoil of the Wars of the Roses. Poetry was no longer written in England, because there was no longer anyone with the taste or the leisure to read it. In Wales, on the other hand, where the wars were of somewhat less concern, poets of the stature of Lewis Glyn Cothi, Huw Dafi, and Guto 'r Glyn still wrote for the families to which they were attached ; and in Scotland, unaffected by the wars, Henryson and Dunbar wrote poetry of distinction. Even in England, the lower orders of society, who were unconcerned in the quarrels of the nobility, sang their songs and carols and ballads, and thereby preserved a native lyrical tradition which, later, Wyatt was skilful to match with the more polished tradition of Italy.

The older poetry of Chaucer, Gower, and Lydgate was printed in various editions early in the sixteenth century, and the Elizabethans recognized in Chaucer a poet whom they might seek to emulate. But the changes in the language which had taken place since 1400 made him a difficult model, and they realized that, if they would create a national literature as the Italians had done, they could not do this by trying to use Chaucer's language. Neither was the more recent poetry of Skelton to their purpose, for he pleased 'onely the popular eare', and was rejected for the same reasons as the 'metre-ballad-mongers' were rejected. Thomas Churchyard had begun his long and undistinguished career before the accession of Elizabeth, and in the 1560s and 1570s Turberville, Gascoigne, Breton, and Whetstone published poems ; but even by the time when Sidney was writing his *Apologie*, in the early 1580s, he felt compelled to admit that he found 'the very true cause of our wanting estimation is want of desert ; taking upon us to be Poets in despight of *Pallas*'.

To Sidney and his friends about this time English literature seemed to be in a state of decay. But very soon the anonymous New Poet would be everywhere acclaimed for his *Shepheardes Calender* as the man who promised a new age in English poetry. Because they so clearly understood the problems which must be faced, the Elizabethans were at once able to recognize the master for whom they had been waiting. Whatever criticisms they may have made of Spenser's poetry in detail they never had the least doubt that he was 'England's Arch-Poet', the man who had done for English what Virgil had done for Latin, or Ariosto for Italian. For this reason at his death the poets gathered in Westminster Abbey and threw their verses, with the pens that wrote them, into his open grave; for this reason long afterwards Milton told Dryden that Spenser was his original — the man who gave him a lofty poetic ambition.

Sidney himself was concerned in his *Apologie* rather to defend poetry generally against the attacks of the Puritans than to claim any notable achievement by English poets; to assert that such achievement was desirable, not to announce its existence. Among the poets who have already written his selection is cursory. To Chaucer, like all Elizabethans, he gives the pre-eminence, and (as was usual at that time) he preferred *Troilus and Criseyde* to all the other poems. 'Truly, I know not whether to mervaile more, either that he in that mistie time could see so clearly, or that wee in this cleare age walke so stumblingly after him.' Of more recent poetry he refers to the *Mirrour for Magistrates* and the poems of the Earl of Surrey. He makes no mention of Wyatt, perhaps because, like Puttenham, he found very little difference between him and Surrey. Of poems by living writers he mentions only the *Shepheardes Calender*, to which he gives qualified approval.

Puttenham, who began his *Arte of English Poetry* about 1565 but continued revising until it was published in 1589, gives a much fuller account of the English poetry that might be read. He prefers Chaucer to the other early writers, and holds a low opinion of Skelton. Among the more

recent he names Surrey and Wyatt as 'the two chief lan-
ternes of light to all others that have since employed their
pennes upon English Poesie'. These contemporaries of his
own include several of the contributors to the *Mirrour for
Magistrates* ; Sidney, Dyer, Fulke Greville, and Walter
Ralegh (none of whose poems was yet published) ; Spenser,
Gascoigne, Breton, and Turberville. On the two last he
makes no comment, but he praises Gascoigne 'for a good
meeter and for a plentifull vayne' ; and he couples Spenser
with Sidney and Sir Thomas Chaloner as writers of pastoral.

William Webbe, in his *Discourse of English Poetrie*,
which was published three years before Puttenham's book,
had given Spenser much higher praise as one who 'in my
judgement principally deserveth the tytle of the rightest
English Poet that ever I read' ; and Webbe's reading was
wide enough for him to include the names of more than
thirty poets. Of recent writers he prefers Gascoigne, after
Spenser, and he quotes E. K.'s appreciation of him from the
notes to the November eclogue of the *Shepheardes Calender*.

> Master George Gaskoyne, a wytty Gentleman and the very
> cheefe of our late rymers, who, and if some partes of learning wanted
> not (albe it is well knowne he altogether wanted not learning), no
> doubt would have attayned to the excellencye of those famous
> Poets. For gyfts of wytt and naturall promptnes appeare in him
> aboundantly.

Spenser most probably agreed with this estimate of Gascoigne,
which is both fair and characteristic of the age : he was a
naturally gifted poet who had not studied his art with the
diligence needed to become a great poet. This fault Spenser
had no intention of committing. In the eclogue which
E. K. is here glossing Spenser had 'set out the perfecte paterne
of a Poete, which finding no maintenance of his state and
studies, complayneth of the contempte of Poetrie, and the

16

causes thereof'. The causes of this contempt had been defined by Sidney as want of merit; Spenser considers them to be want of an intelligent audience. Very properly therefore Spenser dedicated the first considerable work of the New Poetry to the man who became its chief encourager and patron; for only this fortunate conjunction of poet and patron made the work of Spenser and the new poets possible.

Up to this time, during the first twenty years of Elizabeth's reign, all who surveyed the history of English literature discovered much the same pattern. First there had been the poets of the fourteenth and early fifteenth centuries, with the dominating figure of Chaucer to give assurance that English poetry had once achieved greatness. Then, after an interval, came the courtly makers of the reign of Henry VIII, with Surrey and Wyatt pointing the way towards the English Renaissance, only to be followed by the hesitant, scanty, and unsatisfactory poetry of the middle decades of the century, when Gascoigne alone had seemed to come near to fulfilling the earlier promise. The Elizabethans saw that since the pioneer work of Surrey and Wyatt English poetry had been disappointing; and they did not make the mistake of directly linking the later achievement to the poetry written in the early years of the century. Men's attention had been distracted from poetry in the religious crisis of this century, and the poet was unnoticed.

> *Piers*, I have pyped erst so long with payne,
> That all mine Oten reedes bene rent and wore :
> And my poor Muse hath spent her spared store,
> Yet little good hath got, and much lesse gayne.
> Such pleasaunce makes the Grashopper so poore,
> And ligge so layd, when Winter doth her straine.

There was therefore urgent need of a new Maecenas to support and encourage a new Virgil.

Indeede the Romish *Tityrus*, I heare,
Through his *Mecaenas* left his Oaten reede,
Wheron he earst had taught his flocks to feede,
And laboured lands to yield the timely eare,
And eft did sing of warres and deadly deede,
So as the Heavens did quake his verse to here.

The precedent of Virgil, who wrote pastorals at the outset of his career, and was then led by the encouragement of Maecenas to write the epic of the founding of Rome, was inevitably a favourite among the nationally self-conscious poets of the Renaissance. A poet who sought to write his heroic poem was expected to try his hand at pastoral, just as he was expected to begin his poem with an echo of Virgil's opening phrase, which was itself modelled on the opening of the Odyssey. Such details are significant because they show that awareness of a European tradition which is so constant a feature of the Renaissance — which is, indeed, its primary inspiration. So, when national ambition and patriotism led men to found the new vernacular literatures they looked to the examples of Greece and Rome, and more especially to Rome since, as they understood, Rome had derived most of her culture from Greece. Thus the Roman poets, Virgil, Horace, and Ovid, were seen as men facing and overcoming the same problems that were confronting the poets of the Renaissance in every country of Western Europe. Their experience was supplemented from modern Italy, whose literature, at least since the publication of the *Orlando Furioso*, was admitted to be worthy to stand beside the two ancient literatures.

The achievement of Ariosto, not of Dante, had established Italian literature as comparable to Latin, just as in England Spenser, not Chaucer, was accepted as our Virgil. Dante's work was known to educated Englishmen, but none was translated into English in the sixteenth century. Probably

Trissino's version of the *De Vulgari Eloquentia* had its influence on English as on Italian discussions of poetic diction; and certainly Spenser's practice in the *Shepheardes Calender* is not much different from what Dante had recommended. In the *Convivio*, written a few years after the other treatise, Dante defended his use of Italian in preference to Latin — and he had begun the *Divina Commedia* in Latin. Italian, he said, was his native language, in which he conversed with his family, and in which he always thought; it could bring poetry to many — nobles, princes, and (especially) ladies — who were ignorant of Latin; it was, besides, a most excellent, clear, and copious language. To these practical reasons Dante adds the patriotic motive which was to be so strong in the sixteenth century: he wished to show that Italian was as good as other vernaculars, such as Provençal; and he sought to give greater stability and honour to his native tongue through his poetry — a noble ambition which he triumphantly fulfilled. Sidney expressed the normal Elizabethan view of Dante in comparing him to Chaucer as one of 'the first that made the language aspire to be a Treasure-house of Science'. He was a pioneer from whom later poets could learn, rather than a model to be copied. For the Elizabethans, Petrarch and Ariosto provided more acceptable models, and stimulated their rivalry. Thus, as early as 1580 Gabriel Harvey, in a letter to Spenser, compares his *Faerie Queene* to the *Orlando Furioso* 'which . . . you wil needes seeme to emulate, and hope to overgo, as you flatly professed yourself in one of your last Letters'.

Castiglione, whose influence on Elizabethan taste and manners can hardly be exaggerated, shared Dante's views on the use of language, and would not accept the classicism of Bembo, who sought to base literary Italian on the Tuscan of Boccaccio and Petrarch. Dante, though himself a Tuscan, had expressly rejected the claims of his own dialect, and had preferred Bolognese, though his ideal Italian was an amalgam of all the dialects. These arguments were renewed and adapted for Englishmen.

Already in 1545 Roger Ascham, in addressing his *Toxophilus* 'to all gentle men and yomen of Englande', had defended his use of English in terms which recall Dante's.

If any man woulde blame me, eyther for takynge such a matter in hande, or els for writing it in the Englyshe tongue, this answere I make hym, that whan the beste of the realme thinke it honest for them to use, I one of the meanest sort, ought not to suppose it vile for me to write.

Ascham was a classicist who detested the Italian influence on English poetry that he saw in the work of Wyatt and Surrey, or in translations from Italian; and he thought that English should be used only for mean and practical matters. This insular conservatism was contrary to the spirit of the age, and Sidney's introduction of the critical ideas of the Italian Renaissance heralded our own. Spingarn calls Sidney's *Apologie*

a veritable epitome of the literary criticism of the Italian Renaissance; and so thoroughly is it imbued with this spirit, that no other work, Italian, French, or English, can be said to give so complete and so noble a conception of the temper and the principles of Renaissance criticism.

The Elizabethans staked a claim for English poetry in the tradition of Europe: Philip Sidney, and his sister after him, enabled them to do so. The talent was there certainly; but the general excellence of the many rather than the supremacy of the best distinguishes the poetry of the age. In this the Elizabethans differ much from the Romantics. Some would argue, though not (I think) correctly, that five Elizabethans could not be chosen to match Wordsworth, Coleridge,

Byron, Shelley, and Keats. But during the Regency where is the great mass of sonnets, songs, pastorals, elegies, epistles, narrative poems, odes, satires, posies, epigrams? Nathan Drake at that time estimated the number of Elizabethan poets at two hundred and thirty-three — and this is far short of the total. Where are two hundred and thirty-three Regency poets — or even thirty-three — whose verse is still worth reading? This contrast between the general levels of excellency is to be found also in the works of the individual poets. The Romantics seem to have been most uncertain when they were writing well or ill. In reading Wordsworth we are liable to be brought up all standing with

> My drift I fear is scarcely obvious ;

and the more glutinous maunderings of Keats are no less likely to interrupt our delight in his poetry. The Elizabethans had faults too, but they are not these faults. They do not suddenly stumble on prose or slither into vulgarity. They at least keep up the illusion of poetry.

They accepted the Horatian maxim of combining instruction with delight :

> Omne tulit punctum qui miscuit utile dulci.

But they were unashamedly practical about it, just as Tasso was in his famous simile about sweetening the cup of medicine for children. So Spenser defends himself for writing the *Faerie Queene* instead of a philosophical treatise, by reference to 'the use of these dayes, seeing all things accounted by their showes, and nothing esteemed of, that is not delightfull and pleasing to commune sence'. They have better poetic manners than the Romantics : if they have designs upon us they take care not to make them palpable. They were not intent upon explorations of the subconscious : they were trying to produce beautiful objects of a particular kind.

Their poetry was based on alert observation of the human pageant ; it was, as Aristotle had said it should be, an imitation of life — but an ideal imitation, for 'Nature's world is brazen, the Poets only deliver a golden'. Further, these poets always considered the reader, because they always imagined quite clearly and practically for whom they were writing. Romantic poets believed that they were writing for mankind, that they were blowing trumpets to an earth which was unawakened. (That it much preferred to be left in that blissful state escaped their notice.) Elizabethan poets would have considered Wordsworth's intention absurd, and Shelley's ill-mannered. They wrote for people who wished to read their poetry, the Romantics for mankind, who did not. The Romantics seem often to have written with the naïve illusion of adolescents who suppose that the world cares about the state of their souls :

> Bliss was it in that dawn to be alive,
> And to be young was very heaven.

But J. S. Mill's prognostication of a millennium when mankind would indeed be universally engaged in reading the *Ode to Duty* or *The Idiot Boy* has not yet, unfortunately, come upon us. The Elizabethans wrote for Penelope Devereux, or Lucy Harington, or Magdalen Herbert, for a gentleman or noble person, for the court, for the benchers of the Middle Temple. Their audience was not vaguely perceived through a mist of universal benevolence : they could kiss its hand, or hear the tones of its voice. From this arises the paradox that the Romantics, writing for the patronage of the unknown man in the bookshop, are much more personal than the Elizabethans, writing, as often as not, for someone with whom they had dined a few days ago. For the Romantic, with everyone to write for, and therefore with no one to write for, wrote for and about himself in a way 'unprecedented in literary history', as Wordsworth remarked ; whereas the

Elizabethan tried to produce a poem to suit a particular occasion and a known taste. Rousseau's dogma that the only interesting study is of myself would not have commended itself to an Elizabethan, because he recognized that he was involved in mankind — which included himself. The pleasures of introspection were, presumably, not unknown to him, but he preferred the ironical, dramatic appreciation of self. Thus he could see his own life as a whole, to be completed by the death which he so often greeted with some splendid and still-quoted phrase. So John Donne, that quintessential Elizabethan, rose from his death-bed to pose for his picture, wrapped in his shroud, and standing on the wooden urn which he had had made. 'Upon this *Urn* he thus stood with his eyes shut, and with so much of the sheet turned aside as might show his lean, pale, and death-like face.' They did not all play to the gallery as shamelessly as this, but they were always capable of a detached observation of themselves. This power of seeing their own personality from outside, as others saw it, made them such fine dramatists, freeing their imaginations from those limits of self that made almost all Romantic drama still-born. Congruously with this view of themselves they regarded poetry as in essence dramatic : to be judged therefore not by reference to the poet's biography, but by its effect on the audience. The taste and discrimination of the audience thus becomes of considerable importance. Mankind in general has neither taste nor discrimination. Elizabethan patrons had.

Much Elizabethan poetry was private poetry, written for an audience to be counted on the fingers. The new invention of printing had not yet persuaded poets that whatever they wrote must be exposed to the public gaze on the bookstalls, and the old tradition of passing poems round in manuscript survived. Shakespeare's sonnets were handed about among

his private friends ; Donne wrote for a small group of intellectual friends and deplored the possible necessity of publishing ; and the commonplace-books that were kept in country
houses still preserve many poems which might otherwise be
lost. There were also the professional poets writing for a
larger audience, who first appear at this time — men like
Drayton who were disposed to sneer at poets such as Donne
'whose verses are deduced to chambers . . . kept in cabinets,
and must only pass by transcription'. To accuse the courtiers
of intellectual snobbery in treating their poetry as private
and declining to publish it is absurd. Why should they
publish what had been written for friends? They did not
suppose anyone else would care to read it, though when they
were asked to contribute poems to anthologies and song-books
they did not refuse. Much of this poetry contained private
references unintelligible to outsiders ; occasionally there were
intimacies of revelation that were not for the eye of any but
the closest friends. Thus the stanzas of Stella's reply in the
Eighth Song of *Astrophel and Stella*, the song which is the
dramatic climax of the whole sequence, were not included in
the first unauthorized printings, and we may believe that they
were known only to his sister (and perhaps two or three others)
who included them in the later, authorized, edition. Private
poetry continued to exist, as it still does, alongside the public
poetry. Sidney, Greville, and Dyer, or later, Donne, Edward
Herbert, and Henry Wotton, might amuse, delight, or shock
one another with their verses ; but they understood and
enjoyed the poetry of the professionals, Spenser and Daniel,
Chapman and Jonson, and were as ready to discuss poetry
with them as with one another. There was a most lively
interest in poetry, and in the technique of poetry : the poets
were always eager to learn more of their craft, and to profit by
informed criticism.

Thus patronage meant for the poet the assurance of an interested and intelligent audience. A poet could write in the knowledge that his poetry would be judged objectively, much in the manner in which we still judge architecture. Further, a poet might expect that in his patron's house he would meet other poets, and that he might there write and talk about poetry as long as he liked, in the company of sympathetic but critical companions. One such occasion is described by Lodowick Bryskett in introducing his *Discourse of Civil Life*. 'The occasion of the discourse grew', he says, 'by the visitation of certaine gentlemen coming to me to my little cottage which I had newly built neare unto Dublin.' In the company was Edmund Spenser, who excused himself from talking at length on moral philosophy on the ground that, as they knew, he had 'already undertaken a work tending to the same effect, which is in *heroical verse*, under the title of a *Faerie Queene*'. The Elizabethan poet was not given some cash and told to express himself: he was invited to Wilton and asked his opinion about the suitability of the hexameter in English, whether he favoured the admission of words of Northern dialects, what was his view on the insertion of comic scenes in a tragedy. Sometimes he might be commissioned to write a poem or an entertainment — a Prothalamion for the betrothal of the Earl of Worcester's daughters; an elegy on the death of Elizabeth Drury; a masque to entertain the Queen at Wanstead, or the Earl of Bridgewater at Ludlow Castle; an epitaph on a child of the Queen's Chapel, or a sonnet to commend the *Faerie Queene*.

When Wordsworth was at Cambridge the Master of St. John's died, and, according to custom, the coffin was brought into Hall 'stuck over by copies of verses English or Latin', just as would have been done any time in the previous two hundred years or more.

My Uncle [Wordsworth says] seemed mortified when upon enquiring he learnt that none of these verses were from my pen, 'because', said he, 'it would have been a fair opportunity for distinguishing yourself'. I did not, however, regret that I had been silent on this occasion, as I felt no interest in the deceased person, with whom I had had no intercourse and whom I had never seen but during his walks in the College grounds.

Such a reason for refusing to write an elegy would have been as incomprehensible to Spenser or Donne as to Wordsworth's uncle, for they would never have supposed for a moment that it was any more necessary for a poet than for a monumental mason to feel an 'interest in the deceased person'. Both poet and mason were invited to produce a suitable object for commemorating the dead, not to burst into tears. Donne had never seen Elizabeth Drury, but the defects in his celebration of her virtues do not in any way derive from that circumstance. Ben Jonson told Donne that 'if it had been written of the Virgin Marie it had been something' — not 'if it had been written of Anne Donne, or Magdalen Herbert', by whose deaths Donne was deeply moved. Thomas Carew, called upon to write an elegy on Maria Wentworth, chose to be witty and flippant and thereby broke the rules of decorum. To write in an elegy :

> So though a Virgin, yet a Bride
> To every Grace, she justifi'd
> A chaste Poligamie, and dy'd,

was unsuitable because it was not elegiac ; but no one expected or desired from Carew a personal lament.

This concept of decorum, the most important in Elizabethan criticism, is natural to poets who have an audience clearly before their imaginations. Carew could hardly have written these lines if he had been thinking of the Earl and Countess of Cleveland, or of anyone else who mourned their

young daughter : he was merely thinking how he might
contrive a witty conceit, without regard to the occasion. It
could be said of him, as Dr. Johnson said of Shakespeare : 'A
quibble, poor and barren as it is, gave him such delight, that
he was content to purchase it, by the sacrifice of reason,
propriety, and truth'. To this temptation the Elizabethans
were always open, and the Jacobeans always fell. There are
quibbles or puns in Spenser's *Prothalamion*, where Spenser
says of Lady Elizabeth and Lady Katherine Somerset,

> Yet they were bred of Somers-heat they say ;

and again where he alludes to the Earl of Essex's family name
of Devereux, and bids the Earl to have

> Endlesse happinesse of thine owne name
> That promiseth the same.

But on a gay and joyful occasion such fancies were quite
proper. For by decorum is meant the fitting of the style to
the matter ; or the fitting of a speech in a play or a novel to
the character who speaks ; or the suiting of the manner of a
poem to the occasion for which it is written, or to the person
to whom it is addressed. Ben Jonson criticized Sidney
because (he said) he 'did not keep a decorum in making every
one speak as well as himself'. E. K. praises Spenser in the
Julye eclogue, where Thomalin makes a covert allusion to
Aaron 'whose name', says E. K., 'for more Decorum, the
shephearde sayth he hath forgot, lest his remembrance and
skill in antiquities of holy writ should seeme to exclude the
meanenesse of the Person'. Sir John Harington defends
Ariosto against the charge of obscenity on the ground of
decorum : 'there is so meet a decorum in the persons of those
that speake lasciviously, as any of iudgement must needs
allow'. And he goes on to remark of Chaucer : 'I could
recite many places, not onely in his millers tale, but in the

good wife of Bathes tale, & many more, in which onely the decorum he keepes is that that excuseth it and maketh it more tolerable'. Decorum could be kept in the *Miller's Tale*, or even, as Thomas Storer observes, in the Errata to his *Life and Death of Thomas Wolsey Cardinall*, for 'there is no reason that a Booke should be without faultes, when the person of whom the booke intreateth had so many in his life'.

Through the rules of decorum good taste was made reasonable and objective : shepherds were to speak like shepherds, not like nobles, and were not to display an improbable erudition by knowing the name of Moses' brother. Kings were to speak and act like Kings, on whom not even a Falstaff might presume. Rough and lecherous characters that disport themselves on the way to Canterbury might talk bawdy without offence. When Spenser addressed Queen Elizabeth he did so in the superb and stately phrases of the dedication of the *Faerie Queene* ; when Michael Drayton addressed Anne Goodere he shifted his personality and hers into the pastoral world where friendship would no longer seem presumptuous or embarrassing ; but Sir John Harington could properly address his wife, Mall, in terms of intimate affection. The sureness of taste which distinguished the Elizabethans could not have derived from a theory which values poetry by spontaneity and originality, and which therefore invites a judgment of poetry by its inception rather than by its achievement. They preferred to follow a fine precedent rather than to strive to be different. A sonnet does not cease to be a good sonnet because it is an inaccurate translation of a French paraphrase of an Italian sonnet which was itself based on a conceit borrowed from a Latin version of a Greek original. Much — perhaps most — of Elizabethan poetry is in this way consciously made to partake of

the literary traditions of Europe. The Elizabethans had the
same scrupulous care for the finished work of art that had
led the dying Virgil to beg his friends to burn the uncompleted
Aeneid; Sidney himself asked that the *Arcadia* should be
destroyed. The 'fragments' so plentifully scattered about
the pages of the Romantic poets are not to be found in the
works of the Renaissance. Still less would an Elizabethan
have faked a fragment, as Keats did with *Hyperion*, or have
published work in progress, or drafts of cantos.

To strike Romantic attitudes in such ways would have
been derided by the company at Penshurst or Wilton. There,
poetry was regarded, as it had been in the Florence of Lorenzo
de' Medici, or at the court of Urbino, as a civilized accomplishment, one of the things that a gentleman should be able
to discuss with intelligence, and to compose without affecta-
tion. This very comparison was indeed made by Nicholas
Breton, who compared the Countess of Pembroke to that
Duchess of Urbino who presides with such grace and charm
over the delightful talk in the pages of Castiglione. Philip
Sidney, for all his passionate conviction, never loses the
aristocratic ease and elegance of manner which seemed to
him and to his contemporaries proper to the discussion of
poetry. He begins his *Apologie* with a smile at the enthusiasm
of an Italian riding-master at the court of the Emperor
Maximilian. He refers to his own admission 'before ever I
durst aspire unto the dignitie . . . into the company of the
Paperblurrers' — those 'fellows in foolscap uniforms turned
up with ink' to whom Byron refers in much the same tone
of voice. And he ends with a gaiety that is far removed
from the solemnity of Wordsworth's 'I wish to be remembered
as a teacher or as nothing'.

The Elizabethan courtier wished to be remembered for a
variety of reasons, as soldier, scholar, poet — as a complete

and civilized man ; and, following an ancient assurance of the poets, he looked to poetry to eternize his name. Patronage was thus, for the patron, a means of ensuring survival in the memory of later generations, and the poets were not slow to take advantage of this vanity. The ladies also encouraged the poets for similar reasons, and rightly expected the beauty complimented in a thousand sonnets to live still

Where breath most breathes, — even in the mouths of men

— as indeed it does. Such had been the boast of Horace ; and to this Thomas Drant refers in dedicating to the Earl of Ormond his translation of the *De Arte Poetica*.

Well was it for Horace that he was cherisde of Maecenas, for he obtained throughe hym opportunitye to studye : better was it for Maecenas that he cherised Horace, and procured him that opportunitye, for he lifted up his name, and made hym immortall. Wheras, nathles the wyt of the one, and the port of the other, all theyre wyde fames hadd longe ere this time bene drenched in the dust, and rakte up with theyr cynders, had not the Poet bene stayd by his patrone, and the patrons glytterynge honor by the Poete displaide.

He goes on to mention among the famous patrons of letters Ptolemy, the Medici, Bembo, and Francis I. There is a similar discourse on the tradition of patronage in Geffrey Whitney's *A Choice of Emblemes, and other Devises*, where he says (among much else) this : 'For our succession, shall see what we have seene, and behoulde hereby what famous thinges were enterprised and done in our daies, as if they were even nowe standing at our elbowes'. And he compliments his patron, Leicester, because in his zeal and care of those that love good letters he has been following 'the good examples of manie Princes, and great personages, who are renowned therefore, beyond anie other desertes'.

The patrons, though naturally rather less insistent than

the poets, were quite willing to acknowledge this debt of immortality to them. Fulke Greville said that he desired 'to be known to posterity under no other notions than of Shakespeare's and Ben Jonson's master' — as tantalizing a remark as any in all the contemporary notes of Shakespeare. Sidney begged his readers to believe the poets' promises of immortality: 'Thus doing, your name shall florish in the Printers shoppes ; thus doing, you shall bee of kinne to many a poeticall Preface ; thus doing, you shall be most fayre, most ritch, most wise, most all ; you shall dwell upon Superlatives'.

Yet with the change that has taken place in men's attitude to poetry, and to patronage, the important, the essential part played by a few patrons in bringing about the poetic achievement of the English Renaissance, has been forgotten or neglected. One result has been that the flowering of English poetry in the 1580s and 1590s has come to seem miraculous, due to a fortuitous collocation of poetic genius at that time, whereas it was most deliberately considered and planned, and could not have happened at any other time. We remember how much the Florentine Renaissance owed to the Medici, but we forget that a similar debt was owed by the English Renaissance to the Sidneys. At the time the name of Sidney became proverbial for a patron, a synonym for Maecenas ; and (as Daniel observed) patronage was a glory hereditary to their house. Here two from among the multitudinous tributes to Sir Philip Sidney as a patron of letters, may be quoted. First are the words of Tom Nashe from the preface which he wrote for the first edition of *Astrophel and Stella* :

Gentle *Sir Philip Sidney*, thou knewst what belonged to a Scholler, thou knewst what paines, what toyle, what travel, conduct to perfection ; wel couldst thou give every Vertue his encouragement, every Art his due, every writer his desert : cause none more vertuous, witty, or learned than thy selfe.

The other is from Fulke Greville's life of his friend :

The Universities abroad, and at home, accompted him a generall Maecenas of Learning; Dedicated their Books to him; and communicated every Invention, or Improvement of Knowledge with him. . . . His heart and capacity were so large, that there was not a cunning Painter, a skilful Engenier, an excellent Musician, or any other Artificer of Extraordinary fame, that made not himself known to this famous spirit, and found him his true friend without hire; and the common *Rendevous* of worth in his time.

Thus the gay, scurrilous, racy journalist, who made his living by his pen, and the aloof, pious, intellectual courtier, who could afford £20,000 for restoring Warwick Castle, united in their praise of this man's taste and of his fame as a patron. The tributes to his sister, who carried on his task after his death, to her two sons 'the most noble and incomparable pair of brethren', and to others of the Sidneys and Herberts, do but continue the story. Philip and Mary Sidney were not the first or the last patrons of letters in England; but they lived at a time when patronage fitted the current opinions on the nature of poetry, and when the poets most needed the enlightened and critical encouragement that they provided. So they took the occasion to shape and guide the poetry of the Elizabethan age towards a fullness of achievement that, in the 1570s, only they foresaw.

CHAPTER 2

The Education of a Patron
I—England, France, and Germany

THERE is no need here to recount the earlier history of patronage in England. Chaucer owed much to the favour of John of Gaunt and to the taste of Richard II ; Gower tells us how he met King Richard on the Thames, and was commanded to write the *Confessio Amantis* ; King Henry VIII welcomed the poets to his court, as he welcomed all artists and scholars, whether Englishmen, Germans, or Italians, whom he could entice thither. In the first twenty years of Elizabeth's reign, apart from the Queen herself, there were courtiers who were glad to win reputation for patronage of the arts, and among them the Earl of Leicester held an honoured place. Thomas Drant, Archdeacon of Lewes, was not the most distinguished of those who addressed him as Maecenas, but he may speak for the others in some jog-trot lines to Leicester.

> If Englande had such curious wittes,
>   that could in stately verse,
> The factes, the feates of worthy wightes,
>   and royall gestes reherse :
> Your lordshyps honour, should be made,
>   the myrour of our tyme,
> Because you love to laye your looks
>   upon a poets ryme.

These lines were published in 1566 : when a dozen years later Sidney met Edmund Spenser and discussed with him, among much else, Drant's rules for twisting English words to fit

33

classical metres, they probably met in Leicester House. There is at least this much continuity, and Sidney would hardly have denied the influence of his uncle's tastes upon his own.

To Philip Sidney, rather than to Leicester or any other, the Elizabethan poets paid homage ; for Sidney brought back to English poetry the light of the Renaissance which had gleamed for a few years in the poetry of Surrey and Wyatt. So, for example, Daniel, addressing the Countess of Pembroke in verse of a very different quality from Drant's, attributes to Sidney the beginning of the New Poetry, and the end of the Old :

> this tyrant of the North
> *Grosse Barbarisme*, whose powre grown far inlarg'd,
> Was lately by thy valiant brothers worth
> First found, encountred, and provoked forth :
> Whose onset made the rest audacious,
> Whereby they likewise have so well discharg'd
> Upon that hideous beast incroching thus.

We should therefore try to discover what differentiated Sidney from the other patrons of poetry ; to learn why he succeeded where others had failed. To this end we must discuss the gifts of mind and person that distinguished him, and describe the training and experience that developed them. How did the boy of seventeen who set out for France in the spring of 1572 achieve, in three years' residence on the Continent, a reputation from Italy to the Low Countries, from France to Poland, that no other Englishman would rival till the days when Marlborough went there to war, and that only Byron among the English poets has ever equalled ? The story is astonishing, almost incredible ; and yet the evidence remains. What concerns us here is not that Sidney was accepted by experienced statesmen as the future leader of Protestant Europe, but that he seemed, to many an eminent and learned man old enough to be his father, a worthy patron

to whom they might dedicate their books. William the
Silent might look to a future when Sidney's convictions
would bring England to his aid, though his friendship and
Louise de Coligny's were altogether disinterested. But
Henri Estienne and Andreas Wechel, Charles de L'Ecluse
and Peter Ramus, Cesare Carafa, and (beyond all others)
Hubert Languet, had, from the very beginning, no doubts
at all of his quality, and already saw in him a general Maecenas
of learning.

Such men honoured Sidney for no material advantage :
they did not need it, and he could not provide it. Yet it is
difficult to understand how the fresh and eager charm of his
personality,

> A sweet attractive kinde of grace,
> A full assurance given by lookes,

could so master the mature and critical judgment of these
scholars and men of affairs. Charm, certainly, is one of the
most powerful, as it is one of the most elusive and indefinable
of human qualities ; but there must have been more. The
envied gift of poetry had not yet shown itself in him, and
even if it had these men neither knew English nor were yet
persuaded to consider it worth knowing. He had a lively
and enquiring intellect, a quickness of understanding, that
must have made him an excellent listener ; he was funda-
mentally a scholarly, reflective man rather than a man of
action, but at the same time one who believed that reflection
was only to be valued as it led to action. He was serious, even
from childhood, as Fulke Greville tells us.

Though I lived with him and knew him from a child, yet I
never knew him other than a man : with such staiedness of mind,
lovely, and familiar gravity, as carried grace, and reverence above
greater years. His talk ever of knowledge, and his very play tending to enrich his mind : So as even his teachers found something

in him to observe and learn above that which they had usually read, or taught.

Greville's admiration found in Sidney those graver qualities which he most valued ; but Sidney felt that such seriousness was a fault.

> I am ready to admit that I am often more serious than my age or my pursuits require ; yet I have certainly proved by experience that I am never less subject to melancholy than when I am earnestly applying the feeble powers of my mind to some high and difficult task.

He need not have been so much concerned, for there is gaiety and humour in all his work, making his *Apologie for Poetrie* a civilized and delightful essay, not a ponderous tract ; turning an entertainment for the Queen into an occasion for merriment at the pretentious pedantry of Rhombus, 'one not a little versed in the disciplinating of the juvenal frie' ; flickering all about the passion and jealousy and despair of his sonnets. He was never frivolous, but perhaps the secret of his charm, like Rosalind's, is to be sought in the combination of seriousness and good sense with a gaiety and delicacy of manner — a *grace* (so his friends called it) that is bright and untarnished still.

With such qualities he was likely to be welcome wherever he went, but he was not so fond of company as to be incautious or impulsive in his friendships. In the famous letter of advice to his brother Robert, when about to travel, he warns him that the choice of his friends and instructors is most important of all : he adds that the way to win such friendships as he had known was 'either much experience, or much humblenes'. For himself, when he first travelled abroad, humbleness had sufficed : that, and the gentle charity which Bryskett (who accompanied him) noted many years later. 'But say to thy selfe', he begs the reader of his

Discourse, 'say to thy selfe with that worthy bright light of
our age Sir Philip Sidney, Let us love men for the good
that is in them, and not hate them for their evill.' Living as
he did in an age which of all ages held the noblest and richest
ideal for man, Philip Sidney most nearly embodied that
ideal. He was Castiglione's courtier made flesh, and wherever
he went among men he was received with admiration and
delight. They saw in him, as Ophelia saw in Hamlet,

> The courtier's, soldier's, scholar's, eye, tongue, sword,
> The expectancy and rose of the fair state,
> The glass of fashion, and the mould of form,
> The observed of all observers.

That he fell something short of perfection is only proof
of his humanity, saving him from the ostracism that Aristides
and his like so well deserve. Once he unjustly accused
Edward Molyneux of opening his letters to Sir Henry Sidney
and threatened him with his dagger : but Molyneux forgave
him, and wrote an appreciation of him for Holinshed's
Chronicle. He quarrelled with the Earl of Oxford over the
right to a game of tennis, and by the standards of his day
(though not of ours) was in the wrong. He was inclined to
neglect his correspondence even with Languet. And, in the
end, he threw away his life by the heroic but unnecessary
gesture of going into battle without his cuisses, because Sir
William Pelham was without his. Such faults as he had were
thus the product of his idealism, of his impatience with the
world as he found it, of the eagerness with which he gave
himself to the task of the hour. But for all his enthusiasm, he
shared with the men of his age the precious gift of ironical self-
observation, so that he can report the gossip of ladies of the
court about himself in a sonnet, or end a letter of earnest advice
to his brother with 'Lord, how I have babled !' Through
this detachment he was able to accommodate himself to

D   37

men older and more experienced than he was with such ease and grace during his travels on the Continent.

He was seventeen and a half when he first left Britain, after an orthodox education at Shrewsbury and Christ Church. He had entered Shrewsbury School a few days before his tenth birthday, and on the same day as Fulke Greville, the most intimate of all his friends. There they came under the care of Thomas Ashton, a Fellow of Trinity College, Cambridge, and one of the greatest of Elizabethan schoolmasters. He was a Calvinist, and the Catechism of Calvin is among the books which were purchased for the young Philip Sidney. Most of the instruction at school was in the classics, but it is unlikely that Sidney had much studied Greek before he left Shrewsbury for Oxford. Of the Latin poets, he would read Virgil and Horace, Ovid and Terence ; and we know that he had a copy of a book on quantitative scansion and prosody, Tigurinus' *De Syllabarum et Carminum Ratione.* No doubt he remembered this early grounding in the subject when years later with Drant and Dyer, Spenser and Harvey, he discussed the adaptation of classical metres to English. He already had some knowledge of French, and perhaps, like his sister Mary, had received instruction at home from a French tutor.

In the holidays, or when the school was closed during an outbreak of plague in 1566, Sidney stayed with friends and relatives of the family near at hand ; for at this time his parents were much in Ireland, where Sir Henry Sidney was Lord Deputy. More than once he stayed in the house of Sir Richard Newport of Eton, near Wroxeter. Sir Richard's daughter, Magdalen, who was born in 1568, married Richard Herbert of Montgomery Castle, and by him became the mother of two poets, Edward Lord Herbert of Cherbury, and George Herbert. She was also the admired friend of John Donne, to whom he addressed some of his best poetry, and on whose death in 1627 he preached a noble sermon in St. Paul's. Another of Sidney's hosts was Sir Andrew Corbett of Moreton Corbett, who was related to the Sidneys and was also a friend of Thomas Ashton.

Sidney left Shrewsbury in 1567 or 1568 and entered Christ Church. He had already visited the University on the famous occasion in the summer of 1566 when the Queen was entertained there by the Chancellor, Leicester ; so that he must have come to Oxford suitably impressed with its splendour, if not with its learning. He was fortunate in his tutors, being at first the pupil of a fine Latin scholar named Thomas Thornton. We may be charitable enough to suppose that Thornton, who was then only twenty-eight, was alert to detect the quality of Sidney's mind without the recommendation of his being nephew to the Chancellor. He contributed verses to the University's memorial volume on Sidney's death, and the inscription on his tomb in Ledbury Church records, among other matters of pride, that 'he was a sure refuge for young poor scholars of great hopes and parts, and tutor to Sir Philip Sidney'. That he had been tutor to so illustrious a pupil may well have seemed, even sixty years later, a chief claim to remembrance ; just as to Fulke Greville friendship with Philip Sidney required in his epitaph an equal place with distinguished service to Queen Elizabeth and King James.

While he was still in residence Sidney wrote to Sir William Cecil, who had always the highest opinion of 'my darling master Philip', to urge Thornton's claims to a Canon's stall in the Cathedral : when Thornton obtained this shortly afterwards Sidney was placed under the tuition of the Dean, Thomas Cooper. Dr. Cooper was an older man, one of the most distinguished of Oxford scholars, who had recently published his Latin Dictionary, and he was soon promoted to the See of Lincoln. Sidney's third tutor was Nathaniel

Baxter, who attained some repute as a Puritan pamphleteer and minor poet. Long after Sidney's death he wrote a curious, discursive poetical hotch-potch called *Sir Philip Sidney's Ourania*, a work (in its author's opinion) 'containing all Philosophie', and which treats of subjects as diverse as the Conjunction of Venus and the use of mercury as a cure for syphilis. He explains the origin of water-spouts, and describes the burial customs of pygmies; notes a curious use of limpet-shells, and discourses on the immortality of the soul. Baxter dedicated the book to a number of ladies, first among them being the Countess of Pembroke. In the course of the poem Baxter encounters the shade of Sir Philip Sidney, who most obligingly commends him to the Countess:

> My dearest sister, keep my Tutor well,
> For in his element he doth excel.

This ghostly testimonial may, like many another, have been less enthusiastic than its recipient supposed; for it is by no means clear in what element Baxter excelled. It was certainly not in writing poetry. But though Baxter was hardly in the same class as Thornton or Cooper, Sidney was fortunate to have come under the influence of two good scholars, and we cannot doubt that he was a serious and industrious student.

Among the poor scholars whom Thornton helped was the historian and antiquary William Camden. Thornton brought him across the street from Broadgates Hall during Sidney's time at Christ Church, so that he got to know Sidney there. And, since to know Sidney seems always to have been to love and admire him, Camden missed no occasion for praising him in his works. Sidney was contemporary with many other men who were to make their name in the world. Richard Hakluyt, probably on the strength of a friendship formed at Christ Church, dedicated to Sidney in 1582 the first of his books, *Divers Voyages touching the Discoverie of America, and the Ilands adjacent unto the same.* Hakluyt, who did more than any other man to make the English aware of their imperial destiny, refers to Sidney's kindness to him and to his family, and to his 'favour towards these godly and honourable discoveries'. Sidney always felt the call of the New World and must have been excited while they were at Oxford by Hakluyt's informed and vivid talk of maps and voyages and explorations.

Another distinguished contemporary at Christ Church was Richard Carew, the future collaborator with Camden and author of one of the first of the long series of English County Histories, *The Survey of Cornwall.* Besides his historical work, Carew began a translation of Tasso's *Gerusalemme Liberata*, the first in English, which was, however, soon set aside for the triumph of Fairfax's version. Carew, as a cultivated country gentleman, was always ready to defer to a professional scholar such as Camden ; and he remembered with engaging modesty the nervousness of a great occasion in his undergraduate days, when 'upon a wrong conceyved opinion touching his sufficiency' he had been 'called to dispute extempore (*impar congressus Achilli*) with the matchless Sir Philip Sidney in the presence of the Earls Leicester, Warwick and divers other great personages'. He came to regard Sidney as the nonpareil of English writers, whether for prose or verse, and learnt from him to praise *The Excellency of the English Tongue.*

Many other contemporaries of Sidney's at Oxford who were to acknowledge his distinction probably first knew him there. Walter Ralegh, who, with more brilliance and less humility than Sidney yet shared many of his tastes, was at Oriel. Henry Savile, a friend of Sidney's in later years, and a man of deep learning, was already a Fellow of Merton, as was his lifelong friend Thomas Bodley. Richard Hooker, another close friend of Savile's, was at Corpus. One of those who engaged in theological disputes with Thomas Thornton, Sidney's first tutor, was the gifted and eloquent Edmund Campion, who had won the favourable notice of the Queen and of Leicester during the visit to Oxford in 1566; but, while Sidney was at Oxford, Campion withdrew to Ireland, there under the patronage of Sir Henry Sidney and the Irish Speaker, James Stanihurst, to write his *History of Ireland*. Richard Stanihurst, the Speaker's son, was another contemporary whom Sidney must have known at Oxford. He was a member of University College, and a few years later won notoriety for his preposterous translation of the first four books of the *Aeneid* into English hexameters, which Nashe aptly described as 'a foul, lumbering, boisterous, wallowing measure'. Yet Stanihurst had considered the problems of the English hexameter with some intelligence, as his preface shows, and he knew of the discussions on this subject in which Sidney, Harvey, and Spenser shared.

In vain do we try to assess the effect on Sidney of his time at Oxford: as for other men before his day and since, these years left him with firm friendships among his contemporaries, and with the respect of his elders. Oxford must have confirmed both the Puritanism and the sound scholarship which he had first learnt at Shrewsbury from Thomas Ashton. The whole course of his life tended to intensify in him the convictions of Puritanism, and in that very process to turn him away from pure scholarship. For he believed always, as did most of the men of his time, that (as he put it) 'the highest end of the mistres knowledge . . . stands in the knowledge of a mans selfe, in the Ethicke and politick consideration, with the end of well dooing and not of well knowing onely'. The paragon of England was quintessentially an Englishman. To his empirical mind the hair-splitting disputations that were then so large a part of the training in the University seemed trivial and valueless, so that he found it necessary to warn his young brother against 'the chief abuse of Oxford, *qui dum verba sectantur res ipsas negligunt*', a criticism scarcely less apposite in the days of the Logical Positivists than in the days of the Ciceronians.

After leaving Oxford Sidney spent some time (how long, we do not know) at Cambridge: his acquaintance with Spenser and Gabriel Harvey may date from this period, though its significance did not appear for several years. Fulke Greville, who had gone from Shrewsbury to Cambridge, makes no mention of Sidney's being there; but Gabriel Harvey implies, and Laurence Humfrey asserts, that he was there for a time. George Whetstone even goes so far as to claim that Sidney 'was in his time for his continuance reputed the best scholar in Cambridge'. And certainly Cambridge published her memorial volume before either of the two that came from Oxford. Both Universities therefore could claim, with Shrewsbury, that the formal education of Philip Sidney was of the best that England could offer. The care of him by his parents, to whom he was the light of his family, and the interest of his uncles of Leicester and Warwick, whose joint heir he was, encouraged him to profit by this education as much as he might. So, when he left for the Continent to enlarge his experience of men and of tongues, his mind was exceptionally well trained to be receptive of learning in all its forms.

On May 25th, 1572, the Queen granted Sidney her licence 'to go out of England into parts beyond the seas, with three servants and four horses, etc., to remain the space of two years immediately following his departure out of the realm, for his attaining the knowledge of foreign languages'. He travelled in company with the newly created Earl of Lincoln, who was sent on a mission to the court of Charles IX. The Earl was a friend of Sir Henry Sidney's, and, as the husband of the Earl of Surrey's Geraldine, may well have had a further, romantic interest for Sidney. Another of the company was that Lord Rich whom Sidney was afterwards to scorn as the unworthy husband of Penelope Devereux. Sidney's personal attendants were Lodowick Bryskett, Griffin Madox, and an unnamed servant. Bryskett, whose name is always thus anglicized from Bruschetto with a Churchillian disregard for the oddities of foreign speech, was the son of an Italian Protestant refugee from Genoa. He was about nine years older than Sidney, a cultivated and intelligent man, who made a career for himself in the civil service in Ireland, where he was known to Sir Henry Sidney. Madox had served Sir Henry during his years as Lord President of Wales, and, like Bryskett, was well able to share and encourage Sidney's literary tastes. He spoke and wrote Welsh, which (as will appear) was a matter of some interest to Sidney. Bryskett, though born in England, thinking of himself as an Englishman, and writing English as his native language, was a good Italian scholar who, fifteen years later, converted two poems of Bernardo Tasso's into elegies for Sidney.

The party arrived in Paris on June 8th, and Sidney went to the house, in the Faubourg St.-Germain, of the English Ambassador, Sir Francis Walsingham, who also was an old friend of his father's. The Earl of Leicester wrote to commend Sidney to Walsingham in terms that show his anxious affection for his nephew.

He is young and raw, and no doubt shall find those countries and the demeanours of the people somewhat strange unto him; and therefore your good advice and counsel shall greatly behove him for his better direction, which I do most heartily pray you to

vouchsafe him, with any friendly assurance you shall think needful
for him.

This avuncular disparagement contrasts oddly with the
reception accorded to Sidney. He must have had a natural
aptitude for learning languages (except the throaty cacophony
of German, which he could not endure), and no doubt the
grounding he had received in French was better than any
he might receive under more modern methods of instruction.
Bryskett (who was there) says,

> He was so admired among the graver sort of courtiers that when
> they could at any time have him in their company and conversation
> they would be very joyful, and no less delighted with his ready and
> witty answers than astonished to hear him speak the French
> language so well and aptly having been so short a while in the
> country.

Languet paid a similar compliment to his command of French,
'I have watched you closely when you were speaking my
own language, but I hardly ever detected you pronouncing a
single syllable wrongly'. There seems little reason to suppose
that Frenchmen were any more polite about the efforts of
Englishmen to speak their language then than now. A more
remarkable tribute than Bryskett's (who was in attendance
on Sidney, and partial to him from the first) comes from
Théophile de Banos, recalling his first meeting with Sidney,
'I remembered, that day when I first saw you, and wondered
at your excellent gifts both of body and mind—I remembered,
I say, old Pope Gregory, who declared that the English whom
he saw coming to Rome were angels : non Angli, sed Angeli'.

Peter Ramus was in Paris this summer, a scholar with a
Continental fame as a critic of the scholastic interpretations
of Aristotle, a man of fifty-seven, and a practised judge of the
quality of men's minds. Yet when, a few years later, de
Banos wrote the Life of his famous friend and master, he

dedicated it to Sidney not merely because of his own but because of Ramus's affection and respect for Sidney. How astonishing it is that a boy of seventeen, visiting France for the first time in his life, with little or no knowledge of the work of Ramus, should, in the space of a few weeks, have made such an impression. But so it was, and there is no doubt that Ramus considerably influenced Sidney in several ways. De Banos mentions his custom, when head of the Collège de Presles, of assisting poor young men of good intelligence with their studies (as did Thornton at Oxford), 'from among whom several very learned men are yet living who acknow-ledge Ramus as their father and Maecenas'. Perhaps this notable example of patronage moved Sidney, a few years later, to pay for the education of Abraham Fraunce, who became a noted Ramist, at Cambridge. The Ramist logic remained one of the chief intellectual interests of Sidney and his circle, so that, besides Fraunce, Gabriel Harvey and William Temple wrote on the subject. Thus de Banos' comment, made in 1576, that Sidney 'not only loved Ramus as a father when alive, but esteemed and reverenced him after death', remained true.

We can see something of the courtesy of dedicating a book in the letters de Banos wrote to Sidney about this dedica-tion, which are preserved in the British Museum. (Sidney's replies unfortunately are lost.) It was one of the earliest books dedicated to him, and though he was but twenty-one years of age, clearly he had strict views of the propriety of the matter. The book was printed by Andreas Wechel at Frankfort, and when two thousand copies had already come off the press (a measure of the interest in Ramus) Sidney expressed a wish that some change should be made in the dedication : a change, so it seems, that would pay greater compliment to the nobility of Sidney's family. In a somewhat obsequious letter de Banos apologizes for any error, but says that he had asked Languet's advice; later he sends the corrected page to Sidney to show that he has been able to comply with his request. The book, de Banos says, was printed at his own expense, and was selling well in Germany: he has arranged for a number of copies to be sent to England. In a letter of January 25th, 1576, he says that he is sending a copy to Sidney by 'sieur Hervet', who is at Antwerp. (Possibly this may be Gabriel Harvey who, in a poem addressed to Sidney, refers to de Banos as 'a great and excellent part of my mind', and implies that he not only knew de Banos' work, but knew the man himself. But there is no other evidence of Harvey's visiting the Continent.) In the same letter de Banos says that he had recovered most of Ramus's books, which were supposed to have been destroyed after his murder, and that he hopes to recover the rest. He also enquires whether Sidney would accept the dedication of any unpublished work of Ramus's that may be printed.

Why should de Banos have dedicated this book to Sidney? He neither expected nor received any payment for it, as humbler authors did. Sidney's name, in 1576, could not have much aided the sales of a Life of a famous French scholar, published in Germany. There must have been many of Ramus's contemporaries, or of his former pupils, with a far better claim to such a compliment than the Englishman who could have known him for at most ten weeks. We can but acknowledge the fact, and in doing so try to glimpse the personality that so quickly and so surely laid this tribute upon all within its power.

No letter of Sidney's written during this summer in Paris survives, so that we have no means of knowing what impressions he formed of the graver sort of courtiers who welcomed his company. Others have alleged that he met Ronsard and

de Baïf or other members of the Pléiade, who were certainly
in Paris at the time ; and a friendship with Tasso has been
claimed for him on no better grounds than that Tasso was
then in Paris in the suite of Cardinal d'Este, and that Hubert
Languet knew him there. In an elegy included in the Oxford
collection of poems on Sidney's death Richard Latewar calls
upon Tasso and du Bartas to lament Philisides, and there may
be some significance in his naming these two alone of foreign
poets. Du Bartas certainly celebrated Sidney, and as a poet :

> And (World-mourn'd) *Sidney*, warbling to the *Thames*
> His Swan-like tunes, so courts her coy proud streams,
> That (all with-childe with Fame) his fame they bear
> To *Thetis* lap, and *Thetis*, every-where.

Sidney had translated the first week of du Bartas' ponderous
work, but the translation is now lost. Whether Sidney met
du Bartas or not, he had little, except a pious Protestantism,
to learn from one of the dullest of French poets ; and that he
had no need to learn from such a teacher. His knowledge of
French poetry and French critical theory came from the
Pléiade : a brief acquaintance with Ronsard, even if it could
be proved — it is by no means improbable, since Leicester
knew him — would have been of less value than a careful
reading of his poetry. Similarly with Tasso : it would be
pleasant to think of the young Sidney talking with the greatest
poet of the age, whose genius was least foreign to English
taste. But it is of more importance that Sidney and Spenser
knew his poetry.

We cannot now discover what poets or men of letters
Sidney met in Paris, but there is no doubt that he must have
been made aware how large a part the discussion of literary
problems, and experiment, and interchange of verses could
play in the creation of a new literature. He lived in the house
of Walsingham, who, besides being a skilled and astute

diplomat, had something of a reputation as a patron of learning. He had studied at Padua, where on December 29th, 1555, he had been elected chancellor of the *Anglica natio* in the University, and had a wide acquaintance among Continental men of letters. Walsingham was not the man to restrict Sidney's studies to diplomacy and politics, but would encourage an interest in the intellectual life of Paris. Only eighteen months before, in November 1570, de Baïf, with the musician Thibault de Courville, had founded the Académie de Poésie et de Musique whose purpose was to reform French prosody, especially by the introduction of classical metres, and to bring about a closer union between poetry and music. De Baïf also accepted the phonetic reforms which had been proposed by Ramus. Spingarn long ago suggested that Sidney's 'Areopagus' was modelled on de Baïf's Academy, and this seems likely enough, provided that a jesting phrase of Spenser's is not once again made the charter of foundation for a mythical English Academy. Whether or not Sidney met de Baïf or de Courville, Ronsard or Jean Dorat, he certainly knew of their discussions and their poetry. He was receptive and exceptionally intelligent, and what he learnt, not the means by which he learnt, matters most. Italy and Italian literature were to mean more to him than France and French literature — in this he was like other Englishmen of his time — but these ten weeks spent in Paris had an enduring influence on him, and through him on English literature. To French example Hall attributed the use of compound epithets,

> that new elegance
> Which sweet Philisides fetch't of late from France,
> That well beseem'd his high-stil'd Arcady,
> Tho others marre it with much liberty.

But there is no advantage in tracing Sidney's love of the compound epithet, which he used with such felicity, to one

French influence, and his interest in classical metre, or in writing poetry for music, to another. What he gained by his stay in Paris was more important, and less easily defined. For he then first lived in a society where the problems of a new poetry were being actively discussed by men of remarkable gifts : he was accepted perhaps into the society of the poets themselves, and without doubt into the society of courtiers and scholars who knew and cared for their work. In that society he at once made a place for himself, and must very quickly have ceased to be the raw youth of his uncle's description. He began to grow up in Paris, and to discover that he too, an Englishman, might inherit the classical tradition of Europe, now renewed and reborn.

For the next few years Sidney's studies were guided by Hubert Languet. When they first met is not certain : Languet himself, in a letter to the Elector of Saxony, dates their close friendship to the following year, when they were together in Vienna, but there is every reason to believe that they had already met in Paris. Languet was a friend both of Ramus and of Walsingham, whose many kindnesses to him he acknowledges in his letters. And when, after the Massacre of St. Bartholomew, Walsingham hurried Sidney away from Paris, he sent him to the house of Andreas Wechel at Frankfort, where Languet himself had fled. (Languet had somehow helped Wechel to escape from Paris, as three years later Wechel gratefully acknowledged.) Walsingham could not have entrusted Sidney to better care than Languet's, and the friendship, which lasted until Languet's death in 1581, was perhaps the most valuable single influence in Sidney's life. The record of it is to be found in their correspondence, and though Sidney's letters have survived only as chance allowed, Languet's letters to him were published at Frankfort in 1633, by the Elzevirs at Leiden in 1646,

HVBERTVS LANGVET
DE PICTVRA ARCHETYPA
PENES THOMAM HOLLIS ANGLVM
REG·ET ANT·SS·LONDINI SODALEM

HUBERT LANGUET
Engraving by G. B. Cipriani from *Epistolae*, 1776

Indefinitum ne quid libro eſſet in iſto,
Illum etiam pingi placuit qui cætera pinxit.

A. WECHELVS TYPOGR.

ANDREAS WECHEL

and again in Edinburgh in 1776. On their first publication they were recommended in the title-page as 'very useful and necessary to all who study politics and history, also to the councillors of Princes, and those who are entrusted with the keys of the State'. Similarly, Lodovicus Camerarius compares this correspondence to Xenophon's *Cyropaedia*, 'With such piety, learning, and fatherly affection did Languet instruct Sidney in the paths of virtue and honour'.

Languet was one of the most distinguished of that company of Protestant scholars who dignify the controversies of the age. Born in Burgundy in 1518, after formal education in France and at Padua, he studied for three years at Wittenberg under Melanchthon, through whose influence he adopted the reformed faith. He had spent most of his life travelling about Europe, either privately or in the service of Protestant German princes, and had already visited England on a diplomatic mission. For the past nine years he had been in Paris as the representative of the Elector of Saxony, and he knew most of the poets and scholars in the city. The Scottish humanist, George Buchanan, Languet had known already in the 1560s, and in reintroducing himself in a letter of February 10th, 1581, Buchanan refers to their common friendship with such men as Jean Dorat, Sambuc (who published an annotated paraphrase of Aristotle's *Poetics* in 1564), and Charles de L'Ecluse, the famous botanist, whom Sidney was soon to meet in Vienna. Languet's admiration for Sidney was such that he was always delighted to have an occasion for introducing him among his own friends, and to him Sidney owed many valuable friendships. His practical intelligence, his devotion to the Protestant cause, and his unrivalled knowledge of Europe made him the ideal mentor for Sidney; and if occasionally the letters suggest that Polonius had been standing at Languet's shoulder, for the most part they are full of acute observation of the diplomatic affairs of Europe, and of a mature tolerance and worldly wisdom which was not less valuable to the ardent and impetuous Sidney. Languet advised him on his studies, on his choice of friends, even on his diet : 'I am very much afraid of your staying in Italy for the summer, because I know how great a liking, or, I should say, how great a passion you have for eating fruit'. Occasionally Sidney grew impatient of Languet's fussy concern for him, and once, when they were in Vienna, he escaped in the gayer company of Charles de L'Ecluse for a brief visit to Hungary, to look for rare plants and drink Hungarian wine. And Languet constantly had cause to complain about Sidney's neglect of their correspondence. But Sidney had no doubt of what he owed to Languet, and returned his affection with a sincerity which his verses clearly show :

> Languet, the shepheard best swift Ister knew,
> For clearkly reed, and hating what is naught,
> For faithful heart, cleane hands, and mouth as true :
> With his sweet skill my skillesse youth he drew,
> To have a feeling taste of him that sits
> Beyond the heaven, far more beyond our wits.

Sidney was fortunate in many things but never more than when in his skilless youth he met Hubert Languet and won his friendship.

Sidney was introduced into the most exalted company in Paris, and so impressed the young Henry of Navarre that Henry 'having measured and mastered all the spirits in his own nation found out this master-spirit among us and used him like an equal in nature, and so fit for friendship with a King'. At this time also he met Michel de L'Hôpital, the former Chancellor of France, whose wisdom and humanity were shortly to imperil his life. Sidney rightly admired

his integrity and considered that France 'never brought
forth a more accomplished judgment more firmly builded
upon virtue'. He died a few months later when religious
fanaticism had destroyed the policy of compromise which
he thought at any cost preferable to civil war. Sidney probably met some of the Huguenot leaders who were soon
to meet their death; and certainly he was presented to the
feeble and treacherous Charles IX, who on August 9th
created him a Gentleman Ordinary of the Bedchamber and
Baron de Sidenay 'Pour les bonnes et louables vertus qui
sont en luy'.

A fortnight later came the Massacre of St. Bartholomew
when men whom Sidney had but recently come to know and
admire were murdered or forced to fly for their lives. In one
of the more effective scenes in *The Massacre at Paris* Marlowe
shows Ramus confronting his murderers, whose only answer
to his cool rationalism is the violence of

> Why suffer you that peasant to declaim?
> Stab him I say and send him to his friends in hell.

It is difficult for us, who live in an age that takes for granted
more brutal savagery than the Renaissance ever dreamed of,
to appreciate the revulsion with which men and women in
England learnt of the Massacre. To Sidney, sheltering in the
Embassy while his new friends were killing or being killed
in the streets, it must have seemed that the utmost of horror
had been reached. We can hardly wonder that after such
an introduction, at the age of seventeen, to the ferocity
of the Papists, Sidney should have regarded them as the
enemies of all civilized and humane existence. For they
were so far from showing shame at the Massacre that they
exulted in it as in a victory, and commemorative medals were
struck in Paris and by the Pope. Two years later, in Venice,
Sidney was unwilling to meet Guy du Faur de Pibrac, because

he had written the official defence of the Massacre. In 1580 among the arguments he used to dissuade the Queen from the proposed marriage with Anjou was this, that he is

a Frenchman and a Papist, in whom (howsoever fine wits may find further dealings or painted excuses) the very common people well know this, that he is the son of a Jezabel of our age, and that his brother made oblation of his own sister's marriage the easier to make massacres of our brethren in belief.

This loathing of Popery gave him that passionate devotion to the Protestant cause that led such men as William of Orange to see in him a future leader of a union of Protestant states ; but it never interfered with his generous judgment of men. Even in necessity he was most reluctant to accept the Queen's offer to him of the recusant fines. As he wrote to Leicester : 'Truly I like not their persons and much worse their religions, but I think my fortune very hard that my reward must be built upon other mens punishmentes'. In another letter he promises to help the recusant Lady Kytson so far as it is in his power to do. He was tolerant of men's religious opinions, and as he incurred some suspicion by associating with Papists such as Baron Slavata in Italy, so he counted English Papists among his friends. One of them, Henry Constable, wrote *Foure Sonnets to Sir Philip Sidney's Soule* with no sense of incongruity, and John Davies of Hereford later enjoyed the hospitality of Wilton, transcribing in his beautiful hand Sidney's version of the Psalms. Papists, like Pagans, might write good poetry or hold valid critical opinions, whereas Puritans might be narrow-minded paperblurrers of the most contemptible sort. For himself, the hard clarity of Calvin's logic suited him, as did a similar quality in the mind of Ramus ; but in poetry he never made the mistake that so many Puritans make, of emphasizing the *utile*, the propaganda, at the expense of the *dulce*, the delight. To him poetry was first of all an aesthetic pleasure, and only because it was so did it bring instruction. 'And that mooving is of a higher degree then teaching, it may by this appeare, that it is wel nigh the cause and the effect of teaching.' Sidney was much too civilized a man to fall into the ancient heresy of demanding that poetry should be 'socially engaged', of insisting that the poet should accept his readers' dogmas and prejudices. Fanaticism in others could never disturb his self-control, that quality of character which Elizabethans admired beyond any other, and admired so much in Sidney himself.

There is nothing to show that Sidney was ever in any personal danger at the time of the Massacre, and Walsingham's house seems to have provided secure sanctuary for Englishmen then in Paris 'and even to many strangers then in peril and virtuously disposed'. One of them, Timothy Bright, a Cambridge physician, remembered seeing Sidney on that occasion, for the only time in his life, and twelve years later dedicated to him a medical book. There Bright recalls the high hopes men had already, in 1572, formed of Sidney, hopes which by 1584 Sidney had far surpassed (he says) by the achievements of his life.

There may have been no danger for Sidney, but Walsingham wisely ran no risks for him, and sent him out of Paris immediately, without waiting for instructions from England. These came in a letter from the Council of September 9th, requesting Walsingham to obtain a safe-conduct for Lord Wharton and Mr. Philip Sidney to return home. By then Sidney was already on his way to Germany in the company of the Dean of Winchester, Dr. John Watson, and he reached Frankfort safely. There, he went to live in the house of Andreas Wechel, another refugee from Paris, and one of the scholar-printers who are such admirable representatives of

Renaissance Europe. Possibly Sidney had already met Wechel in Paris, or perhaps Walsingham sent him to his house because his good friend Languet had gone there. However that may be, Sidney remained in Wechel's house throughout the autumn and winter, no doubt studying and learning much from the two scholars whose company he shared with Bryskett and Madox. Three of his letters from this time survive, all dated in March 1573, but they make no mention of his studies or of his companions. In one he refers to some 'works' that he is having sent to Leicester; but what these were cannot now be known.

Languet may already have left for the Imperial court in Vienna, where he was sent on business for the Elector of Saxony. Early in the summer Sidney joined him there, travelling by way of Heidelberg, Strasburg, and Basle, and staying some time in each city. At Heidelberg he first met Henri Estienne (or Henry Stephens as Englishmen chose to call him), another famous scholar-printer, and, as always, Sidney immediately impressed Estienne with his qualities — so much so that Estienne hurried after him to Strasburg in order to make him a present of a volume of Greek maxims written out in his own hand. Like Wechel, Estienne had succeeded a distinguished father in the task of editing and printing the newly discovered Greek and Latin texts; he had studied in Italy, and for a time worked in Venice with Paolo Manuzio; he had, as a student, enjoyed the patronage of Daneau who taught him his Greek at the Collège de France. Towards the end of his life he dissipated his energies in restless wanderings about Europe, became jealous and quarrelsome, and hindered rather than helped the cause of scholarship, especially by refusing access to his library to his brilliant son-in-law Isaac Casaubon. But at this time, in his middle forties, he was at the height of his powers, and eager to encourage and advise the gifted young Englishman. They met again in Vienna, and in a long dedication to Sidney of the Greek Testament which Estienne printed at Geneva in 1576, he relates the course of their friendship in terms which help to show how it was, as Spenser said of Sidney,

> That all mens hearts with secret ravishment
> He stole away, and weetingly beguyled.

The difficulty of describing charm such as Sidney possessed must be my excuse for a rather long extract from this dedication.

We are now in the third year since I made you a gift of a Greek book, or rather booklet, as a pledge of our then new friendship ; and now you shall have another Greek book as a small present from me to confirm that friendship. That first booklet I myself gave into your own hands at Strasburg ; but this small present I cannot give you in the same way for

> betwixt us be
> Many a shadowy mountain and sounding sea.

That other little book, written by the same hand that gave it into yours, pleased you very well : the novelty of the minute and elegant writing — which provided a sort of challenge to keenness of sight — seemed to make it acceptable. But I trust that this book will be no less welcome to you, although in print, for I think that the type in which it is set is not a bad imitation of my own hand. Besides, in that other book the workmanship could be said to surpass the matter, but in this, by contrast, the matter far surpasses the workmanship. For there you received excellent maxims certainly, and packed with wisdom — but with human wisdom ; whereas here you will receive not only wise maxims but those that were pronounced by the lips of Him who is Prince and Founder of Wisdom to all mankind. . . . But whatever the difference between that gift and this, both were prompted by the same mind, a mind most desirous of pleasing you and of showing its good will towards you, — and even more so now (to tell the truth) than it was then. For somehow or other every time I see you and enjoy your company I feel more and more affection towards you. I first chanced to see you at Heidelberg, and a little afterwards at Strasburg, and then again, after a long time, at Vienna ; but at Strasburg the love which I had felt for you at Heidelberg greatly increased, and at Vienna the love I felt for you at Strasburg grew still more. Not that it is at all surprizing that my love for you should have grown in this way, since your gifts of mind, which had aroused it, seemed also to have grown. And may they never cease to grow until you have achieved so much and so well that the fame of your England shall increase through you.

With such a tribute from such a man did Philip Sidney receive the first of the many books that were dedicated to him. Estienne assumes that Sidney would take note of the typography, as well as of the contents of the book : and for this edition he wrote the essay on the style of the Greek Testament which was formerly well known as a first attempt to apply standards of literary criticism to the Holy Scriptures. Perhaps he already recognized Sidney's interest in such matters, though it is unnecessary to suppose that Sidney prompted it.

Estienne continued to show Sidney proof of his friendship, as when he presented him with a copy of his great edition of Plato in 1578. In 1581 Estienne edited the works of two late Greek historians, Herodian and Zosimus — it was the *editio princeps* of Zosimus, of whom Gibbon observed that 'his prejudices and ignorance undoubtedly render him a very questionable judge of merit' — and dedicated the volume to Philip Sidney. He was concerned lest Sidney should be dissipating his intellectual gifts in the futile life of the court, and begins his dedication with three lines adapted from an epistle of Horace warning him against throwing away the gifts Apollo gave. The histories he sends will, he hopes, provide a series of cautionary tales, and will rescue him from 'those Sirens of the Court, to whom, as you well know, many of your age and of high birth fall prey'. The engaging naïvety that allowed Estienne to hope that Sidney would be turned from the frivolities of court life by the tedious and ancient scandals related by Herodian and Zosimus is very characteristic. Yet it is affecting to find a celebrated scholar caring so much for his young friend : wishing that he would concentrate on his studies, and struggle to preserve that 'literary leisure' which the ageing Estienne so seldom achieved.

While in Strasburg Sidney made the acquaintance of Johann Sturm, foremost of the educational pioneers of the sixteenth century, who had been a correspondent of Roger Ascham. Ascham called him 'the dearest frende I have out of England', and from him derived much of his own theories of education. Sturm knew Lord Burghley and took the opportunity to write to him by a messenger of Sidney's. In a letter of July 18th Burghley thanks Sturm for his kind reception of Philip Sidney, and clearly Sidney once again won the admiration and friendship of a distinguished scholar. His school at Strasburg was famous for more than forty years, and for a time Calvin himself had taught there. Sturm's purpose was to train a man to take his place in the government of the commonweal, like Elyot, or Dr. Arnold, but he was less concerned than Castiglione or Languet with the graces of personality. His practical outlook on education recommended him to Englishmen : Burghley, who was very doubtful about the value of a Continental tour, admired his work ; Thomas Hoby, the translator of Castiglione, went to hear him lecture in 1547; and when Philip Sidney's brother Robert went to the Continent in 1579 Languet arranged for him to stay with Sturm.

From Strasburg Sidney continued his journey to Vienna, travelling up the Rhine as far as Basle before turning east. Some time late in this summer Languet welcomed him to Vienna, where he had been for several months, and introduced him among his friends. Théophile de Banos was introduced to him by Languet as to 'the true image of nobility', and readily accepted him both as an admirer of Ramus and for his own qualities. Charles de L'Ecluse, at this time director of the Imperial Gardens, and one of the most famous botanists of the century, met Sidney through his old friend Languet, and the two became close friends and correspondents. Clusius (as he was known to the cosmopolitan world of learning) is fittingly commemorated in the name of the exquisite *Tulipa Clusiana*; for he was one of the first to grow tulips in Europe, and was almost certainly responsible for their introduction into England. In 1582 Richard Hakluyt wrote: 'Within these four years there have been brought into England from Vienna in Austria divers kinds of flowers called Tulipes and these and others procured there a little before from Constantinople by an excellent man called M. Carolus Clusius'. He had a vast correspondence throughout Europe, and we find him playing an important part in the introduction of the potato, of tobacco — he sowed the seed at Vienna in 1577 — and of the horse-chestnut. He noted first seeing oranges in Hungary, where Sidney may also have seen them, and his insatiable curiosity led him to experiment with seeds collected from every part of the opening world. He himself investigated the European flora and wrote many books, among them the *Historia rariorum plantarum*, which is one of the pioneer works of scientific botany. For de L'Ecluse was a botanist in the modern sense, not a herbalist: his interest was in plants as living creatures, and not merely for their usefulness to man.

Charles de L'Ecluse was Languet's contemporary and, like him, had studied under Melanchthon at Wittenberg where he too had been converted to Protestantism. His religion made his position at Vienna difficult when to the tolerant Maximilian succeeded the bigoted Rudolf II, but he remained there until 1588. He spent the last years of his life, from 1593

CHARLES de l'ECLUSE
Engraving by J. J. Boissard from *Icones diversorum hominum*, 1591

TWO *IMPRESE*
Drawings by Abraham Fraunce from Bodleain MS. Rawl. D. 345

till his death (at the age of eighty-three) in 1609, as Professor of Botany at Leiden. There, at the entrance to the Botanic Gardens, is a huge laburnum, supported in its old age by iron struts and crutches, which was planted by Charles de L'Ecluse in 1603. Probably it was one of the first laburnums to be seen in Northern Europe, and the ancient familiar tree is a suitable memorial to a man who did so much for the gardens of Holland and England.

In Vienna, Charles de L'Ecluse was especially friendly with the Emperor's physician, Crato von Krafftheim, to whom he had been introduced by Languet some years before. Crato was in his fifties at this time, and had been a pupil not only of Melanchthon but of Luther himself, so that his talk must have been of considerable interest to Sidney. He seems, like everyone else, to have enjoyed Sidney's company, and, after Sidney left Vienna, kept up a correspondence with him. In one of his letters, dated March 20th, 1575, he asks Sidney to send him any English book he may have on medicinal plants to add to his library. Unfortunately none of Sidney's letters to him are known to exist.

Sidney's escapade, when he went into Hungary with Charles de L'Ecluse, has been briefly mentioned. At the end of August he told Languet they would be away but three days, and Languet gave him a letter of introduction to Dr. Pür-kircher of Pressburg. But they stayed for at least a month : the first of Languet's extant letters to Sidney, dated September 22nd, 1573, which was sent to him at Wiener Neustadt, reveals Languet's pathetic awareness that Sidney had been playing truant.

> Like a bird that has broken out of its cage [he wrote] you make merry, and wander all over the place, forgetful perhaps, of your friends, and careless of the dangers which often happen in journeys of that kind. . . . I am sorry that you have no one with you who

might talk to you about different subjects on your journey, or instruct you about the manners and institutions of the people you visit, conduct you to learned men, and, when necessary, act as your interpreter. I could perhaps have procured you such a companion, had you told me what you were going to do.

No doubt it was to escape from this oppressive paternalism that Sidney broke out of the cage of Languet's affection, and it is good to think of him having a holiday for once. The visit seems to have been a success, for a few years later de L'Ecluse and Pürkircher told him that they had been drinking his health in Austrian wine and hoped shortly to do so in Hungarian, in commemoration of their previous travels. Languet continued to grumble about Sidney's unkindness on this occasion, and in a letter of February 13th, 1574, he admits his fear lest at Padua Sidney should have 'only some obscure nook left in your friendships for me. It would be better for me if you returned to your rough old gardeners, with whom you lived last year.' The phrase, which must allude to de L'Ecluse, suggests that Sidney may have lodged with him in the house of Dr. Aichholz, Chancellor of the University, who was always prompt to send friendly messages to Sidney in the letters written to him from Vienna.

The visit to Hungary was not entirely frivolous, for Sidney there met the tall and comely Lazarus Schuendi, who had been appointed commander-in-chief against the Turks in Hungary some years before by the Emperor Maximilian. He was a brave, intelligent soldier, and Languet hoped that Sidney might get his first experience of warfare under his command. Languet sent on a letter from Sidney to Schuendi in November of this year, with a request that Schuendi would acknowledge it. Sidney never served under him, but a few years later Count Hanau sent him Schuendi's treatise on the defence of the Empire against the Turks.

In Vienna, Sidney met the Florentine medallist, Antonio Abondio, who made a portrait of him which he kept at his house, where the sentimental Languet used to go to see it, 'and then immediately I pay the penalty for it, because it only renews the pain I felt when you went away'. On hearing this while in Venice, Sidney relieved Languet's distress by sending him his own copy of Abondio's portrait. Later Abondio seems to have made another portrait of Sidney, for in a postscript in a letter of Charles de L'Ecluse of December 4th, 1575, Abondio 'sends his humble duty, and tells me that he will complete your portrait as soon as he recovers from the illness which has afflicted him almost the whole of this last summer: he will send it to M. Languet for forwarding to you'. Unfortunately these portraits are no longer known. Other friends from this first stay in Vienna who continued to write to Sidney were Jean Vulcob and Bouchetell. Vulcob was at the Imperial court in the service of the King of France; and Bouchetell served Vulcob in some capacity.

From his first leaving England Sidney must have intended to visit Italy, and he would be encouraged to this by most of his new friends, who owed much of their own culture to their years in Italy. Languet, it is true, had misgivings and made Sidney promise not to visit Rome, where the Papacy would contaminate his soul, even if it did not endanger his body. This promise Sidney kept, though reluctantly, and he afterwards blamed Languet for his insistence. But he was not to be deterred from crossing the Alps by any warnings, not even by Burghley's distrust of Italy, where young men 'shall learn nothing but pride, blasphemy and atheism'. He must have decided on arrangements for his travel to Italy before setting out for Hungary, for when he returned, at the end of September, he heard from Languet that Thomas Coningsby, a friend who had recently joined him in Vienna, had already left for Venice.

CHAPTER 3

The Education of a Patron
II — Italy and the Imperial Court

SIDNEY stayed on for a few more weeks of the autumn of 1573 in Vienna until, about the end of October, after shedding many tears on parting with Languet, he left. In his *Pastorall Aeglogue* written after Sidney's death, Bryskett draws a charming picture of their travels together. Lycon recalls to Colin (Bryskett) the happy days when

> through many a hill and dale,
> Through pleasant woods, and many an unknowne way,
> Along the bankes of many silver streames,
> Thou with him yodest ; and with him didst scale
> The craggie rocks of th' Alpes and Appenine ;
> Still with the Muses sporting, while those beames
> Of virtue kindled in his noble brest,
> Which after did so gloriously forth shine.

How delightful it is to think of the little party riding over the Alps and coming down into Italy through the incomparable country of the Dolomites, brilliant now with the colours of autumn, and hearing for the first time on the lips of everyone they met what Shelley, on his first coming there, would call 'the clear and complete language of Italy'. So on down through the Veneto to Venice, the most human of all man's cities, where the pace of life is still the pace of man's walk, where almost all sounds are human sounds. The contrast with other cities was not then so great as it is now, when elsewhere we are hustled off the streets and squares by the loud and stinking traffic of the twentieth century ; but the excitement of coming across the water to Venice cannot but have stirred Sidney and his companions, at this time especially when the splendid victory of Lepanto was fresh in men's minds.

To Venice and Padua most Englishmen came at this time, partly because of the more liberal tradition there — the *Patavina libertas* was a long-standing glory of the University of Padua — and because Protestants could live unmolested by the Inquisition. Probably there were other reasons why the English then, and always, tended to prefer Venice to the other cities of Italy, and to have a taste for Venetian painting and Venetian glass above all other ; but these affinities are not easily to be discovered. Perhaps Englishmen saw in Venice a more gorgeous and colourful London, for it was not then ridiculous, when travel by water was normal and frequent, to compare the Thames with its palaces to the Grand Canal. Again, the Venetians, like the English, loved to build fine houses in the country to which they could retire from the city ; and so to Palladio, who worked in the rather English countryside of the Veneto, and not to Florentine or Roman or Neapolitan architects, the English architects of the succeeding age looked as their master.

Sidney must have arrived in Venice about the beginning of November, for on the 6th he signed a receipt for money paid to him by Thomaso Balbani, on a letter of credit from the Italian banker in London, Vetturelli. Nearly a year later, on October 21st, 1574, Vetturelli asked Sir Henry Sidney for payment of £190 advanced to Philip Sidney then going from Venice to Germany. Almost the whole of this time was spent in Venice or Padua, with a very brief excursion across Italy to Florence and Genoa. (Then, presumably, Bryskett scaled

65

with him the craggy Apennine.) There are thirteen letters of Sidney's preserved from this period, all of them addressed to Languet; but apart from these there are tantalizingly few records of what must surely have been one of the most important years in his life.

When he arrived he was welcomed by Thomas Coningsby and a cousin, Richard Shelley, who had been living in Venice long enough for the Venetians to transform his name, with characteristic gaiety, into Signor Conchiglia — Mr. Shellfish. In recommending Shelley to Languet a few months later Sidney described him as 'a man of erudition, who knows Greek, Latin and Italian well, and has some slight acquaintance with French; but he is sadly addicted to Popery'. Sidney was also kindly received by two men to whom Languet had given him introductions, the Count of Hanau and Arnaud du Ferrier, the French Ambassador. Du Ferrier was a cultivated man of liberal views, who became a friend of the great Venetian statesman and opponent of Papal domination, Paolo Sarpi, 'the most deep and general scholar of the world', as Sir Henry Wotton very properly called him. (There is no reason to suppose that Sidney ever met Sarpi, who was but two years his elder, and who at this time, immediately after his entry into the priesthood, was living at Milan.) Du Ferrier had friends also among the poets and critics in France, such as Guy du Faur de Pibrac, who reconstituted de Baïf's Academy a few years later as the Académie du Palais, and who in 1574 came with Henri III to Venice. Languet described Pibrac to Sidney as 'a man of such intelligence, learning and eloquence that his equal is not to be found in France', and urged him to overcome his antipathy to the defender of the Massacre of St. Bartholomew. They met a few times, and Pibrac spoke well of Sidney to Languet when he saw him the following year. Another Frenchman whom Languet wished

Sidney to meet in Venice was Pomponne de Bellièvre, who had organized the flight of Henri III from Poland, and became his Chancellor.

Wolfgang Zindelini, tutor to the Prince Palatine Christopher, was in Venice from 1573 to 1591, and he and Sidney became friendly at this time. Later he was a correspondent of Sir Henry Savile's and in 1646 Ludovicus Camerarius owned two volumes of his letters written during these years in Italy; they were never published and perhaps no longer exist. Zindelini, who came from Constance, seems at this time to have been enjoying the life of a student at Padua, where, so the German humanist poet Melissus suggests, a Paduan beauty named Laelia engaged much of his attention. To judge from Languet's reproachful letters to him, Sidney also enjoyed the pleasures of Italian social life: 'you have made so many elegant friends, whose manners please you more than mine'. Languet even teases Sidney by suggesting that he is becoming Italianized — 'you Italians', he says in one letter. Sidney was too courteous and too sensitive to remain impenetrably English among the Italians, and in a letter of advice to his brother about to travel he makes the point with his usual good sense: 'Marrie, my heresie is that the English behaviour is best in England, and the Italian in Italy'. In the letters which he addressed to the anxious and rather disapproving Languet there is, naturally enough, very little information about his way of living or of the friends he made, and we must gather what hints we can find elsewhere. Thus, in the same letter to his brother, he gives his impression of the Italians:

For the men you shall have there, although some in deede be excellentlie lerned, yett are they all given to soe counterfeit lerning, as a man shall learne of them more false groundes of things, then in any place ells that I do knowe, for from a tapster upwardes they

67

are all discoursers. In fine certaine qualitties, as Horsemanship, Weapons, Vauting, and such like, are better there then in those other countries, for others more sounde they do little excell neerer places.

'They are all discoursers', he says, but he does not mean by this that they are mere chatterboxes, for in another letter to his brother he defines 'discourser' — 'which name I give to who soever speakes *non simpliciter de facto, sed de qualitatibus et circumstantiis facti*'. In other words, he found, as others have found, that the Italians are naturally delightful talkers who do not restrict their conversational powers to a bald narration of facts : he is warning his brother not to sit open-mouthed listening to the Italians, but to keep his wits about him. He was but passing on the advice which Languet had given him soon after his arrival in Italy: 'You will admire the intelligence and sagacity of the people. They are in truth quick and intelligent, and yet most of them carry more on the surface than they have within, and they very generally spoil their attainments by display, and make themselves offensive.'

However much he enjoyed the company of Italians — and the constant companionship of the Italian Bryskett would help him to adapt himself quickly to their society — Sidney seems to have had more friends among the French and Germans in the cosmopolitan society of Venice and Padua. One Italian, Cesare Carafa, a Protestant member of the famous Neapolitan family, was a man of his own kind who remained a fast friend. He was something of a poet, who wrote in Latin and Spanish as well as in Italian ; and it was said of him that 'He applied his mind equally to the learning of knightly exercises, of the sciences, and of letters, and in all of them made such wonderful progress that he was held in the highest esteem by the principal men of letters of his day'. Carafa, like Sidney, no doubt modelled his conduct on Castiglione's ideal courtier, the pattern of the Renaissance gentleman. Through such friendships as this Sidney established a name in Italy, where the English were still customarily regarded as Northern barbarians. Bruno said that while he was in Milan he had heard of Sidney's reputation ; and Manelli, in dedicating to Robert Sidney his translation of Tacitus' *Agricola*, says that he has 'long known how high a place of honour the name of Sidney holds throughout Europe ; for courteous manners, great generosity, and the excellence of a mind filled with every kind of learning have made Sir Philip Sidney known in Italy, France and Germany'.

We hear of few Italian friends, and Sidney admitted that he had made none in his first two months in Venice ; and yet he seems to have had access later to the very exclusive ruling society. He was friendly with at least one member of the Venetian family of Grimani, to which two sixteenth-century Doges belonged. He heard the news of the defeat of Count Lewis of Nassau in April 1574 from the Council of Ten, who in the same month granted to him, Bryskett, and three servants a licence to carry arms in Venetian territories. However, Sidney refused to be impressed by 'all the magnificent magnificences of all these magnificos', and, though he gladly acknowledged the supremacy of the Italians in painting, is disappointingly silent about the architecture and painting of Venice. We should be rash to assume either indifference or ignorance because in writing to Languet he chiefly discussed politics : we might as well conclude that Languet, whose portrait had been painted by Titian, cared nothing for painting.

When he had been some weeks in Italy Sidney promised, in answer to Languet's request, to send his portrait : in a later letter he says that he is still undecided whether to give the commission to Tintoretto or Paolo Veronese 'who hold

F   69

by far the highest place in the art'. (Titian was still alive but at his great age would probably have seemed unsuited to paint the nineteen-year-old Sidney.) In the end Sidney decided that Veronese should do the portrait, and he gave his first sitting on returning from Padua to Venice. On February 26th, 1574, he wrote to tell Languet of it : 'This day Paolo Veronese has begun my portrait, for which I must stay here two or three days longer'.

When the portrait was finished, Sidney sent it to Languet in the care of his cousins Richard Shelley and Robert Corbett, and on June 11th Languet wrote to acknowledge its receipt.

I kept it with me some hours to feast my eyes on it, but my appetite was rather increased than diminished by the sight. It seems to me to represent someone like you rather than you yourself, and, at first, I thought it was your brother. Most of your features are well drawn, but it is far more youthful than it ought to be. I should think you were not unlike it in your twelfth or thirteenth year.

A year later, when he had again seen Sidney, Languet showed more appreciation of the portrait.

As long as I enjoyed the sight of you, I made no great account of the portrait which you gave me, and scarcely thanked you for so beautiful a present. I was led by regret for you, on my return from Frankfort, to place it in a frame and fix it in a conspicuous place. When I had done this, it appeared to me to be so beautiful, and so strongly to resemble you, that I possess nothing which I value more. M. Vulcob is so struck with its elegance that he is looking for an artist to copy it. The painter has represented you a little sad and thoughtful. I should have been better pleased if your face had worn a more cheerful look when you sat for your portrait.

Such were Languet's comments on what must surely have been the finest portrait painted of any Englishman of the sixteenth century ; but it is lost now, or obscured somewhere under the title of 'Portrait of a Young Man', and we cannot judge for ourselves. Neither do we know whether the copy

Vulcob wished to have done was ever executed, or if so, where it is. If either exists, it is most likely to be in France; for Languet, who was unmarried, died in the house of du Plessis-Mornay, who was a friend and admirer of Sidney, and Vulcob, who had known Sidney in Vienna, and to whom du Ferrier had written enthusiastically about Sidney from Venice, was a French courtier. We may, at first, be a little surprised that Sidney preferred to have his portrait painted by the great decorative painter Veronese, who painted few portraits, rather than by the more sombre and serious Tintoretto, who painted so many; but his choice shows his or his friends' perception, for his fair and rather feminine complexion and his very youthful looks would admirably suit the style of Veronese.

For most of his time in Italy Sidney was studying hard, especially at the University of Padua. It is not possible to discover whether he matriculated, since the records for this period are lost; but the point is of little importance. He learnt to speak Italian well, which seemed to Languet an absurd and unnecessary accomplishment for an Englishman; but German he could not, or would not, learn, in spite of Languet's advice.

It has a sort of harshness — you know very well what I mean — so that at my age I have no hope that I shall ever master it, even so as to understand it; nevertheless, to please you, I will sometimes, especially at dinner, practise it with my good Delius.

Matthew Delius of Hamburg was the author of a Latin poem in four books on wit and elegance on speaking, who was at the time studying in Italy. I do not know that he ever overcame Sidney's dislike of German. Sidney continued his study of Greek, chiefly in order to read Aristotle, of whose works he at this time considered the *Politics* to be most important, though a few years later he told his brother that the *Ethics* was the beginning and foundation of all. He does not refer to the *Poetics* in his letters, but he knew the book well, and probably heard Zabarella, Professor of Logic at Padua, lecturing on it. Zabarella held the view that poetics is an instrument of civil philosophy, whose end is to make others good. This opinion was certainly shared by Sidney and Spenser.

Of the books which he read in Italy Sidney mentions several in his letters. They include studies of the Venetian government and constitution, which was generally considered to be a model for other states, though, as Sidney with his usual astuteness recognized, their 'good laws and customs we can hardly proportion to ourselves because they are quite of a contrary government'. (But it was the one Italian government which he advised his brother to study.) He also read Tarchagnota's *History of the World*, and a book on the Council of Trent, of which he sent two copies to Languet. His interests were primarily in the politics and diplomacy of Europe ; or at least this is the main topic of his correspondence with Languet, since it was on such matters that Languet could give him most valuable instruction. But he mentions, even to Languet, other works that he read : collections of letters by famous Italians, Paolo Manuzio, Bernardo Tasso, Bembo and Tolomei, and Lorenzo de' Medici ; and books on *imprese*, those devices for which he himself later became renowned among Englishmen. In one of these books, Ruscelli's *Le Imprese Illustri*, he would see the *impresa* of Sir Richard Shelley, the Grand Prior of the Knights of St. John, and uncle to Sidney's friend of the same name, who perhaps first awoke his interest in devices.

He asked Languet to obtain the French translation of Plutarch's *Lives*, but Languet hesitated to borrow Vulcob's copy 'because I see that he is his favourite author', as he was of many a Renaissance courtier studying to emulate the heroes of Greece and Rome. (Vulcob presumably had a copy of Amyot's translation from which the noble English version of North was made a few years later.) Languet advised Sidney to read Cicero's Letters, both to improve his Latin style and for their revelation of the causes which led to the fall of the Republic : this he promised to do, and to practise his Latin by translating Cicero first into French, then from French into English, and finally into Latin 'by a sort of perpetual motion'. But though his Latin style is fluent and graceful enough, Sidney, like most Englishmen, found great difficulty in accommodating his pronunciation of it to Continental fads. This was of the first importance when Latin was the common language of Europe, and Languet strongly recommended him to improve his pronunciation. Twelve years later he seems still to have been troubled by it, and asked the advice of the famous Latinist Lipsius, who wrote for him and dedicated to him a short treatise on the subject. With such seriousness did the scholars of Europe concern themselves in the education of Philip Sidney.

Sidney does not write of his reading in Italian poetry or criticism, though his wide knowledge of both is clear from the *Apologie for Poetrie* and other writings of his own, in prose and in verse. He was the first Englishman to make mention of Dante's Beatrice ; his *Arcadia* owed not a little to Sannazaro's ; he seems to have had a special liking for Tasso's poetry. He may have met Tasso in Padua at the Accademia degli Animosi but Zouch's assertion that Sidney knew Tasso cannot now be substantiated. The prestige that Italian literature had among Sidney's friends was considerable. There was little reason for him to tell Languet that he was reading these things, or to fill his letters with descriptions of Venetian palazzi and paintings. Languet, who had studied at Padua, and who had probably read the *Orlando Furioso* before Sidney was born, did not expect such matter to occupy Sidney's letters : he had some prejudices against Italian civilization, and he supposed that Sidney would be chiefly concerned with more serious studies than poetry or music or painting. And so, no doubt, he was.

Sidney was joined in Venice by Robert Corbett, a cousin whom he had known since his schooldays, and whom he now called his very greatest friend. Unlike his other cousin Shelley, Corbett was 'of the right side in religion'. Shelley's addiction to Popery did not prevent his being a loyal subject of Queen Elizabeth : he used to send home from Venice information on the movements of the Spaniards, and he returned freely to England in 1582. (He was of Michelgrove in Sussex, and of the same family as the poet.) When these two, Shelley and Corbett, carried the Veronese portrait to Languet in April 1574, Languet found Corbett all that Sidney had said : loyal, sensible, modest, sincere, and devoted to Sidney. He did not take so kindly to the recusant Shelley. Another Englishman whom Sidney knew in Venice was Edward, Lord Windsor, who died there in January 1575 : his monument is still to be seen in the church of SS. Giovanni e Paolo. Cesare Carafa knew him and wrote to ask Sidney to convey his condolences to the family in England.

Much of what was best in the education Sidney received in Italy must have derived from hours of talk with friends such as these — men mostly of his own age and of similar tastes, enjoying the liberty of growing up away from the constant tutelage of their elders. We cannot describe these things as we can describe a formal education, but we should not therefore underestimate the value of such companionship to a man of Sidney's quality. Languet gave him sound advice on this too : telling him that since his own nature was somewhat serious, he should choose companions who

could make him more gay and lively. He was glad when
Sidney moved to Padua, because in the University town,
he believed, there would be more suitable companions to
talk to about his studies. These included, besides languages,
music, astronomy, geometry, history, and ethics. Languet
knew that Sidney had a special interest in history, 'by which
more than anything else men's judgments are shaped'; and
he considered that a study of 'that branch of moral philosophy
which treats of justice and injustice' would be of the greatest
use to him. Sidney already knew Greek and Latin, French
and Italian, and at some time or other, though this may not
have been until later, he learnt Spanish.

This facility in languages, which only deserted Sidney
when he was confronted by the German concatenation of
consonants, must have enabled him to profit from the lectures
he heard, and from the conversation of the elegant Italian
friends whom he met in Padua. His natural seriousness, his
knowledge that he must learn fast, since he must soon (as
Languet unnecessarily reminded him) tear himself away from
literary leisure, would ensure that he wasted very little time
in frivolity : we may be permitted to hope that he found time
enough to enjoy himself. And indeed we need scarcely
doubt it, for if gravity was a quality in him that Languet
and Greville especially noted, his writings never leave the
impression of a solemn, unsmiling man. Far from it, for
there is always the hint of a smile behind his seriousness,
which his friends in Italy must have known as a part of the
delight of his company :

> To hear him speake and sweetly smile,
> You were in Paradise the while.

Not intellectual gifts alone, but the irresistible personal
grace that accompanied them, made men seek his friendship
wherever he went : as Languet told him, 'so long as you

remain true to yourself, wherever you go you will find men to love you and show you kindness'. It was no more than the truth ; but whereas in France and Germany he had been in the company of men much older than himself, who, recognizing his qualities, sought quite disinterestedly to share with him the learning of their experience, in Italy he was generally in the company of his own contemporaries, and learning with them. In consequence, we have less information about his year in Italy, because young men in their early twenties are as interested in themselves as in their most gifted companions, and are more careless about writing letters, or recording their impressions : the older men, in France, and Germany, and Austria, remembering their experience of thirty or forty years, at once recognized in Philip Sidney qualities that were unique.

In October 1574, a few weeks before his twentieth birthday, Sidney left Italy to return to Vienna. He was taken ill immediately after his arrival, but soon recovered under the tender care of Languet, and set out on a visit to Poland. He was back in Vienna by November 27th when he wrote to Leicester, giving him the latest news from the Imperial court, where he remained throughout the winter. Another young Englishman who was later to make a name for himself was in Vienna at this time, Edward Wotton, and Sidney and he became good friends, learning the finer points of horsemanship together from the Emperor's riding-master, John Pietro Pugliano.

Skilful horsemanship was greatly admired in Sidney's generation, and the mastery of it was one of the necessary accomplishments of a gentleman. Sidney shared this opinion, naturally enough: he advised his brother Robert to read two Italian books on the subject, and to 'mark the bitting, saddling, and curing of horses' — a characteristic note of that practical thoroughness with which he studied any subject. In the *Arcadia* Sidney portrays the ideal of horsemanship which he learnt from Pugliano.

But he (as if Centaurlike he had bene one peece with the horse) was no more moved, then one is with the going of his owne legges : and in effect so did he command him, as his owne limmes, for though he had both spurres and wande, they seemed rather markes of soveraintie, then instruments of punishment ; his hand and legge (with most pleasing grace) commanding without threatning, & rather remembring then chastising, at lest if sometimes he did, it was so stolen, as neyther our eyes could discerne it, nor the horse with any chaunce did complaine of it, he ever going so just with the horse, either foorth right, or turning, that it seemed as he borrowed the horses body, so he lent the horse his minde : in the turning one might perceive the bridle-hand somthing gently stir, but indeed so gently, as it did rather distill vertue, then use violence. Him self (which me thinkes is straunge) shewing at one instant both steadines & nimblenes ; somtimes making him turne close to the ground, like a cat, when scratchingly she wheeles about after a mouse : sometimes with a little more rising before, now like a Raven leaping from ridge to ridge, then like one of Dametas kiddes bound over the hillocks : and all so done, as neither the lustie kinde shewed any roughnesse, nor the easier any idlenesse : but still like a well obeyed maister, whose becke is enough for a discipline, ever concluding ech thing he did with his face to me-wards, as if thence came not onely the beginning, but ending of his motions.

Sidney's own skill was yet another cause for the admiration with which he was regarded. Christopher Clifford dedicated to Sidney his book *The Schoole of Horsemanship* 'both because of your great knowledge and experience in Horsemanshippe, and in all other vertues, whereby ye draw to you the harts of everie one that knowes you, and also for your speciall curtesie showed unto me'. Again, in the proud sonnet with which Sidney celebrated his success in a Tournament held in 1581, he tells how

Horsemen my skill in horsemanship advance,

77

though he attributes his success to Stella's presence. But however much he delighted in his horsemanship, and in men's praise of it, he never exaggerated its importance, and laughed at the excessive enthusiasm which he had observed in Pugliano. This sane and balanced judgment of his, as much as the natural grace with which he achieved whatever he attempted, won the admiration of his fellows. Probably no compliment would have pleased him more than that of an anonymous eighteenth-century writer : 'It may be justly said, without Hyperbole or Fiction, as it was of Cato Uticensis, That he seemed to be born to that only which he went about'.

During these months in Vienna Sidney must have resumed his friendships with such men as Charles de L'Ecluse and Théophile de Banos, Crato von Krafftheim and Antonio Abondio, but since he was every day in Languet's company there is none of that invaluable correspondence to inform us of his life there. Late in February he accompanied Languet for a few days' visit to Prague. From there Languet sent him with a letter of introduction to his master, Augustus, Elector of Saxony, in which he mentions Sidney's high birth, and the favourable reception he had had at the hands of the Emperor. He adds : 'he has an excellent mind, and almost more experience in affairs than his years can support'.

The time had now come for Sidney to return to England, and Languet wrote other letters on his behalf — to Dr. Ursinus at Heidelberg, to Count Lewis of Wittgenstein at the court of the Elector Palatine, to Wechel and to Dr. Glausburg. (Ursinus, who was a professor of theology at Heidelberg, was an austere scholar who inscribed over the door of his study : *Amice, quisquis huc venis, aut agito paucis, aut abi, aut me laborantem adjuva.*) Languet lent him money for his journey, and Sidney, to Languet's distress, insisted that Edward Wotton also should sign the bond. Sidney was in

Prague on March 2nd, when he sent Thomas Jordan some Latin poems that he had promised him, written by someone whose name he did not know but whom he believed to be a Frenchman. (Jordan was a Polish physician, at this time perhaps the chief medical authority in the service of the Emperor and living at Brno.) On March 5th Sidney reached Dresden, where Edward Wotton joined him for the journey home. At Strasburg Sidney renewed his acquaintance with Sturm and Lobetius, a learned lawyer well known to many Englishmen, including Sir Henry Sidney. He revisited Wechel at Frankfort, and at the time of the Fair the devoted Languet came there from Prague to see him once more. The Count of Hanau, who had had to leave Vienna in the autumn while Sidney was in Poland, had written to him to say he hoped they might all three meet there, and probably he too came to say farewell.

Sidney reached England on the last day of May 1575, almost exactly three years after leaving home. He made it one of his first duties to write to the Count, to give him news of his safe arrival, and of his finding his family and friends in good health, 'since I cannot but think that any good news about my affairs will be welcome and pleasing to you'. In this same year, Thomas Drant, in a poem addressed to Leicester, refers to the high hopes with which Sidney was welcomed home from his Continental tour :

> Sic redeat toto laudatus ab orbe Philippus,
> Spes generis tanti, praestans Sydneia proles.

Philip Sidney was still six months short of his twenty-first birthday, but Drant's claim is no more than the truth : that the world united in his praise.

We can scarcely hope, after nearly four centuries, to discover how the raw and inexperienced boy who set out for

France in the summer of 1572 could have been so rapidly transformed into a man with a European reputation. It is simply a fact which we must accept. After all, even now, most of us, if asked to name one man to represent the ideal pattern of the Englishman, would name Sir Philip Sidney; and it was so that his contemporaries, whether at home or abroad, regarded him. Thus when Lipsius first met him, a few years later, he observed : *'Anglia est flos regionum, et tu flos Angliae'* — 'the flower of England', and, truly, for all the depth of his learning in the culture of Europe, he was always essentially English. He sought, like so many of his contemporaries throughout Europe, to be the complete man, the Courtier of the Renaissance. Castiglione's famous book, as well as the books of Guazzo, della Casa, and others, was an essential part of his education. Probably he had read it in Hoby's translation before ever he left England, and if so he would have learnt that among the graces of a courtier must be good taste and a critical understanding of letters ; also, if he were favoured by the Muses, the accomplishments of a poet.

Back in England again, with the good-will of Protestant Europe, and 'the hope of all learned men', Sidney wished and expected to engage in practical affairs, to shape to virtuous action the earthly learning and experience which he had now acquired. Languet wrote imploring him not to give up his Latin studies amid all the time-wasting temptations at court, even though to continue them was generally regarded as pointless for a man of his position. He was almost at once taken up with the magnificent Progress of Queen Elizabeth of that summer, during which she was entertained by the Earl of Leicester from July 9th to 27th at Kenilworth Castle. Laneham's enthralled and breathless account of the entertainment still makes it vivid to us, in a way that George Gascoigne's more formal record of his own compositions cannot. Sidney must have compared this reception of the Queen with the Venetians' welcome to Henri III the year before. Then there had been water-pageants and ceremonial speeches; many complimentary poems were addressed to the King, and a tragedy by Frangipani was performed in the Sala del Gran Consiglio. One of the poems, a Capitolo by Andrea Mene-chini, was dedicated to Sidney's friend Arnaud du Ferrier with what must be the greatest proliferation of superlatives ever known. Most splendid of all was the triumphal arch erected on the Lido and painted with ten pictures by Tintoretto and Paolo Veronese. The *Princely Pleasures* cannot but have seemed naïve and provincial after this, with the jog-trot verses of Gascoigne, Hunnis, and Ferrers instead of sonnet, capitolo, and canzone; with the Coventry play, 'Good bangz a both sidez', instead of a tragedy on the classical model. They were a characteristically English mixture, where Hercules is accompanied by 'armonious blasters' eight foot tall carrying five-foot trumpets; where King Arthur and the Lady of the Lake go cheek by jowl with Jupiter and Pallas; and Triton's wreathed horn is 'foormed of a wrinkld wealk'. Besides, to contrast with these more sophisticated parts of the proceedings, were the Bottom-like rustics at a country wedding; Captain Cox with his marvellous repertory of songs and stories, who 'at afternoonz can talk az much without book, az ony inholder betwixt Brainford and Bag-shot, what degree soever he be'; and, most hilarious of all, the singer Goldingham, supposed to represent Arion on a dolphin's back, suddenly finding himself hoarse, tearing off his disguise, and crying out that 'he was none of Arion, not he, but even honest Harry Goldingham'. How Shakespeare would have loved all this! And Shakespeare, then eleven years old, might very well have been brought over those few miles from Stratford to see the Queen. No doubt Sidney, like the Queen, laughed at the clowns ; but perhaps, remembering Venice and his foreign friends, he winced a little.

Sir Henry and Lady Sidney were at this time in attendance on the Queen — Laneham sometimes entertained Lady Sidney in her chamber with dancing, playing, and singing ; and with them was their thirteen-year-old daughter Mary, whom the Queen had invited to court after the death, early in the year, of her younger sister Ambrosia. Mary was already attracting the attention of poets, one of whom addressed her at Woodstock (where the court went in September) in lines that are better prophecy than poetry :

> Though young in years, yet old in wit, a gest due to your race,
> If you hold on as you begin, who is't you'll not deface ?

A little before this Sir Henry had returned, very reluctantly, to Ireland as Lord Deputy. Philip accompanied him across England, and father and son were entertained with 'wine and cakes and other things' to the cost of 7/2 by the Corporation of Shrewsbury, who at the same time welcomed Robert Corbett on his return from the Continent.

After seeing his father off, Philip Sidney returned to London for the autumn, and spent his time in the social round, to the neglect, among other things, of his correspondence with Languet. Not until late in November did he find time to write to Languet, excusing himself on the grounds of the Queen's Progress and his father's departure. As nearly three months had passed since these excuses could even have appeared plausible, Languet was not much mollified, and very justly reproached Sidney.

Had you sacrificed one dance a month you could have satisfied us abundantly. Last year you were here with us for only three or four months. Recall to mind how many excellent authors you read, and how much good you derived from reading them : if in such a short time you were able to learn so much that was of value in the right ordering of your life, surely the memory of it should have withheld you from drowning yourself in mere pleasures.

The undertone of disappointment in this letter must have touched Sidney, and it was clearly necessary that someone should remind him of his abilities and opportunities. For, after three years of intensive study abroad, and absence from his English friends, it must have been tempting to relax, and to give himself up to amusement.

Other friends wrote to him in London, addressing their letters to Leicester House in the Strand, where he seems to have spent most of his time. De Banos wrote to him about the dedication of his Life of Ramus, which was published in January 1576; Charles de L'Ecluse wrote several times, and on March 19th sent him a book on the plants of Spain, finding it again necessary to complain of Sidney's neglect of his correspondence; Cesare Carafa wrote from Venice; Wacker, diplomat, dramatist, and Latin poet, from Vienna; Joachim Moller from Prague. Moller had met Sidney in Vienna in 1574, and Languet recommended him now as a learned and pious man whose knowledge of German affairs might be useful to the Queen. Languet's letters were full of political news, of his hopes and fears for the Protestants. His devotion to Sidney led him to advise him both on his studies and on his conduct to those in authority at home.

See that you cultivate Cecil's friendship: he is fond of you, and will make everything easier for you. The best way for you to win his goodwill, is to love his children — or at least to pretend that you love them. But remember that he is an astute old man, who has learnt much from long experience of public life, and will easily see through the pretences of young men.

Sometimes, as here, the advice has a worldly cynicism, which, to a less honest generation, may seem surprising in its candour.

Sidney had intended to revisit Paris before returning to

England, but changed his plans at the last moment, and went instead through the Low Countries. But now he received an invitation to Paris from no less a person than the Duc d'Alençon, who suggested that he should stay some months there in order to study the French as he had studied the Germans and Italians. Languet advised him to accept, chiefly (as it seems) because this would give them a chance of meeting again ; but Sidney declined, and never visited France after the Massacre. It is difficult to imagine Sidney as the guest of the unsatisfactory creature whose suit for Queen Elizabeth a few years later moved him to such eloquent indignation ; but Alençon was a poet and a patron of painters and sculptors, and the compliment of an invitation from the heir-presumptive to the throne of France is evidence of Sidney's repute.

There is little to show how Sidney occupied his time during the winter and spring after his return from the Continent. About this time he won the friendship of Walter, Earl of Essex, who had known Sidney since childhood and may have seen him in the Queen's train at Chartley the previous summer. Sidney's first meeting with Penelope Devereux, the Earl's twelve-year-old daughter, meant little to him, as he regretfully admits in the thirty-third sonnet of *Astrophel and Stella*. She was so young, even in an age when Juliet at fourteen could be reproached by her mother for being slow to marry ; and Sidney failed to see the woman's beauty in the child's face. But Essex had begun to think of Sidney as a future son-in-law when he took him to Ireland, where he was sent as Earl Marshal the following summer. Sidney joined his father in Connaught some time in July and was with him when news was brought of the sudden illness of the Earl. Essex sent for Philip Sidney, but dying before he reached Dublin, left him this last message :

Tell him I send him nothing, but I wish him well, and so well that if God do move both their hearts I wish that he might match with my daughter. I call him son ; he is so wise, so virtuous and godly ; and if he go on in the course he hath begun, he will be as famous and worthy a gentleman as ever England bred.

Sidney returned to England to attend the Earl's funeral, which took place at Carmarthen on November 26th. The proposed marriage between Philip Sidney and Penelope Devereux was a matter of public interest, but we need not suppose that Sidney himself seriously considered it. Essex had stressed the importance of affection between the two parties — by no means a usual assumption in a society where marriages were regarded as contracts between families rather than individuals — and to the sophisticated Sidney Penelope must still have seemed but a little girl. Also, from certain observations of Languet's, it appears that he was anxious to remain free for some time yet of the ties of marriage.

In Ireland, Sidney had his first brief experience of campaigning, and saw his father's vigorous prosecution of the war against the rebels. Personal experience at this time, for he was never again in Ireland, probably taught him that in Ireland 'truelie learning goeth very bare, yet are theyr Poets held in a devoute reverence'. The paradox fascinated him, for to the rationalistic mind of the Renaissance poetry was a privilege of learning, whether in its writing or its enjoyment. Sidney feels that he must apologize for being moved by the old ballad of the Percy and Douglas, 'which being so evill apparelled in the dust and cobwebbes of that uncivill age, what would it work trimmed in the gorgeous eloquence of Pindar ? ' The same problem was exercizing Addison's mind nearly a century and a half later, but, less willing than Sidney to admit to perplexity, he seeks to satisfy a classical taste by a comparison of the ballad with Virgil's *Aeneid*.

I will not claim that Sidney gave much thought to poetry

G

or learning in the eighteen months that followed his return to England. He was in need of relaxation and found it in the vivid life of the court. He neglected his correspondence so shamefully that his friends on the Continent were perplexed and saddened, but Languet's suggestion that his engaging manners had been insincere provoked an indignant retort. For some men, delight in the company and conversation of their fellows seems to inhibit correspondence with friends who are elsewhere; while others, too shy or perhaps too slow to be good conversationalists, much prefer the private intercourse of letters. One of Sidney's acquaintances, Jacobus Monau of Bratislava, was (we are told) 'born not merely to maintain, but to strengthen friendships by his assiduity in writing letters'. No one would have said the same of Sidney, yet everyone was immediately captivated by him when he came and talked. But the life of the court — in 1576 he was appointed Cup-bearer to the Queen — could not satisfy a man of his gifts. He looked for a post more worthy of his ambition, and the death of the Emperor Maximilian in the autumn of the year provided an occasion for serious employment. Sidney was chosen by the Queen to go on an embassage to the new Emperor Rudolph, to condole with him on the death of his father, and to congratulate him on his accession; on the way he was also to condole with the Elector Palatine, Lewis, and his brother Casimir, on the death of their father.

The Queen's choice was probably determined by her knowledge that when Sidney had spent some months in Vienna he had made a favourable impression on the old Emperor, and had shown an intelligent understanding of diplomacy. The mission on which he was now to be sent was largely ceremonial, but Sidney would be expected to report on all he learnt during his travels, as were many who travelled even on private business. He was also to explore the possibilities of a Protestant League. The occasion would be the first practical test of the training that he had received, chiefly under the guidance of Languet, and it was of the utmost importance to his future career that he should perform his duties with dignity and wisdom. Preparations for the mission took up the months of December and January, and the visit that he made to Dr. Dee on January 16th in company with the Earl of Leicester and Edward Dyer may have been in some way connected with these. From him Sidney and Dyer at one time took lessons together in chemistry. For, though Dee's restless intellectual curiosity led him into the outlandish regions of astrology (of which Sidney was contemptuous), it also made him the most eminent mathematician and geographer of his time.

The Instructions to Sidney were drawn up and dated February 7th: a fortnight later his father gave him £350 to supplement the Queen's allowance. Soon afterwards he left for Antwerp, accompanied by his chosen friends, Fulke Greville and Edward Dyer, and by two older counsellors, Sir Henry Lee and Sir Jerome Bowes, both of whom were experienced diplomats. Lee was the Queen's Champion, and nephew to the poet Sir Thomas Wyatt; Bowes was a Puritan of indomitable temper, who had been on a diplomatic mission to Moscow. Sidney was away from England for a little over three months, and though the diplomatic results of his mission do not here concern us, the renewal of old friendships, and the forming of new, are of importance. From Brussels, where the English Ambassador, Dr. Thomas Wilson, had made arrangements for the party's welcome, Sidney went to Louvain to meet the gallant and treacherous Don John of Austria. Don John was at first condescending in his manner to the young Englishman, but was soon won over by Sidney's charm, so that, in Fulke Greville's words, 'the beholders

87

wondered to see what ingenuous tribute that brave and high-minded Prince paid to his worth'.

Sidney went through Heidelberg, where he saw Prince Casimir but not the Elector, and on to Prague, where the Imperial court was then in being, and where he had audience of the Emperor on Easter Monday. In Prague he found Edmund Campion, whom he had known at Oxford, and who was now Professor of Rhetoric in the Jesuit College. Sidney went to hear him preach, and also met him privately, with the result that Campion absurdly hoped that Sidney might be converted to Roman Catholicism, as he disclosed in a letter written to John Bavand.

A few months ago Philip Sidney came from England to Prague as Ambassador, magnificently provided. He had much conversation with me — I hope not in vain, for to all appearances he was most eager. I commend him to your sacrifices, for he asked the prayers of all men, and at the same time put into my hands some alms to be distributed to the poor for him, which I have done. Tell this to Dr Nicholas Sanders, because if any one of the labourers sent into this vineyard from the Douai seminary has an opportunity of watering this plant, he may watch the occasion for helping a poor wavering soul. If this young man, so wonderfully beloved and admired by his countrymen, chances to be converted, he will astonish his noble father, the Deputy of Ireland, his uncles the Dudleys, and all the young courtiers, and Cecil himself.

The astonishment of Campion himself, if his judgment had not been clouded by his own conversion, and by the second-hand verbiage which it seems to have imposed upon his style, would have been no less: he might then have recognized in Sidney a leader of the Puritans, using all his tact and charm to learn from Campion's own lips how far conversion had led him on the path of disloyalty.

For some twenty days Languet was in Sidney's company, travelling with him from Prague to Nuremberg, Heidelberg,

and Cologne, where they parted, but with a firm promise
from Languet that he would visit England again before long.
Languet now for the first time met Greville and Dyer, and
was delighted with them, if only because they shared his
affection for Sidney. Languet introduced to him the younger
Joachim Camerarius, physician, botanist, and man of letters.
Sidney much enjoyed his company, as he often told Languet,
and they continued to correspond in later years. Philip
Camerarius, a younger brother of Joachim, has preserved
the record of a conversation with Sidney during his visit
to Prague, when 'as one day he talked privately with me and
some others, he entertained us with very memorable discourses'. Unfortunately the conversation which most clearly
remained in the mind of the historian was on the subject of the
absence of wolves from England. Various absurd suggestions
had been made, but Sidney ascribed the absence of wolves,
in a matter-of-fact account, to a law which allowed certain
convicted persons to redeem themselves by the slaughter of
so many wolves. Sidney also talked to them about Ireland,
and his conversation, we are told,

was verie pleasing to the companie that sate at table with him, and
no man would make any question thereof, especially when we saw
it approved by Hubert Languet, a man of most exquisit judgment,
and exceeding wel travelled in the knowledge of things, and in the
affairs of the world.

What a charming picture it is, the old and respected Languet
smiling his approval of the eager and resplendent Sidney,
while the company listen to a sensible explanation of the
absence of wolves from England : we must be grateful even
for this glimpse.

One book was dedicated to Sidney at this time, a somewhat tedious anthology, in four books, of topographi-
cal Latin verse, edited by Lambert Daneau, and entitled

Geographiae Poeticae. Daneau was the son of the Greek scholar whose patronage of Henri Estienne has been mentioned: he was at this time living at Geneva, where he would hear of Sidney from Estienne. The rather feeble verses of dedication imply that he had not met Sidney ; but they may have known each other later in Leiden, where Daneau went in 1581 as Professor of Theology. Presumably, therefore, it was Sidney's reputation as a patron of learning that led Daneau to dedicate the work to him. He sent Languet two copies to be forwarded, with a request that Sidney would acknowledge them. Languet, in his covering letter to Sidney, says that he does not know Daneau at all, but that when he and Sidney were in Germany in the spring of 1577 he had heard that Daneau intended to dedicate to him a commentary on the second Epistle of St. Paul to the Corinthians. This Languet had managed to prevent, because he knew that Daneau's theological opinions would not be approved at the English court.

Daneau was far from being a polished Latinist, but the verses of Paulus Melissus, the Protestant German scholar and courtier, may stand comparison with those of any of the humanists of the Renaissance. Melissus, whose real name was Paul Schede, might have known Sidney in Paris, but more probably only now met him at Heidelberg, where he was librarian to the Elector Palatine, and thus in charge of the finest library then existing in Germany. Certainly the earlier of his two poems addressed to Sidney dates from 1577, and there is no mention of Sidney in the editions of the *Schediasmata* published in 1574 and 1575. Melissus was born at Melrichstadt in Franconia in 1539, had studied at Jena, and afterwards at Vienna under Jean Sambuc. He was an accomplished musician, and even before first visiting France had been much interested in the Pléiade's experiments with the musical settings of poems. Sambuc recommended him to Ramus, by whom he was introduced to Ronsard, whose poetry he already much admired. On Ronsard's death Melissus, who was at the time in London, composed an Ode in his memory. He was a friend and correspondent of the musicians Claude Goudimel, who was murdered in the Massacre of St. Bartholomew, and Orlando di Lasso, who worked at the Bavarian court. In 1572 he published a translation of the Psalms into German, arranged for French chants. He was a gifted and cultivated man, with many literary friends, especially in France, and was the first to interpret Ronsard and the new French poetry to the Germans. He and Sidney must have had many things in common, for Melissus, in spite of his gifts as a Latin poet, was eager to see a vernacular German literature created.

In the first of his poems to Sidney, written at the time of his embassage, and in the first line of the poem, Melissus refers to Sidney's reputation as a patron, addressing him as one famed in the worship of the Muses :

Sydnee Musarum inclite cultibus.

He wishes he could accompany Sidney on his return to England, and in a pleasant conceit imagines Sidney's eloquence, which had charmed the Emperor, similarly assuaging the stormy seas. But they must part, Melissus to cross the Alps on a three-years visit to Italy, and Sidney to travel down the Rhine on his way home to London.

Languet knew that Sidney was very eager to meet William the Silent, the outstanding Protestant leader of the time, but discouraged him from making a private visit without the Queen's permission. While he was still hesitating he received the Queen's command to stand proxy for her as sponsor for William's infant daughter. He spent the last few days of May in the company of the Prince and his wife, and of Phillips van Marnix, Count of Ste Aldegonde, who was then staying with them at Gertruidenberg. We have the opinion of that truly great man William the Silent, which two years later he invited Fulke Greville to report to the Queen.

With himselfe he began *ab ovo*, as having been of Charles the fift's Privie Counsell, before he was one and twenty years of age : and since [as the world knew] either an Actor, or at least acquainted with the greatest actions, and affairs of Europe ; and likewise with her greatest men, and ministers of Estate. In all which series of times, multitude of things and persons, he protested unto mee [and for her service] that if he could judge, her Majesty had one of the ripest, and greatest Counsellors of Estate in Sir Philip Sidney, that at this day lived in Europe : to the triall of which he was pleased to leave his own credit engaged, untill her Majesty might please to employ this Gentleman, either amongst her friends or enemies.

Even more remarkable evidence of the Prince's good-will is the suggestion of a marriage between one of his sisters and Sidney. Though the marriage never took place, doubtless because of the Queen's disapproval, Sidney's admiration for William never faltered. Neither did he devote himself to any cause with more ardour than to the liberty of the Netherlands, for which he gave his life. In the last year of his life he had many friends there, especially among the remarkable company of scholars gathered together at the new University of Leiden. To Sidney, who believed that men should acquire knowledge in order to act virtuously, the Prince's founding of the University in commemoration of the siege of 1574 must have seemed most noble. He would have acclaimed the University's title to its proud motto, *Praesidium Libertatis*, no less than we, in whose time a new tyranny closed the University for fear of so stalwart a tradition of liberalism.

Sidney's liberalism extended far beyond the bounds of Protestant resistance to the bloody oppression of Papists ; and he numbered among his friends the authors of the two outstanding liberal pamphlets of the time, François Hotman and du Plessis-Mornay. Philippe de Mornay, Sieur du Plessis Marly, had arrived in England on a mission from Henry of Navarre in the spring of 1577 and remained some eighteen months. Languet, who had met du Plessis-Mornay in 1570, foresaw that the two young men would become close friends. Mme du Plessis-Mornay says in her *Mémoires* that her husband's chief confidants in England were Sir Francis Walsingham and Sir Philip Sidney, 'the most accomplished gentleman in England'. A daughter was born on June 1st, 1578, and named Elizabeth : her godfathers were Sidney and Henry Killigrew. Soon after this, du Plessis-Mornay left England, but he and Sidney continued to correspond with some regularity : at least, in a letter of July 1583 du Plessis-Mornay concludes, wrongly, from a mere three months' silence on Sidney's part, that he had married.

Du Plessis-Mornay was perhaps the most distinguished intellectual leader of the Huguenots, a man of wide knowledge and determined conviction, a serene and upright character. He wrote much, whether in French or in a spare and effective Latin, and many of his books were translated into English. Sidney himself began the translation of *A Woorke concerning the trewnesse of the Christian Religion*, and when the wars in the Netherlands called him away before he had finished the task he left instructions to Arthur Golding to complete it. The book was published the year after Sidney's death, and was thus the first published book to contain any of his writing. Others of du Plessis-Mornay's books were translated by Samson Lennard, who went with Sidney to the Netherlands, and was with him at Zutphen ; and by Mary Sidney, under the title of *A Discourse of Life and Death*.

Sidney had returned from his first diplomatic mission with enhanced reputation, and in the following years many

Continental scholars and men of letters visited him in England. Languet bought books for him at the Frankfort fairs, and sent him copies of books on the authors' behalf, such as Daneau's *Geographiae Poeticae*, and a Latin translation of Plato made by a French scholar, Jean Serran. Languet asked Sidney to find a good family, Edward Wotton's perhaps, in which the son of a friend might live in order to learn English ; after his brief visit to England early in 1579 Languet took Robert Sidney back to the Continent with him, and gave endless care and concern to that attractive but wayward young man's education. Few of Sidney's own letters have survived but from many references in Languet's and others' we know that he maintained a considerable correspondence with his French, German, Italian, and Dutch friends. Through him especially the interchange of ideas with the Continent took place. The flow was not entirely setting from the Continent to Britain, since we too had something to contribute to the common pool of knowledge. But in literary matters we had, as yet, little to give and much to learn : with these things Sidney and his friends now chiefly concerned themselves.

CHAPTER 4

Experiments for a New Poetry

WHILE Sidney was abroad his sister Mary had married, in April 1577, the Earl of Pembroke, and from now until he left England for the last time, many of the happiest and most productive periods of his life were spent in her company at Wilton. After his death she gathered there the poets and men of letters to continue her brother's work, so that (as Aubrey says) 'In her time Wilton house was like a College, there were so many learned and ingeniose persons'. So far as we know, the Earl himself took little part in the literary discussions that were to be so frequent in his house, but since he was a cultivated man, who in later years had his own company of actors, he could scarcely have been ignorant of his family's tradition of patronage before they migrated from Wales.

Henry Herbert, second Earl of Pembroke, was born about 1534, and even if he no longer needed to speak Welsh, like his cousin of Montgomery Castle, we need not assume that he had lost all interest in his ancestry. To have done so would have been characteristic neither of the men of the age nor of men of Welsh descent in any age. In the previous century two poets of excellent accomplishment, Lewis Glyn Cothi and Guto'r Glyn had celebrated the fame and achievements of his family. When his second wife, Katherine Talbot, died in 1575, William Middleton wrote for her a long and elaborate elegy in Welsh. The first of his ancestors to take the surname of Herbert, Sir William ap Thomas of Raglan, married a famous lady named Gwladus, daughter of that Davy Gam, esquire, whose death at Agincourt is reported to Henry V in Shakespeare's play. (On the field of Agincourt she lost not only her father but her first husband, Sir Roger Vaughan, by whom she was ancestor of Henry Vaughan the poet.) Lewis Glyn Cothi praises this Gwladus as 'the Star of Abergavenny, the strength and support of Gwent and the land of Brecon'; and he lived long enough to extol her sons and grandsons. Of her sons the most famous was William Herbert, who married Anne Devereux, daughter of Lord Ferrers of Chartley, and who in 1468 was granted the Earldom of Pembroke. Though he had four legitimate sons, the Earls of Pembroke of the sixteenth-century creation descend from an illegitimate son.

After the battle of Bosworth, Lewis Glyn Cothi addressed a congratulatory poem to Henry VII, whose ascent of the English throne fulfilled ancient Welsh prophecies. It is worth remembering, what the Elizabethans were never so tactless as to forget, that the House of Tudor was of Welsh origin. Hence derived the renewed prestige of the Arthurian legends, which led Henry VII to call his eldest son Arthur, and which probably prompted Spenser to choose this, rather than classical myth, for the machinery of his heroic poem. (But Tasso too had mentioned the Matter of Britain as one of the most suitable themes.) Sidney himself, according to Ben Jonson, 'had ane intention to have transform'd all his Arcadia to ye stories of King Arthur', and Milton long contemplated an Arthuriad for his heroic poem. At this time men began to insist on the British element in our culture, rather than on the English, so that it became fashionable to refer to the Welsh as 'Cambro-Britons', the Welsh branch of the native inhabitants of Britain. So too the Empire founded by the English would be known always as the British Empire, a phrase coined by the Welshman John Dee. We too easily forget how great a part Welsh families played in the sixteenth and seventeenth centuries, Herberts, Vaughans and Cecils, Aubreys and Donnes.

Philip Sidney, whose father had been Lord President ; whose sister married into a family that had only been English for a couple of generations ; who had been accompanied on his travels by a Welshman, Griffin Madox ; and who must often enough, when at school, have heard the Welsh spoken (whether or not he understood a word of it), could not disregard the influence of Wales. So, in the *Apologie for Poetrie* he shows his understanding :

In Wales, the true remnant of the auncient Brittons, as there are good authorities to shewe the long time they had Poets, which they called Bardes, so thorough all the conquests of Romaines, Saxons, Danes, and Normans, some of whom did seeke to ruine all memory of learning from among them, yet doo their Poets, even to this day, last ; so as it is not more notable in soone beginning then in long continuing.

Appropriately, therefore, *The Historie of Cambria, now called Wales*, translated by Humphrey Lhoyd, was dedicated to him. Sir Henry Sidney's antiquarian interests led him to study Welsh history, and when the manuscript came into his hands on Lhoyd's death in 1585, he persuaded David Powell to edit and publish it. Another book of Lhoyd's had been the occasion of one of the more light-hearted passages in Languet's correspondence with Sidney. Languet had the book in Vienna, and though he professes his admiration for it, he fell asleep while reading and knocked over his lamp, which burnt the unbound book.

I was on the point of sending you the scorched remains of my poor Cambrian, that you might desire your Griffin his countryman to perform his obsequies, while you offered a laugh to appease the

97

ghost. But please tell Griffin to write him an elegy in Welsh and send it to me.

The elegy does not survive, but Sidney in replying to Languet could tell him that Madox had made a sort of funeral oration.

The connections between Welsh and English poetry have been all too little studied, even in poets of Welsh descent such as Donne, the Herberts, and Vaughan : the study would be well worth the making. Sidney, with his insatiable thirst for learning, knew that here was a source of knowledge : how much he was able to use it I cannot say. Perhaps by example or suggestion he prompted Spenser when in Ireland to have some of the Irish poetry (which Sidney also mentions) translated. These men sought poetry wherever they might find it, in the mouths of the ballad-singers, in little-known languages, 'even among the most barbarous and simple Indians where no writing is', as well as in the classics of antiquity and of the Renaissance. Mary Sidney's marriage to the Earl of Pembroke gave to her and her brother opportunities for learning much about the poetry of Wales : it would be as foolish to deny that they made use of them as to assert that they spent five evenings a week reading the poems of Lewis Glyn Cothi together. At the least, they knew that fine poetry had been written in Wales by poets attached to the households of princes and nobles, and that there had been a friendly and dignified relationship between poet and patron.

When Sidney first visited his sister at Wilton we do not know, but he was certainly her guest there in December 1577, together with the Earls of Leicester and Warwick. In a letter of December 16th, written from Wilton to the Earl of Sussex, another of his uncles, he mentions a small act of patronage.

I was bolde of late to move your Lordeshippe in the cace of the poore stranger musicien. He hathe alreddy so furr tasted of yowr Lordeshippes goodnes as I am rather in his behalfe humbly to thanke yowr Lordeshippe yet his cace is suche as I am muche constrained, to continew still a suiter to yowr Lordeshippe for him.

The name of the foreign musician cannot now be discovered, but it is pleasing to find Sidney, on his first recorded visit to Wilton, thus interesting himself in his support.

Fulke Greville and Edward Dyer may also have been at Wilton this Christmas, and with these two, especially at Wilton, Sidney's discussions on the future of English poetry took place. The life of a courtier never prevented Sidney from pursuing his literary studies, as both Languet and Estienne warned him that it would, but rather increased his pleasure and delight in them. So Dr. Thomas Moffett observed, who was physician to the Earl of Pembroke's family, and who knew Sidney well: Sidney (he says) 'considered that day most propitious to him upon which he might withdraw for a time from the noisy squabbles at court and . . . might read and dispute with a few University men, in some place where he was made welcome'. Most of all, as he tells us himself, he loved to read and dispute with his beloved sister, with Fulke Greville, and with Edward Dyer. These two had been with him on the embassage earlier in the year, but had been his friends already for some time. Greville, as has been said, entered Shrewsbury on the same day as Sidney, and remained his most devoted friend till death. He is one of the most eminent of Elizabethan courtiers, as he is one of the most profound of our poets. Southey said of him, 'Had his command of language been equal to his strength of intellect, I scarcely know the author whom he would not have surpassed'. He was, besides, a man of immense wealth, and as a patron of letters he had a considerable reputation. He remained a bachelor all his life 'the better to hold his fortune together', and met his death, at the age of seventy-four, at

99

the hands of a disappointed servant who murdered him on learning that Greville had excluded him from his will. Throughout his life he preserved a detached and cynical attitude towards the great world, in which for so long he played a leading part, and towards women. With the severe discipline of Calvin always instructing an exceptionally acute and fearless mind, he allowed neither the world nor women to deflect him from meditating on the meaning and value of life. Out of his meditations he made some of the most sombre and thoughtful poetry in the language, and was never taken from poetry by a public career, as were others of his contemporaries. Both Queen Elizabeth and King James thought highly of his political ability, so that, as Naunton says, 'he had the longest lease, the smoothest time without rubs, of any of [Queen Elizabeth's] favourites', and under King James he was for eight years Chancellor of the Exchequer. In Queen Elizabeth's time he was always at the centre of the intellectual life of the country, whether with Sidney and Dyer, or later living with Francis Bacon in Essex House. Afterwards, when to the premature loss of Sidney had been added the rebellion and execution of Essex and the death of the Queen, Greville seems to have withdrawn a little, and to have lived on the memories and experiences of the first fifty years of his life. In the end he summed up that life in the well-known epitaph composed for his tomb in St. Mary's Church at Warwick : 'Servant to Queen Elizabeth, Counsellor to King James, Friend to Sir Philip Sidney'. He was a man of outstanding intellectual power, with an equally sound judgment of the Queen's interests and of his own, and a commendable skill in avoiding any conflict between the two. He seems seldom to have relaxed the cold self-discipline with which he governed himself, except in the company of Philip and Mary Sidney.

EDMUND SPENSER
Portrait at Pembroke College, Cambridge

FULKE GREVILLE, LORD BROOKE
Engraving after the portrait at Warwick Castle

Edward Dyer, who was eleven years older than Sidney, was more genial and less gifted than Greville. The son of a country gentleman in Somerset, he entered the service of the Earl of Leicester as a confidential secretary, and quite early became acquainted with the Earl's nephew and heir. Lady Mary Sidney had a high opinion of his judgment and loyalty : in a letter to her husband's secretary, Edward Molyneux, in 1574, she advised him, 'in all your proceedings in my Lord's causes take the wise noble Mr. Dyer's friendly counsel, who, I know, doth most dearly tender my Lord's honour and well-doing, as much as a faithful friend may do'. Dyer had written poetry at least as early as 1575, probably before either Sidney or Greville, but now only about a dozen short poems can with any certainty be called his. He drew on English models, not on Italian, and had already developed his own individual style before the meetings at Wilton. Gabriel Harvey once called him, rather oddly, 'in a manner oure onlye Inglish poett', by which, presumably, he intended a compliment to Dyer's native quality. We cannot well judge from the little we have left, but in his own day men knew and praised much more of his poetry, as quotations from lost works in Puttenham's *Arte of English Poetry* and in *Belvedere* prove. Besides a reputation as a poet Dyer had already achieved some fame as a patron. In this year, 1577, John Frampton dedicated to him his *Joyfull Newes out of the newe founde Worlde* (a translation from the Spanish of an American herbal) with these words :

I founde no man that I know in that respect more worthy of the same [*i.e.* the dedication] than your worshippe, nor yet any man, to whom so many Schollers, so many travellers, and so manye men of valor, suppressed or hindered with povertie, or distressed by lacke of friends in Courte, are so muche bounde to as to you.

Frampton continued to dedicate books to Dyer at least until 1596, and others also welcomed his patronage.

With these two friends then Sidney planned his campaign
to make English poetry comparable with the poetry of Renaissance Italy, or of the ancient world. To them, by the will that
he made as he lay dying at Arnhem in 1586, he left his books.
After his death, under the leadership of Sidney's sister, they
continued the work which they now began.

Attempts have often been made to shape their informal
discussions into the proceedings of a formal literary academy;
but to do so is wholly to misunderstand the spirit of the
meetings, and the nature of English poetry. Thanks to these
friends' unacademic attitude, English poetry of the Renaissance never became pedantic and frigid; it was never divorced
from life, because, serious as was the concern of these men
with poetry, with aesthetic and technical matters, their concern with life underlay all their thinking. The grace and ease
of manner on which Castiglione so much insists in *The
Courtier*; the smiling elegance that distinguishes Sidney's
Apologie for Poetry; the gentle irony that is one of Spenser's
especial delights — these things are almost always to be found
in Elizabethan poetry. So Spenser's light-hearted phrase, in a
letter to Harvey, about Sidney and Dyer who 'have proclaimed
in their ἀρείῳ πάγῳ a general surceasing and silence of balde
Rymers', is not to be taken as evidence of proposals for an
English Academy, but as a hyperbole that exactly illustrates the
serious intention and gay manner with which these talks
were conducted. Gabriel Harvey understood the phrase so,
and added his own ironical comment on an Areopagus composed of two young men:

Your new-founded ἄρειον πάγον I honoure more than you will or
can suppose, and make greater accompte of the twoo worthy
Gentlemenne than of two hundreth *Dionisii Areopagitae*, or the
verye notablest Senatours that ever Athens dydde affourde of that
number.

The name was applied by Spenser in a moment of amused observation, so characteristic of the Elizabethans, or of Italians. It is the *sorriso italiano*, that ability to be whole-heartedly serious in what we are doing, and then, a moment after, to stand aside and smile at our seriousness : the mood of Michelangelo's sonnet on the discomforts of painting the roof of the Sistine Chapel :

> Ho già fatto un gozzo in questo stento,
>
> I've grown a goitre cooped up in this den.

Through this gift of detachment Spenser, in the most passionate moment of his incomparable *Epithalamium*, can turn his imagination away from the bridal chamber to the unconcerned creatures of the night, to bid them be silent :

> Ne let th'unpleasant Quyre of Frogs still croking
> Make us to wish their choking.

Just so does Donne bid the busy old fool, the unruly sun, to go chide late school-boys, not interrupt his love-making.

In two pastoral poems which Sidney wrote 'upon his meeting with his two worthy friends and fellow-poets, Sir Edward Dyer and M. Fulke Greville', the chief impression conveyed is that they were enjoying themselves. (And that, after all, is what poetry is for.)

> Join mates in mirth to me,
>> Grant pleasure to our meeting ;
> Let Pan, our good god, see
>> How grateful is our greeting.
>>> Join hearts and hands, so let it be,
>>> Make but one mind in bodies three.

And again :

> Well was I, while under shade
> Oaten reeds me music made,
> Striving with my mates in song ;
> Mixing mirth our songs among.

> Greater was this shepherds' treasure,
> Than this false, fine, courtly pleasure.

Similarly in the delightful dedication of the *Arcadia* Sidney calls his sister to bear witness how the book was composed, 'being done in loose sheets of paper, most of it in your presence, the rest, by sheets, sent unto you, as fast as they were done'. He gladly accepts the consequence of so amateurish a way of writing : 'Reade it then at your idle times, and the follies your good judgment will finde in it, blame not, but laugh at '.

Such was the mood and such the company in which the New Poetry originated. And because Sidney was himself a skilled and gifted poet he was so well able to be a stimulating patron of others. Castiglione had said that the courtier should write both verse and prose, so that, even if he himself attained no distinction as a writer, he could better understand the writing of others. 'For it happeneth very seldome, that a man not exercised in writing, how learned soever he be, can at any time know perfectly the labour and toile of writers, or tast of the sweetnesse and excellency of styles.' So much the more then could Sidney understand the needs and problems of writers. William Gager of Christ Church, in the Epilogue to his play *Meleager*, which was performed before Leicester and Sidney in Oxford in 1585, wrote of him as the man who (being himself the best of poets) alone favours the new poets :

> Qui solus novis
> Favet poetis, ipse vates optimus.

At first Sidney and his friends strove in song, composing poems one against the other as, long afterwards, Shelley and Keats and Leigh Hunt sat down together to write each a sonnet on the Nile. Fortunately, we can still trace this poetic rivalry from which so much would follow. Mrs. Humphry

Ward first (in recent times) pointed out the parallels between some of Sidney's sonnets in *Astrophel and Stella* and some of Greville's in *Caelica*. The similarities and contrasts, which are very numerous in the earlier poems in *Caelica*, will be obvious to anyone who reads them ; but, since they so well illustrate the difference in style and temperament between the two poets, and show also the method by which they practised the art of poetry, some must here be briefly examined.

Most writers have assumed that Sidney wrote his poems first, and that Greville then wrote his by way of comment or parody. There is no evidence for this, and I suspect that at times the two friends were writing in the same room together, at the same table — as Sidney wrote the *Arcadia* for Mary, with her sitting by him. The poems, or most of them, cannot be exactly dated, but Greville's poems in *Caelica* are arranged more or less chronologically, and the first eighty-three must have been written before Sidney's death. As the title-page of Greville's *Certaine Learned and Elegant Workes* informs us, his poems were 'written in his Youth, and familiar Exercise with Sir Philip Sidney'. Even the title of his miscellaneous poems, *Caelica* (as Miss Yates has pointed out), asserts a contrast with Sidney's. Sidney addressed his mistress as Stella, a single star ; Greville therefore must call his Caelica, the heavens themselves. Stella is to some degree identifiable with Penelope Devereux, though, at least in the first thirty-two sonnets, she is an excuse for writing sonnets rather than the object of the poet's devotion. (In any event, it is quite wrong to make too close an identification of Philip Sidney with Astrophel and of Penelope Devereux with Stella. The poet entitled his sequence *Astrophel and Stella*, not Philip and Penelope, and the characters are so far fictional.) Caelica cannot be identified at all : she was not one star, but a galaxy, not one lady, but several. Besides, she is also called

Cynthia and Myra. At times she is certainly Queen Elizabeth ; at others Myra seems to bear some likeness to Mary Sidney, and the simple anagram may have been intended to suggest this.[1] Greville's attitude to women was very far from the Petrarchan adoration, and it is a waste of time to look for any serious love affair behind his poetry. Much more often his poems suggest a mocking voice, making merry with Sidney's idealism, or with women's vanity. Naturally, therefore, the ladies of the court had their revenge, and, as Francis Bacon says, Greville

would say merrily of himself; 'That he was like Robin Goodfellow ; For when the maids spilt the milkpans, or kept any racket they would lay it upon Robin ; so what tales the ladies about the Queen told her, or other bad offices that they did, they would put it upon him'.

Such treatment no doubt confirmed his resolution to remain a bachelor. If ever he felt affection for any woman it was probably for the Countess of Pembroke, his Myra, to whom the tenderest of his poems are addressed : he calls himself Myraphill, by analogy with Astrophel. So too Richard Latewar, in his memorial poem for Sidney, calls Greville Mirafilus — Mirafilus who was nurtured by the same Muses as the lamented Sidney, and who is well known for his devotion to him :

Musis nutritus iisdem

Mirafilus, fidoque tui bene notus amore.

Mirafilus quo non vivus praestantior alter.

In these poetical compliments to Mary Sidney, 'the subject of all verse', Dyer also joined with his poem *Amarillis*.

[1] Sidney called himself Philisides, an obvious conflation of his own name. Then Philisides suggests a lover of stars, and is translated into Astrophel, more correctly Astrophil. Therefore the lady beloved of one whose name means star-lover must be called 'Stella. These ingenious tricks with names commended themselves to Sidney's contemporaries in every country. So his French admirers made play with the similarity of sound between Sidney and Cygne, and made puns about Swans.

We need not assume, because Greville and Dyer complimented their young and beautiful hostess in verse, that they were in love with her : to do so is a vulgar confusion of fiction with fact. To seek biographical implications in Elizabethan poetry is always rash, and in Greville's *Caelica* merely silly. Caelica, and Cynthia, and Myra, and Amarillis, like most ladies, real or imaginary, possessed a variety of charms, 'as, item, two lips indifferent red ; item, two grey eyes, with lids to them ; item, one neck, one chin, and so forth'. Caelica's hair, as Greville somewhat ungallantly mentions, was a wig. In truth she bore just about as much, or as little, resemblance to the Countess of Pembroke as did Daniel's Delia.

These problems are of no importance. What interests us is not the relationship between Sidney's friends and his sister, but between their poems and his, many of them written in her house at Wilton. Both Sidney and Greville wrote poems based on the complementary conceits of the poet giving his eyes to the blind God of Love, and of Love then being dazzled by the eyes of the poet's mistress. (The poems are variations on a familiar theme which Shakespeare also developed.) In the sixty-fifth sonnet of *Astrophel and Stella* Sidney addresses Cupid in the true Petrarchan manner :

> For when, nak'd Boy, thou couldst no harbour find
> In this old world, grown now so too too wise,
> I lodg'd thee in my heart, and being blind
> By nature born, I gave to thee mine eyes.

Greville begins the twelfth poem of *Caelica* thus :

> Cupid, thou naughtie boy, when thou wert loathed,
> Naked and blind, for vagabunding noted,
> Thy nakedness I in my reason clothed,
> Mine eyes I gave thee, so was I devoted.

The contrast is immediately apparent. Greville mocks the loathed vagabond, and blames his own folly in being generous to Love. Sidney will say nothing stronger than that Love was unkind so to repay his good turns, and he makes no excuse of folly. Sidney lodges Love in his heart : Greville clothes Love's nakedness in his reason — and there, surely, the ironical Greville had been looking over Sidney's shoulder. The bold, imperative opening of Greville's poem is as characteristic of him as of Donne, writing fifteen or twenty years later ; like Donne too is the self-scorning detachment of 'so was I devoted'.

In the eighth sonnet of *Astrophel and Stella* Sidney plays with the conceit of Cupid coming from Greece to these North climes, where he seeks ease and warmth in Stella's joyful face.

> But she, most fair, most cold, made him thence take his flight
> To my close heart ; where, while some firebrands he did lay,
> He burnt un'wares his wings, and cannot fly away.

Greville's eleventh sonnet uses the same fancy, but again with an ironical twist, attributing the coldness of Northern women to the conflict between principle and desire :

> Feare keeping lust there very long at gaze.

This poem ends with a very characteristic shrug of the shoulders at the human predicament, of which Greville was always acutely aware. Even in so tender a poem as *Caelica* xxii the same ironical observation of feminine caution comes in at the end :

> Was it for this that I might Myra see
> Washing the water with her beauties, white?
> Yet would she never write her love to me :
> Thinks wit of change while thoughts are in delight?
> Mad girles must safely love, as they may leave,
> No man can print a kisse, lines may deceive.

The contrast here between 'wit' and 'thoughts' is the same as the contrast between 'reason' and 'the heart' in the other poem quoted. And it is doubtless no accident that this cynical ending follows an echo of some lines of Sidney's in the second book of the *Arcadia* :

> She once stark nak'd did bathe a little tine ;
> But still (me thought) with beauties from her fell,
> She did the waters wash, and make more fine.

But which borrowed from the other I will not guess. This is not the place to collect and contrast parallel passages, especially since they are both numerous and apparent ; we need only observe the close collaboration in writing that existed between the two men.

Dyer was the other member of Sidney's 'happy, blessed, trinity', and even among the few poems known to be his, two show that he also wrote in rivalry with his friends. His one surviving sonnet,

> Prometheus, when first from heaven high,

was included in the *Arcadia* of 1598, with an answering sonnet by Sidney :

> A Satyr once did run away for dread.

His poem *A Fancy* was imitated in *Caelica* lxxxiii, where Greville even follows Dyer in punning on his own name. Dyer had written :

> My song, if anie aske whose greivous Case is such,
> *Dy er* thou let his name be knowne : his folly shewes to much.

So Greville wrote :

> Let no man aske my name, nor what else I shoulde be ;
> For *Greiv-Ill*, paine, forlorne estate doe best decipher me.

Ingenuity of this kind always delighted the Elizabethans, for they found in devising such tricks something of the enjoyment of using a new and exciting medium. When these poems were written cannot be decided. Sargent thinks that Dyer's *Fancy* was written when he was out of favour at court, between

1572 and 1575 ; Bullough that both his and Greville's may have been written about 1580 when Sidney and his friends were out of favour for their outspoken opposition to the French marriage. Certainly they cannot be later than that time, and Dyer's at least, written in Poulter's measure, is likely to be quite early. Probably the first rivalry among the three poets should be dated some time in 1577, when they returned together from the Continent : we may suppose that they continued to meet quite frequently and to discuss poetry during the next two or three years. Dyer had written poetry before this ; but Greville was led by Sidney, as he said, 'to steale minutes of time from my daily services, and employ them in this kind of writing'.

Greville's style is as different from Sidney's as his mood and temper : lacking Sidney's grace and elegance, and marked instead by a spare and sinewy strength. He was a more stern Puritan than Sidney, at least in his later years, and was inclined to dismiss poetry as an art of recreation, incapable either of enriching man's understanding, or of making him better. Thus it was no more than 'pleasing sauce to dainty food' — a very different thing from a touch of sweetness on the cup of medicine. In diction, therefore, Greville tended to follow the same practical, Puritanical way, and for him

> Those words in every tongue are best,
> Which doe most properly expresse the thought ;
> For as of pictures, which should manifest
> The lief, we say not that is fineliest wrought,
> Which fairest simply showes, but faire and like :
> So words must sparkes be of those fires they strike.

He expressed this judgment some years after he began writing poetry, but from the first his style is marked by just these qualities. We may be certain that he had strong and clearly considered opinions to contribute to the early discussions.

He would have been quite unwilling to follow literary fads and fashions, to be diverted from what he wished to say by too elaborate a consideration of how he was to say it. As he wrote in his Life of Sidney: 'For my owne part, I found my creeping genius more fixed upon the Images of Life, than the Images of Wit'. This severity must have been a salutary check on the livelier enthusiasms of Dyer and Sidney.

These three then wrote poetry together, each in his own way. Dyer, as the oldest, was most attached to the native tradition established by Surrey and other contributors to *Songs and Sonnets*. Greville had an unadorned, plain style which sometimes suggests Daniel, and at others Donne — like them, but long before them, he eschewed classical allusions and Petrarchan conceits, except in parody. Sidney brought to English poetry all he had learnt from French and Italian — the compound epithet, the setting of words to music, the attempt to use classical metres, the employment of figures of rhetoric, the elaboration of conceits; emblems, pastoral, sonnet, and an incredible multiplicity of metres and forms. The difference in style between the three poets made their rivalry especially fruitful in experiment. Sidney knew that poetry was disparaged in England simply because it was not good enough, and he sought the only remedy by these concerted attempts to improve it.

My meaning . . . is not to take upon me to teach Poets howe they should doe, but onely finding my selfe sick among the rest, to shewe some one or two spots of the common infection growne among the most part of writers : that acknowledging our selves somewhat awry, we may bend to the right use both of matter and manner ; whereto our language gyveth us great occasion, being indeed capable of any excellent exercising of it.

The evidence for what he and his friends achieved lies in the poetry that they and their immediate successors wrote.

The flowering of English poetry in the last ten years of the century was not some haphazard accident, due to the fortuitous collocation of poetic genius in that decade : it was brought about principally by these men's skill and insight.

There are not many allusions to the discussions they had together, though they must have talked of poetry whenever they met. Sidney refers to their meetings in a couple of poems from which I have already quoted ; Spenser mentions their acceptance of him into their councils ; Gabriel Harvey knew of their work, and was associated with them ; later writers like Crashaw and Aubrey still looked back with envy to the meetings of the poets at Penshurst or Wilton. No minutes were kept of their meetings ; no Boswell was at hand to record their talk ; they wrote no autobiographies. Such things were foreign to their purpose, which was not to glorify themselves, but to give to England a poetry and a literature worthy of her. Even in our present neglect of Renaissance literature apart from the drama, there is no need to emphasize the triumph of their success : at one bound English was established among the great literatures of Europe, and men could foresee that it would become the language of the New World.

I anticipate : and must return now to Wilton House in the late 1570s. Much of Sidney's experimental work of these years is to be found in the *Arcadia*, with its almost infinite variety of verse-forms. There are to be found attempts at various classical metres in English ; there are Italian forms, such as *terza rima, sestina, ottava rima*, and sonnet ; there too are the first of all English madrigals. The *Arcadia* and the *Shepheardes Calender* are the workshops of the New Poetry : fascinating places to explore, so long as we are not disappointed if we find here and there trial pieces which their designers learnt to discard, and experiments in a technical

virtuosity that no one else has dared to attempt; for alongside
of these we shall find work of sheer perfection designed and
made with a sureness of touch which conceals the novelty.

Among the things which Sidney had set himself to do was
to fit poetry to music, an ambition which had perhaps been
aroused by his knowledge of the work of de Baïf's Académie
or of the Italian experiments which the French imitated.
Sidney had always had a taste for music, even from his earliest
days. On his way back to school after the visit to Oxford in
1566, somewhere near Chipping Norton, the eleven-year-old
boy was moved by music to his first act of patronage. In
Thomas Marshall's accounts of Philip Sidney's expenses,
which Wallace found at Penshurst, is this entry on September
8th, 1566 :

> Item, given by Mr Philip's commandment to a blind harper
> who is Sir William Holles' man in Nottinghamshire.
> . . . .   12d.

Perhaps this was the 'blind crowder with no rougher voice
than rude style' who sang the ballad of the Percy and Douglas ?
However that may be, there is no doubt of Sidney's lifelong
delight in music. We need not conclude from his remark
to his brother, advising him to keep up his music, that he
himself was ignorant of it. 'Take a delight to keepe and
increase your musick, yow will not beleive what a want I
finde of it in my melancholie times', he wrote ; but this could
very well mean no more than that he enjoyed the solace of
music when he was feeling sad, whether played by himself
or another. In the *Arcadia* he shows that he was by no means
ignorant of the qualities of the various instruments, which
was indeed hardly likely since there was a fine collection of
instruments, for use, not for ornament, at Penshurst. As
Pattison has said, 'In the *Arcadia* all the lyrics are described
as being sung by various characters, and the accompanying

instruments are carefully chosen to underline the mood of the different songs'. We have already found Sidney interesting himself, when at Wilton, in a foreign musician, and he invited professional musicians there to give recitals. Sir Arthur Basset wrote to Sir Edward Stradling on February 6th, 1584, about a musician named Thomas Richards:

> I have given some commendacions of the man and his Instrument knowledge, but cheefly for the rareness of his instrument with wyars, unto sondry of my good friends, namely to my cosen sr Phillippe Sydney, whoe doth expecte to have yor man at Salsbury before the VIIth of Marche next, where there will be an honorable assemblye and receyte of many gentlemen of calling.

Settings of some of Sidney's own poems survive, by William Byrd and Charles Tessier, among others, both of whom seem to have had some connection with Sidney's circle. Tessier dedicated *Le Premier Livre de Chansons* to Lady Rich in 1597, and Byrd in his *Psalmes, Sonets and Songs of Sadnes and Pietie* of 1588 set two funeral songs for Sidney, as well as one of the songs from *Astrophel and Stella*. At the end, when Sidney lay mortally wounded at Arnhem, he asked that his song of *La Cuisse Rompue* should be sung to him, a song which no longer survives.

Whether or not Sidney himself was a skilled musician, he must have had an adequate technical knowledge as well as a lively appreciation of music. He was, as I have said, especially interested in the problems involved in writing songs. His two madrigals were written ten or twelve years before Watson published the book that contains the first English settings. Sidney must have got to know the work of Luca Marenzio and other Italian madrigalists while he was in Venice, and his retentive mind carried the pattern home to England. Whether these two poems of his were ever set I do not know, but it seems very likely, for professional musicians were often asked to set their patron's songs for private performance, as in a masque at Wilton. In 1590 Watson published his *First Sett of Italian Madrigalls Englished*, which contained twenty-three of Marenzio's composition and two by William Byrd 'composed after the Italian vaine, at the request of the said Thomas Watson'. Watson, like Byrd, knew of Sidney's experiments for the New Poetry, though this particular volume may owe nothing to the Sidneys. In addition to these madrigals, which would probably precede any setting that may have been made, Sidney attempted the difficult task of writing words for already existing tunes : to Italian and Spanish tunes, to a Neapolitan villanell, to a Neapolitan song with the refrain 'No, no, no, no' ; to the tune that has become the Dutch National Anthem, Wilhelmus van Nassau.

In the Queen's College manuscript of the *Arcadia* there is an interesting passage, missing from other copies, which well illustrates Sidney's appreciation of the problems involved in writing songs.

Amonge the beste singers of the Sheppardes who had in their youthe bine broughte up in some arte to helpe, the naturall benefitt of yt country muses their grewe a controversie whether this last kinde of verses, wherin every silable is measured, or the other that ar closed upp in a ryme, were the more commendable. Dicus likinge the measured and Lalus the riminge, Dicus sayd that since verses had the cheif ornament if not one[ly] in musicke, those that weare iuste apropriated to musicke did agree wth musick, since musick standinge principally uppon the sounde and the qualite, to aunswere the sounde thay broughte woordes, to aunswere the qualitie thay broughte measure, so that for every sembreif or mynom that had his silables matched acordingely, wth a longe foote and a short foote. . . . So that eyther by the time a poet shoulde knowe how every worde should be measured unto yt, or by the verse assone finde out the full quantitie of ye musicke, besides that yt hathe in yt self a kinde of musicke, since by ye measure one may perceave some verses roninge wth a highe note, fitt for great matters, some wth a lighte foote fitt for noe greater then Amorous conceites. . . . Lalus of the other side . . . sayd Dicus did muche abuse the dignitie of Poetrye to applye yt to musicke since rather Musicke is a servante of poetrye, for by thone the eare onelye, by thother the mynde is pleased and therfore what dothe most adorne wordes leavealed wth a proporcione of number, to that musicke be applyed, wch if yt cannot doe yt well, yt is the musicions faulte and not the poettes.

Because of the quantitative effect of music when sung, to which Dicus refers, Sidney, like de Baïf and his friends, thought it desirable to experiment with quantitative scansion on the Greek and Latin models. Unless we understand this, the numerous experiments in classical prosody will seem freakish and a mere waste of time. They arose not from a pedantic classicism, which was very far from Sidney's thought, but from an attempt to accommodate verse to music.

Two motives prompted the various experiments in quantitative scansion. There was the classicism of men like Ascham who abused 'our rude beggerly ryming, brought first into Italie by Gothes and Hunnes, when all good verses and all good learning to were destroyed by them': to such men rhyme was an obsolete barbarism. Others, like Ronsard and de Baïf, wishing to imitate the Greek custom of singing or chanting poetry, and therefore to make poetry that could be sung, saw that observance of quantity was necessary to this end. These two views were not always clearly distinguished, but for the most part Sidney and his friends followed the Pléiade, not the classical purists. Sidney had learnt the rules of classical prosody at school from Tigurinus' work on the subject, and he knew of Tolomei's attempts to reintroduce them in Italy. Besides, a member of Leicester's circle, Thomas Drant, Archdeacon of Lewes, had already formulated rules for determining the quantities of English syllables. Drant had been at St. John's, Cambridge, when Thomas Watson[1] was Master and Roger Ascham a Fellow : both were already interested in the attempt to abolish rhyme from English verse. He was also the first to translate into English Horace's *De Arte Poetica*, the most influential critical work of antiquity throughout the sixteenth century, when Aristotle's *Poetics*, only recently accessible, had scarcely begun to exert its influence. Like others of Leicester's circle, Drant was strongly Puritan and anti-Papist, and devoted much of his literary energies to these things ; but he had a high opinion of the excellence of poetry, and of the honour of patronage. His rules no longer exist, but can be deduced from references in letters of Spenser and Harvey, and from the practical experiments which they and Sidney made. We should not scoff at Drant as a dunderheaded pedant, for, if Latin poetry had derived its prosody from Greek (as it certainly had), why should not English derive its prosody from Latin ? There is no natural aptitude of one language rather than another for quantitative scansion, and Greeks and Romans no more kept an exact division into short and long syllables when speaking than we do. The poets were eager to get away from the jog-trot of Poulter's measure, or of Skelton's metres. They wished not only to adapt poetry for musical setting but to make it in itself more musical. A quarter of a century later Campion renewed the plea for classical prosody, because, as a musician, he wished verse to be scanned quantitatively, as it necessarily must be (to some extent) when sung. But if English verse was to be scanned by quantity, some means of determining quantity must be devised. This Drant set out to do.

Drant died in 1578, but Sidney (who knew him) had probably begun his experiments before that date, and under his criticism. Spenser received Drant's rules from Sidney,

---

[1] Later Bishop of Lincoln.

and probably, therefore, Spenser had not himself met Drant, but joined Sidney's group late in 1578 or early in 1579. (He first mentions Drant's rules in a letter of October 5th, 1579.) Spenser was in London by the summer of 1579, when he was for a time in Leicester's service. However, he certainly knew Sidney before this, for already on April 10th E. K. wrote to Gabriel Harvey mentioning Spenser's dedication of the *Shepheardes Calender* to Sidney, whom he calls 'a special favourer and maintainer of all kind of learning'. In view of Spenser's strongly expressed opinions on the need for considering the taste of patrons to whom books are to be dedicated, this implies that Spenser was by then well acquainted with Sidney. He may have got to know Sidney while in the service of the Bishop of Rochester at Bromley Palace, no great distance from the court or from Penshurst. He may have met Sir Henry Sidney in the summer of 1577, when, to judge from his account of the execution of Morrogh O'Brien, he must have been in Ireland, perhaps sent there on some business for the Earl of Leicester. They may even have met some years before in Cambridge. We cannot be certain of any dates, except that Spenser knew Sidney well enough by April 1579 to feel sure that he would accept the dedication of the first great work of the New Poetry.

By the autumn of that year Spenser could write to Harvey from Leicester House, assured that he had been fully received into Sidney's circle :

As for the twoo worthy Gentlemen, Master Sidney and Master Dyer, they have me, I thanke them, in some use of familiarity : of whom, and to whome, what speache passeth for your credite and estimation, I leave your selfe to conceive, having alwayes so well conceived of my unfained affection and zeale towardes you.

Spenser intended to dedicate to Edward Dyer a poem entitled *Slomber*, which has not survived, at least in its original form ;

and his commendation of Harvey to his new friends resulted in Harvey soon joining in their experiments.

Gabriel Harvey had risen from humble origins by his intellectual ability to become a Fellow of Trinity Hall; and with this academic success there went (as so often) a somewhat absurd and pathetic eagerness to be accepted in aristocratic society. But Harvey was much more than a mere snob: he had an arrogant egotism that at times came near to megalomania, as he reveals in the privacy of the notes so carefully written in the margins of his books. Sometimes on reading these, we feel that he is asking us to say 'What a fine fellow was Harvey', and we cannot wonder that he provided his enemies with endless matter for mockery. He had, according to Nashe (whose evidence is not necessarily to be trusted), risked offending Sidney during the Queen's reception of the University of Cambridge at Audley End in July 1578. 'He would make no bones to take the wall of Sir Philip Sidney and another honourable knight (his companion) about Court yet attending.' Nashe maliciously attributed Harvey's behaviour to his having his head turned by the Queen's attention, and by her remarking that he looked like an Italian: there is something in Nashe's allegation, for Harvey thought the remark worthy of more than two hundred Latin hexameters, revelling in the compliment. (We need not accept Nashe's further insult, that Harvey at once affected an Italian accent when speaking English, though this was not beyond his conceit.) Harvey celebrated this famous occasion with a book of complimentary verse, *Gratulationes Valdinenses*, in which he included two poems addressed to Sidney. In the first of these he mentions Sidney's reputation on the Continent, and refers to the friendship of Languet, Estienne, and de Banos towards him. A third poem, though not addressed to Sidney, immediately follows the other two and was clearly intended in compliment to him. In this Harvey summarizes Castiglione's precepts for the ideal courtier, portraying the man that Sidney was, and that Harvey clumsily aspired to be. His exhausting efforts to be a gentleman made him a butt, and his reputation has suffered through the vivid lampoons of Nashe ; but whatever his social shortcomings, he was an intelligent and sensible critic, by no means (as he has so often been represented) an insensitive pedant who led men more gifted than himself astray with his classical versifying. On the contrary, he saw the impossibility of it before either Sidney or Spenser. G. M. Young, in his essay *A Word for Gabriel Harvey*, shows how unjust has been the usual estimation of Harvey : after all, the correspondence with Spenser is clear enough, with its vigorous *reductio ad absurdum* of Drant's rules.

In good sooth, and by the faith I beare to the Muses, you shal never have my subscription or consent (though you should charge me wyth the authoritie of five hundreth Maister Drants) to make your Carpènter, our Carpènter, an inche longer or bigger than God and his Englishe people have made him.

He mercilessly parodied the 'reformed versifiers' — portraying the poet in the Bishop of Rochester's garden addressing a laurel tree.

What might I call this Tree ? A Laurell ? O bonny Laurell :
Needes to thy bowes will I bow this knee, and vayle my bonetto :
Why, but thou, the renowne of Prince, and Princely Poeta :
Th'one for Crowne, for Garland th'other thanketh Apollo.

After fifteen lines of this stuff we are not surprised at Daphne's retort to the poet :

But what says Daphne ? *Non omnis dormio*, worse lucke.

Harvey by his ridicule put an end to the experiments in quantitative scansion that for a few months had beguiled Sidney and Spenser.

If Dyer also tried his hand in classical metres none remains today, and there is only one copy by Fulke Greville, a rather successful poem in sapphics. Spenser does not mention him as taking part in the experiments, and we may suppose that he would very soon have seen that they were bound to fail, without recourse to trial and error. His sapphics are obviously written to contrast with Sidney's, that are put into the mouth of Zelmane in the first book of the *Arcadia*. Greville succeeds by skilfully keeping the natural stress, and by using rhyme (which helps to naturalize his verses) where Sidney had striven for a purer classicism by avoiding it.

This controversy over the use of classical metres in English has received a disproportionate amount of attention from the historians of literature ; and both the origins of it, and Harvey's part in it, have generally been misunderstood. These experiments were but a small portion of the many that were made in the process of establishing the New Poetry, and though it was very necessary that they should be made, they were neither the most important, nor the most interesting.

Of the eighty poems in the *Arcadia*, which probably contains most of Sidney's early work, since it was finished (in one form) by the end of 1580, only eight are in classical metres, all of them unrhymed. There are seventeen sonnets, and here we see Sidney experimenting with many different rhyme-schemes. He used the favourite English form of three quatrains followed by a couplet for nine of these sonnets, but later abandoned this form, and did not use it at all in *Astrophel and Stella*. There he preferred the more usual Italian forms. He necessarily discovered the difficulty of having only five rhymes in English, but tried to preserve the contrast between octave and sestet, and to emphasize this by the pattern of the rhymes. He did not attempt to avoid the final couplet, but preferred the rhyme-pattern *cd cd ee* for the sestet, which distinguishes it very clearly from the *abba abba* pattern of the octave that he most often uses. The so-called Shakespearean form, which is rare in Italian, suits English well, because in English there is an almost infinite number of rhyme-sounds, with comparatively few words to each sound ; whereas in Italian there are few rhyme-sounds, but an immense number of words to each sound. In these early sonnets Sidney experiments in other ways : by rhyming throughout on one sound (*bright*), or by repeating two words only as rhyme-words (*darke*, and *light*). This last device he used with much skill in the eighty-ninth sonnet of *Astrophel and Stella*. These experiments were especially important, for they helped him to develop his own command of the sonnet, and to set a standard for the sonneteers of the 1590s.

Equally valuable were his lyrical poems, almost all of them designed for singing. As a base he uses the iambic foot which is so much the best suited to the cadence of English, but he writes lines of three, four, five, six, or seven stresses, and constructs stanzas of considerable complication, quite unlike anything that had gone before in English.

> The Fire to see my wrongs for anger burneth,
> The Ayre in raine for my affliction weepeth,
> The Sea to ebbe for griefe his flowing turneth,
> The Earth with pittie dull his center keepeth ;
> Fame is with wonder blased,
> Time runnes away for sorrow,
> Place standeth still amazed
> To see my night of evils, which hath no morrow :
> Alas, alonely she no pitie taketh
> To know my miseries, but, chaste and cruell,
> My fall her glory maketh ;
> Yet still her eyes give to my flames their fuell.

He also attempted famous Italian stanzas, including a piece of the most exacting virtuosity, a double sestina. In a sestina there are six stanzas, each of six lines, with the rhyme-words of the first stanza used throughout, but rearranged in each in such a way that the rhyme-word in the first line of each stanza is the same as in the last line of the preceding stanza. The poem is concluded with a tercet in which all six rhyme-words must be used, but those used here as rhymes must be the same as in the first three lines of the last sestet. In a double sestina this elaborate rhyme-scheme is repeated in the same order in the seventh to twelfth stanzas as in the first six, and the poem again ends with a tercet, as before.[1] Probably Petrarch was Sidney's model for this remarkable poem, for, though sestinas are not uncommon, few have attempted the double form.

We tend, nowadays, to scoff at these complex and 'artificial' forms, and at such things as echo-poems — Sidney wrote one, in quantitative hexameters! — or acrostics, pattern-poems, and the rest. But, at least when a new literature is being established, they have their uses, by posing difficult problems to the writer, who will gain fluency and flexibility by solving them. There is also the sheer delight in the mastery of technique which is a necessary part of the equipment of any artist, and which is always present in the artists of the Renaissance. We do not jeer at the violinist who displays his technical mastery in a cadenza, nor hiss a coloratura soprano because she has wandered from sober prose ; we even tolerate a fugue, though it may be composed on B-A-C-H. The Renaissance artist enjoyed making things, and sometimes enjoyed displaying his skill, for no better reason than that he had acquired it with much diligence. As a receptacle for salt a paper carton may be as good as the golden salt-cellar that

---

[1] So complicated an arrangement is more easily explained diagrammatically : the rhymes are abcdef ; faebdc ; cfdabe ; ecbfad ; deacfb ; bdfeca ; then repeat (abcdef, etc.) and end with the tercet bdf.

Benvenuto Cellini fashioned for Francis I, but we need not therefore condemn the King because he commissioned Cellini, or Cellini because he invented so extravagant an object to serve so simple a function. Even architects felt that they were entitled to amuse themselves with their materials, whether they did so for religious motives, as in Sir Thomas Tresham's Papist Folly, the Triangular Lodge at Rushton, or for secular reasons, as in John Thorpe's house designed in the form of his own initials :

> Thes 2 letters I and T
> Joined together as you see
> Is ment for a dwelling house for mee.

Not only problems of metre, and of adapting poetry to music exercised Sidney and his friends, but they also gave much thought to the diction of poetry. Sidney was credited with the introduction of compound words, which was strongly advocated by the Pléiade, and he certainly used the device with notable felicity :

> The poore-clad truth of loves wrong-ordred lot . . .
> Then did he slacke his love-enstructed pace . . .
> Brave crest to him her scorne-gold haire did yeeld . . .
> Of which the two life-giving lights are figured in her eyes . . .

Spenser, whose 'sea-shouldering whales' so enchanted Keats, must have shared Sidney's delight in inventing compounds. In other matters of diction they did not entirely agree, for Sidney was much more of a purist than Spenser, as his criticism of the *Shepheardes Calender* shows. 'That same framing of his stile to an old rustick language I dare not alowe, sith neyther Theocritus in Greeke, Virgill in Latine, nor Sannazar in Italian, did affect it.' (There his scholarship was at fault, for Theocritus did affect it.) In other words, Sidney disapproved of archaisms and of dialect words, both of which Spenser used freely, and both of which were approved by the Pléiade. Only once, in the poem on Ister bank, did Sidney use an archaic diction. This poem must have been written between the time when Languet left England, in February 1579, and his death in September 1581, and perhaps shows the brief influence of Spenser during their association. His own more mature style, as in *Astrophel and Stella*, is very pure and direct, closer to the style of Watson and Daniel (who probably sought to imitate it) than to Spenser's. Sidney preferred to adorn his poetry by other means, whether metrically, as we have seen, or more especially by a masterly use of the rhetorical figures. In this he and Spenser were at one, and were the two most skilful poets in this manner. The subject is too technical for an elaborate discussion here, but Sidney's use of rhetoric was annotated in two works by contemporaries : Abraham Fraunce's *Arcadian Rhetorike* and John Hoskyns' *Directions for Speech and Style*.

Fraunce's book was published two years after Sidney's death, before the *Arcadia* was in print. Fraunce quotes freely from the *Arcadia* to illustrate the figures of rhetoric in English, along with examples drawn from Homer, Virgil, Tasso, du Bartas, Boscan, Garcilaso de la Vega, and others. In form his work follows the *Rhetorica* of Talaeus, a friend and colleague of Ramus ; but it was entirely new to choose a work by an English writer for so many of his examples. (Fraunce dedicated the work to the Countess of Pembroke, as might be expected, in an abominable piece of macaronic verse written in a mixture of Greek, Latin, Italian, Spanish, English, and French.) In the result *The Arcadian Rhetorike* is an anthology selected for the purposes of illustrating the figures of rhetoric, and at the same time of glorifying the *Arcadia*, quotations from which always follow immediately after those from Homer and Virgil, and thus take precedence over Italian, French, and Spanish. One example must suffice to show Fraunce's method.

Cap. 28 of Epanorthosis :

The calling backe of a mans selfe followeth, when any thing is revoked, and it is as it were, a cooling of that heate of exclamation whereof wee latelie spake. It is either Epanorthosis, or Aposiopesis : Epanorthosis correction, is, when any thing passed is called back. [He then gives examples from Homer and Virgil, and follows these with a passage from the *Arcadia*.]

Sir Philip Sidney :

In the Countrey of Thessalia (alas ! why name I that accursed Countrey, which brings forth nothing but matter for tragedies ? but name it I must) in Thessalia I say there was (well I may say there was) a Prince : no, no Prince, whom bondage wholly possessed, but yet accompted a Prince and named Musidorus. O Musidorus, Musidorus ! But to what end serve exclamations, where there are no eares to receive the sound ?

John Hoskyns gave his treatise, which was not published till the present century, with an annotated copy of the 1590 edition of the *Arcadia* to the son of a friend of his, to instruct him in the best manner of speaking and writing, which in Hoskyns' opinion was exemplified in the *Arcadia*. Because he had given the *Arcadia* to his pupil, he naturally does not use lengthy illustrations from it in the text of his treatise. Ben Jonson made a large extract from Hoskyns' work in *Discoveries*, and two later writers on style, Thomas Blount and John Smith, based their work on Hoskyns' appreciation of the *Arcadia*. Thus for eighty years or more the *Arcadia* provided the model of good writing.

The Elizabethan critic admired and commented on the skilful use of rhetorical figures when making an appreciation of literature, whether poetry or prose. Sidney and Spenser prove their remarkable skill by almost always using these figures so that they neither perplex nor offend the modern

reader, who is inclined to run away from terms such as antanaclasis or epiphonema. The American scholar Veré Rubel has
analysed a number of Sidney's sonnets, in a study of *Poetic
Diction in the English Renaissance.* Thus in the thirty-third
sonnet of *Astrophel and Stella* we find the following figures :
epanalepsis, zeugma, antitheton, ploce, expeditio, antanaclasis,
hysteron proteron, epizeuxis, ecphonesis, and again antitheton.
We can enjoy the poem without noticing this, and without
the least awareness that such figures exist. They are, after
all, used in our own day. 'All this and a 7 too.' 'Make mine
Myers.' 'This is the gin.' 'Trade not aid.' 'Whose finger
on the trigger?' 'The man in Whitehall knows best.' 'Never
in the field of human conflict was so much owed by so many
to so few.' 'I have nothing to offer but blood, toil, tears, and
sweat.' The advertising copywriter, the inventor of political
slogans, and the orator still use the figures of rhetoric to seize
the attention of their audiences, whether they, or the audience,
know it or not. Sidney and his friends studied these things,
and made poetry out of them ; for Rhetoric was simply an
attempt to codify the excellences observed in the writings of
the accepted classical writers, and thereby to assist the new
vernacular writers to emulate them. It was a means to critically
observant reading ; just as a classification of flowering plants
is a means to a more accurate observation of them. A botanist
is not thereby deprived of an enjoyment of the beauty of
flowers, and a critic on the look-out for the figures of rhetoric
is not thereby made less sensitive, but rather more sensitive, to
the beauty of poetry. And, obviously, these 'rules', which,
like the rules of grammar, were truly known only when they
were already forgotten, helped the poets to fashion a New
Poetry. If you wish to do something, whether tying a fly
or building a cathedral, the best way to learn how to do it is
to see how others, whose success is clear to you, have gone

about it. Sidney and his friends were sensible and practical men, not merely very gifted men : they knew that the creation of a new literature was something about which they could learn much from other literatures, or from older writers in their own.

We cannot now assess Spenser's contributions to discussions of the New Poetry : his own essay *The English Poet* is lost, though there is good reason to suppose that Sidney's *Apologie* contains much that would have been in it. But we need not doubt that a poet of such gifts, well-read in the literature of Europe, and ambitious to be the great English poet of the Renaissance, must have been most welcome to Sidney and his friends ; while his gentle humanity, and quiet, pervasive humour recommended him on personal grounds, so that he was soon accepted into their familiar councils. Because Spenser's own achievement is so much greater than that of Dyer or Greville or Sidney himself, we must not conclude that from the start he dominated their discussions of poetry. He was willing and eager to learn all he could, and Sidney especially, with his unequalled experience of the intellectual life of the Europe of his day, had much to give him. Spenser had read widely, and had talked with his friends at Cambridge ; but Sidney had learnt at first hand what Frenchmen and Italians were thinking about the new vernacular literatures, and his talk cannot have failed to fascinate and excite Spenser.

In the *Shepheardes Calender*, written for the most part, if not entirely, during his intercourse with Sidney, we find Spenser experimenting in much the same ways as Sidney in the *Arcadia*. His metrical invention, so remarkable in all his work, is already shown here. Most of the thirteen different metres, like Sidney's, are based on the iambic foot ; he uses couplets, and stanzas of four, six, eight, nine, and ten lines.

He also writes a sestina, but with the rhymes arranged in a simple progressive pattern, not as Sidney's and Petrarch's in their double sestinas.[1] He does not use *terza rima* or *ottava rima* here, though he used the latter in *Muiopotmos* and *Virgil's Gnat*.

Spenser was more daring than Sidney in his attempts to widen the diction of poetry : he was also more willing to draw on the resources which he found in Chaucer, rather than to use the French and Italian models, though he was far from disdaining these. He delighted in words wherever he could find them, but had an instinctive preference for the native sources of language, even when 'old and rustic'. Sidney, desiring that English poetry should take its place in the European tradition, was inclined to be cautious, and we may suppose that his strictures on the language of the *Shepheardes Calender* were not first made in the pages of the *Apologie*. Spenser must surely have argued in defence of his diction despite Sidney's precedents. Indeed on this very point E. K. (in anonymity dispensing with discretion) most vigorously defends Spenser :

For in my opinion it is one special prayse, of many which are dew to this Poete, that he hath laboured to restore, as to theyr rightfull heritage such good and naturall English words, as have been long time out of use and almost clean disherited.

He goes on to attack those who instead of reviving obsolete words, or borrowing from native dialects, introduce French, Italian, and Latin words into English, until 'they have made our English tongue a gallimaufray or hodgepodge of al other speches'. There Sidney would have agreed with E. K. and Spenser, that the English vocabulary should not be supplemented indiscriminately from foreign sources : he only

[1] Spenser's pattern is abcdef; fabcde; efabcd; defabc; cdefab; bcdefa; bdf.

differed from them when they went on, logically enough, to advocate the use of all available English sources. He would be already familiar with these arguments, on both sides, from Italian writers : from Trissino who followed Dante in wishing to use the native sources of language, and from Bembo and his followers who sought to establish the Tuscan of Petrarch and Boccaccio as the classical and correct Italian. The controversy occupies many pages of the first book of *The Courtier*, but Castiglione himself was on the side of Dante, and of Spenser, as he shows in his preface. Sidney's conservatism was probably due to his recognition that we had no model, such as Petrarch or Boccaccio, to follow, since Chaucer's language was obsolete. Spenser, with the calm confidence of the supreme artist, knew that he could fashion his own diction. Sidney died before he knew that Spenser was justified, but he recognized him at once as the greatest of living poets, the only one to be named with Chaucer.

Metre and diction, pastoral and heroic poetry, sonnets and songs, were some of the topics that Spenser discussed with Sidney and Dyer, as with Harvey and E. K. (whoever he may have been). No doubt they also talked together of the nature and purpose of poetry, in which Spenser closely agreed with Sidney. Both accepted the Horatian dictum that poetry must combine instruction with delight, and both agreed that the delight made the instruction acceptable. Spenser's letter with the first three books of the *Faerie Queene*, addressed to Sir Walter Ralegh, bears many resemblances to Sidney's *Apologie*, not because Spenser had read it (though, most probably, he had), but because they had often discussed these matters together. Sidney is, in a sense, the model for the *Faerie Queene* : to that noble and virtuous gentleman Spenser had dedicated the *Shepheardes Calender*, and 'to fashion a gentleman or noble person in vertuous and gentle discipline' he wrote the *Faerie Queene*. At least, that was one of his avowed purposes; the other was more purely artistic, and at the same time patriotic, 'to overgo Ariosto'. In that too Sidney most certainly encouraged him.

In April 1580 Spenser first mentioned the *Faerie Queene*, in a letter to Gabriel Harvey asking him to return some portion of it that Spenser had lent him. Spenser, therefore, began it at this time, during his close association with Sidney. We could the more easily deny Sidney's influence on Spenser's conception of the poem, if it had not been attested by W. L. in his commendatory verses to the *Faerie Queene*.

> When Spencer saw the fame was spredd so large,
> Through Faery land of their renowned Queene :
> Loth that his Muse should take so great a charge,
> As in such haughty matter to be seene,
> To seeme a shepeheard then he made his choice,
> But Sydney heard him sing, and knew his voice.
>
> And as Ulysses brought faire Thetis sonne
> From his retyred life to menage armes :
> So Spencer was by Sidneys speaches wonne,
> To blaze her fame not fearing future harmes :
> For well he knew, his Muse would soone be tyred
> In her high praise, that all the world admired.
>
> Yet as Achilles in those warlike frayes
> Did win the palme from all the Grecian Peeres :
> So Spencer now to his immortall prayse,
> Hath wonne the Laurell quite from all his feres.
> What though his taske exceed a humaine witt,
> He is excus'd, sith Sidney thought it fitt.

Spenser would hardly have accepted so circumstantial an account of Sidney's influence had he disputed its truth; and there could be no advantage in false flattery of the dead. We

may therefore accept W. L.'s account. This alone would be
sufficient praise of Sir Philip Sidney's perspicacity as a patron
of poets, that he recognized Spenser's genius so early, in spite
of some dislike of his diction, and that he set him to the task
of writing the greatest poem of the English Renaissance.

CHAPTER 5

A Generall Maecenas of Learning

DURING the autumn of 1579 the court, and especially the Puritan party to which Sidney belonged, was much troubled at the renewed proposals for a marriage between the Queen and the Duke of Anjou. Sidney was known, at least since the tennis-court quarrel with the Earl of Oxford in the summer, as an opponent of the marriage ; and in the winter he undertook the invidious task of urging the arguments against it in an open letter to the Queen. Leicester and Walsingham seem to have set him to this : they knew his skill with the pen, and correctly, if not very courageously, observed that the Queen's wrath would be a less severe affliction to the young courtier than to the established statesman. Sidney performed his duty (as he no doubt saw it) with tact, vigour, and dignity, and presented the memorial to the Queen some time early in 1580. Many times it has been said that the Queen was deeply offended, and that Sidney was dismissed from court as a result ; but Fulke Greville, who must have known, says that this was not so.

Yet Sidney must have been aware that his presence at court would not be altogether discreet at this time, and he spent much of the year 1580 in his sister's company at Wilton. He was in London at least as late as January 16th but wrote from Wilton to Leicester's secretary, Arthur Atey, on March 25th. A fortnight later his sister gave birth to her first child, William Herbert, and Sidney stood proxy for Leicester at his baptism shortly afterwards. Languet wrote to offer his congratulations in a letter which shows how closely he shared in the affections of Sidney's family. 'In truth some share of the happiness reaches even me ; for her singular excellence and her generosity to me, though she never knew me, made me not a little anxious on her account, until the news was brought me of her safe delivery.'

Probably at this time Sidney began to write the *Arcadia* for the Countess of Pembroke, which he composed sometimes as he sat with her, sometimes on horseback when out hunting the neighbouring country, sometimes when he was parted from her and living in London or at Penshurst. To her the *Arcadia* remained always a romance, written mostly in her company and always for her delight, and she preferred it so, rather than in Fulke Greville's recension, with chapter headings that invite the reader to interpret the romance as a moral allegory. Her judgment was certainly right, as we can see from Sidney's advice to her to read it at her idle times, and in his promise to his brother Robert to send him his 'toyfull book'. This book, casually put together at odd moments for the private amusement of a dearly loved sister, became a model for English prose style through nearly a hundred years. But its fame is more than this : for it has probably given pleasure to a greater diversity of readers over a longer period than any other work of English fiction. Published in nearly twenty, editions in about a hundred and twenty years, the *Arcadia* provided elegant young ladies with reading that distracted them from household cares ; suggested plots and incidents to Shakespeare ; and (to Milton's scorn) gave a prayer to King Charles on the scaffold. Neither was its fame confined to English readers. It was translated into Dutch, German, and Italian, and Marie de Médicis in 1622 sent Jean Baudoin to England expressly commissioned to learn

English and to translate the *Arcadia*. In order to understand how great a revolution this famous book had made, we need only observe that there was no English-French dictionary published until 1609, and that the *Arcadia* was probably the first literary work of any kind to be translated from English into either French or Italian. Truly Sidney had set English on the way to become one of the chief literatures of Europe, when Frenchmen and Italians wished to read his work. Those who could, read the book in the original : the younger Dousa read it in manuscript, and the French savant Peiresc owned a copy of the edition of 1605. While Sidney lived, Italians were more likely to remark, as did Guarini to Samuel Daniel, that English was a barbarous and illiterate tongue :

> our costes were with no measures grac'd,
> Nor barbarous tongues could any verse bring forth.

He had intended to change that ; and by 1668 an enthusiastic German could enumerate more than thirty foreign editions of the *Arcadia*. Besides all this, the *Arcadia* was added to — even by pious Cavalier children in the 1640s — it was used as a 'cover-story' for a satire on the Puritans, it was imitated, paraphrased into verse, dramatized, turned into the libretto of an opera by Parisetti with music by Alveri, and thence, from the Italian, into German. Mrs. Stanley published a modernized version in 1725, and we may suppose that Richardson knew Sidney's Pamela before inventing his own. The book continued to delight sensitive and discriminating readers as diverse as Charles Lamb, Swinburne, and Virginia Woolf. She indeed owed more to the book than she discloses in her graceful and enchanted essay : for who can doubt, when reading *Orlando*, that even in the twentieth century the legacy of this book has been inherited ?

In Sidney's lifetime the *Arcadia* was known only to his own circle of friends, in manuscript copies passed from household to household. As Molyneux says, 'A speciall deere friend he should be that could have a sight, but much more deere that could once obteine a copie of it'. In its original, simpler form, the Earl of Angus had already seen it in 1581, and in that year Thomas Howell's *Devises* contains the earliest printed notice of the book. There, in a poem 'Written to a most excellent booke, full of rare invention', Howell praises the author,

> Whose prime of youth grave deeds of age displaies,

and seems to urge its publication. Howell, a Welshman of undiscovered antecedents, had been for nearly twenty years in the service of the Herberts, and in this book, which is dedicated to the Lady Mary, Countess of Pembroke, he includes an epitaph on her predecessor, Lady Katherine (Talbot), Countess of Pembroke. *Devises* was the first of the many books dedicated to Sidney's sister, and, though undistinguished, it is not wholly without grace. Howell wrote it, he says, 'at ydle times in your house, to avoyde greater ydlenesse or worse businesse' — phrases that recall those used by Sidney in his dedication of the *Arcadia*. Howell must have been at Wilton during the time of Sidney's meetings with his friends there, and he shares their tastes in poetry, above all for Chaucer and Petrarch, even if he lacks their gifts. This was the last of his three books of verse, and the noticeable improvement it shows over the others may be attributed to the company in which it was written. Howell had not much to contribute to the New Poetry, nor even perhaps to discussions of it ; but he had been writing poetry 'for his owne exercise and his Friends pleasure' for a dozen years or more, and his presence at Wilton cannot have been unwelcome. We may note what he expects of the Countess's patronage — not money, obviously, since he had long been provided for by her husband's family. Something of more value, he believed, would accrue to him :

> If the Reader hereof, behold your name in the fyrst leafe, he will deeme the whole Booke the more fruitfull, and the framer thereof the more skilfull : but if he shall once perceyve your Honor to be Patronesse to this labour, he will eyther love it, bicause he doth honor you, or wil not dare to reproch it, bicause he perceyveth you are as ready, and knoweth you are as able to defend it, as eyther Aiax was to garde Tewcer, or Pallas to guyde Ulisses.

In other words, the taste and judgment of the Countess of Pembroke would ensure an audience for a book that was dedicated to her, in much the same way as, nowadays, the recommendation of a book of poems by two or three of the best-known reviewers will ensure its acceptance.

The reputation which Sidney and his friends had acquired in the late 1570s as patrons of learning and especially of poetry attracted the attention not only of scholars and poets, but also of those Puritans who attacked poetry as vicious and demoralizing. Most notorious of these was Stephen Gosson, who, in the autumn of 1579, dedicated to Sidney his *Schoole of Abuse.* Most have supposed that Gosson did so merely out of a thick-skinned inability to perceive that it would scarcely be acceptable to the leader of the New Poetry ; but surely Gosson, who had himself written plays, and who knew Sidney's Puritan sympathies, thought, in his new reforming zeal, that he should direct his attack at the enemy's conscience. Such men as Gosson do not fail to recognize their opponents, nor, having recognized them, do they evade the fight : rather they seek, by Philistine pugnacity, to overwhelm them. Gosson, as Spenser observed, 'was for hys labor scorned : if at least it be in the goodnesse of that nature to scorne' ; but this only incited him to renew his efforts, and later in the same year to dedicate to Sidney another work called *The Ephemerides of Phialo*, which included an answer to some of the critics of the *Schoole of Abuse*. Gosson's chief interest to us is that his attack on poetry, at least in part, prompted Sidney's reply in the *Apologie for Poetrie*, the finest exposition in English of the critical ideas of the Renaissance, and at the same time one of the best pieces of Elizabethan prose. Sidney most probably wrote his essay soon after Gosson's attack, though it was not published until 1595. There is no need for me here to give an account of it, since its arguments and observations pervade the whole of this book. Thomas Lodge also replied to Gosson with a *Defence of Poetry* but the pamphlet was immediately withdrawn, and Lodge described his next book, *An Alarum against Usurers*, as 'these Primordia of my studies'. This he dedicated to Sidney, trusting that he would recommend the book to others. Lodge's opposition to Gosson may have brought him to Sidney's notice, but it is not clear that Lodge was personally known to him.

More acceptable to Sidney than a Puritan attack on poetry must have been the dedication of a Puritan satire on the Papists, *The Bee hive of the Romishe Churche*, which was translated into English in 1580 by George Gilpin, the English agent to the States, who had carried letters to Sidney from Languet. The Dutch original was by Phillips van Marnix, Count of Ste Aldegonde, the cold and rigorous statesman whom Sidney had met with the Prince of Orange in 1577. The dedication was signed by the publisher, John Stell, who claims no personal knowledge of Sidney, but confesses that he had presumed to publish the book under Sidney's patronage and protection, 'not doubting that it should want credite, if it were not overshadowed with the countenance of some speciall personage'. Stell pays the usual elaborate compliments to Sidney, 'a mirror among men', 'a blossome of true

Nobilitie', and disclaims any intention to profit by the publication. Thus Stell, like Howell, believed that the name of a Sidney would invite readers for his book ; and doubtless, as a publisher, he knew what he was about.

The dedication of such books as these, which are of little interest to us today, shows both the reputation already won by Sidney, and what lesser writers who dedicated books to him expected to gain thereby. For Spenser on the other hand Sidney's patronage meant the encouragement to write in a new manner, to attempt a greater poem than had yet been attempted in England since Chaucer's day. Through Sidney Spenser met other men who were interested in the creation of the New Poetry ; through Sidney, before long, he obtained a post which provided him with a livelihood during the years that must pass before his heroic poem could be ready for publication. For, though Spenser wrote many other poems besides the *Faerie Queene* during the 1580s, he preferred not to publish them until the first three books of his big poem were ready. In this he showed both self-confidence and practical sagacity. The *Shepheardes Calender*, published at first anonymously, had won recognition as the first work of the new poet, from whom the highest things were to be expected. Had he published miscellaneous short poems as he wrote them during the next ten years, he would have risked disappointing these expectations. Instead, he waited until he could present to the eager audience the first instalment of the heroic poem which they awaited, and of whose progress judicious rumours had from time to time been propagated. First the eclogues, on Virgil's precedent, and then the heroic poem : it was the classical progress of the great poet, which had been recommended by Vida. And so, when he was ready, Spenser could introduce his poem with words recalling those that preface the *Aeneid* :

Lo, I the man, whose Muse whilome did maske,
As time her taught, in lowly Shepheards weeds,
Am now enforst a far unfitter taske,
For trumpets sterne to chaunge mine Oaten reeds,
And sing of Knights and Ladies gentle deeds ;
Whose prayses having slept in silence long,
Me, all too meane, the sacred Muse areeds
To blazon broad emongst her learned throng :
Fierce warres and faithfull loves shall moralize my song.

It is a kind of muted fanfare, heralding his poem with that modest assurance which is so characteristic of Spenser. To this moment he had looked forward in those early days with Sidney, the moment of triumph for the ideas they had shared together. Only then would Spenser publish other poems already written some time before, when everyone would gladly accept whatever England's arch-poet had to offer. Only then, too, would he even publish his tributes to Leicester and Sidney, though the volume containing *Astrophel* had been entered to Wolfe on August 22nd, 1587, and though some of his friends upbraided him for not having shown any thankful remembrance towards Sidney. But such deliberately thought-out and well-planned conduct was typical of the age, as of Spenser, who could never have been guilty of ingratitude to 'that most noble Spirit, which [as he acknowledged] was the hope of all learned men, and the Patron of my young Muses'.

Now, in 1580, the problem for Spenser, once set to the task of writing the *Faerie Queene*, was how to earn his living in an occupation worthy of his abilities and of his dignity, while at the same time having leisure enough for writing. We cannot imagine Spenser as a publisher's hack, writing pamphlets to order, like Nashe, and living a hand-to-mouth existence in the back streets near St. Paul's. Sidney knew that something better than this must be found for the poet who was to write the great English heroic poem. Fortunately he was in a position to help him. In the summer of 1580 Lord Grey de Wilton was appointed to be Lord Deputy in Ireland, and as a personal friend of Sir Henry Sidney it was natural that he should seek his advice before going to a country Sir Henry had known so long. This advice was freely and generously given, and we may believe that the Sidneys recommended Spenser to Lord Grey as his confidential secretary. Leicester too, who knew Spenser's qualities, would have spoken for him ; and so when Grey sailed for Ireland in August Spenser went with him. Whether Spenser and Sidney corresponded we do not know : it is perhaps unlikely. But Spenser found in Ireland one who knew Sidney intimately, Lodowick Bryskett. The two became close friends and Spenser eventually became Bryskett's deputy in the Clerkship of Munster. Life in Ireland was not entirely savage, and Bryskett records an occasion when Spenser and a number of other gentlemen, most of them soldiers, came to the little cottage which he had newly built near Dublin, there to take part in a discussion such as Castiglione records. When Bryskett calls upon Spenser to speak, he excuses himself on the ground that in his *Faerie Queene* he has already undertaken a similar task, as many of his hearers, who had seen parts of the poem in manuscript, well knew. Walter Ralegh also sought out Spenser when he was in Ireland, and in Ralegh's company Spenser returned to England in 1590 to oversee the printing of the first three books of the *Faerie Queene*.

Not long after Spenser left for Ireland Sidney returned to London, where he stayed at Leicester House. From there he wrote a second long letter of advice to his brother Robert, then already set out on his Continental tour and causing Languet much anxiety. The letter, written 'in great hast, of method, without method', advised his brother about his expenses, and how they were to be met; and about his studies — history, mathematics, astronomy, horsemanship, fencing, and music. Robert must improve his handwriting, and take care of his health, '*gratior est veniens in pulchro corpore virtus*'. The chief news at home is of Francis Drake's return, 'of which yet I know not the secreat poyntes, but about the world he hath bene, and rich he is returned'. Thus, in the moment of the first news of the voyage, Sidney's mind turns alike to the glory of the adventure and the material success of the adventurer. This was the normal response in an age when men thought it proper that skill and daring should be rewarded. Ralegh, in a single compressed line, summed up the ideal which led men such as Drake, Frobisher, and himself,

> To seeke new worlds, for golde, for prayse, for glory.

Drake had sailed into Plymouth just three weeks before, and Sidney's pride in the achievement of an Englishman was intensified by personal friendship for Drake.

The news of the marvellous voyage soon reached Sidney's friends on the Continent. Languet wrote to him on October 22nd, full of excitement at the news, and added a characteristic note of worldly advice: 'I do ask you to let me know anything you hear about the voyage. Indeed, although I do not know Drake, I honour and admire him, nor do I doubt that his will be a famous name to all posterity. I advise you to cultivate his friendship.' Charles de L'Ecluse, who had met Drake before, was also delighted at the news, and determined to come to England as soon as he could in order to learn at first hand of Drake's botanical discoveries. He arrived in England the following summer, when he discussed the new discoveries with Winter and Eliot, and with Drake himself. While in England the famous botanist visited Derbyshire and the North of England for the first time, and even went on an excursion to Ingleborough. (It is delightful to think of his skilled eyes exploring the limestone pavements of this celebrated site, and discovering there or on the summit, perhaps for the first time, those plants which still bring the botanists every season.) He saw something of Sidney and Dyer while he was in England, and Dyer must have introduced him to John Frampton's translation of Monardes' work on the flora of the New World. Charles de L'Ecluse obtained a copy of the Spanish original from a Portuguese doctor in London, Hector Nuñez, and while he was waiting at Gravesend for a favourable wind to return to the Continent translated the work into Latin. This book was published by Plantin in the following year, 1582, and dedicated to Sidney and Dyer in return for their kindness to him in England. Was it on this occasion that de L'Ecluse first brought tulips into England? If so, may not some of these precious bulbs have been planted at Penshurst or Wilton?

Very likely, for Richard Hakluyt, who mentions the first planting of tulips in England, had known Sidney from Oxford days. Sidney shared with Hakluyt, and many another Elizabethan, a lively interest in the exploration of the New World, and especially in plans for colonization in North America. Already in 1576 Sidney, Mary Sidney, and Edward Dyer are to be found subscribing £25 each to Frobisher's voyage of that year; and when he returned with his bogus gold Sidney wrote excitedly about it to Languet, who with the caution of experience, wrote a somewhat damping reply. Michael Lok, a London merchant trading with the Levant, who had been the underwriter on that occasion, perhaps then first met Sidney. He drew the maps for Hakluyt's first book, which was dedicated to Sidney, and himself dedicated to Sidney the map designed to show English priority in the exploration of North America. (For this same book Hakluyt had employed John Florio, then teaching Italian in Oxford, to make a translation from Ramusio.) This interest of Sidney's in discovery did not fail. He was a friend of Sir Walter Ralegh's and keenly interested in his Virginian project; as a member of Parliament he was, with Drake, on the committee for Ralegh's Virginia Bill in 1584; some of his friends had hoped that he, not Sir Richard Grenville, would have been in charge of the planters who went to Virginia early in 1585. Ralph Lane, who was left as Governor by Grenville, was a friend of Sidney's and wrote to him from Roanoak on August 12th of that year. In the autumn he was only prevented by the Queen's command at the last moment from sailing with Drake to the West Indies. His appointment to the Governorship of Flushing, which came in the letter of recall that reached him at Plymouth, put an end to his concern with the New World by engaging him in the troubles of the Old.

Tempting as it is to follow Sidney in all his activities and interests, in imperial and military and political affairs, I must confine myself to an account of his influence on the literary and intellectual life of the time. Such a division is quite arbitrary, and would have seemed so to Sidney, with his essentially practical outlook on the world : 'for as Aristotle sayth, it is not Gnosis, but Praxis must be the fruit', that is to say, 'All thought exists for the sake of action'. Besides, Sidney's contemporaries rightly reckoned it among his glories that he set an example for learning, not only to scholars, but to courtiers and soldiers. The gifts of a scholar or of an artist were not then supposed to unfit a man for practical affairs, nor was intellectual ability thought of as necessarily opposed to good sense. The ideal of the Renaissance was the complete man, who related the whole of life to one unifying purpose; the older mediaeval confidence in the authority of

the expert had been broken by the new mood of self-reliance.
A man was equipped by the Creator with the power of
reason, and he could learn anything and everything; above
all he must learn to act and to do. Also, each man had
his special gifts which it was his duty (as Languet never tired
of reminding Sidney) to develop for the service of others.
The fact that we have turned aside from these ideals, back to
a timid acceptance of the expert, must not blind us to the
nobility of the Elizabethan ideal, most succinctly phrased by
Daniel,

> What good is like to this,
> To do worthy the writing, and to write
> Worthy the reading and the world's delight?

Then Ralegh could dream of a British Empire to rival Spain's;
and Sidney could set the English poets to rival the Italian.
So, though this is not the place to discourse on Sidney's
active life, we must never forget that the New Poetry in
England owed its characteristic excellences, above all, its
humanity, to the fact that it was brought into being by men
who, whatever the care and concentration they gave to
literature, always remembered that their first concern was with
life. For this reason the practical, hard-headed, empirical
English have produced more of the world's great poetry than
any other people.

Yet some of Sidney's friends on the Continent feared lest
the diversity of his interests might turn him from the world
of letters, and were troubled to see the courtier (as they
supposed) suppressing the scholar. Languet had warned
Sidney of this danger as early as 1575, soon after his return
to England. And when, in 1581, Languet died, Henri Estienne
was prepared to take his place with fatherly advice, and
to warn Sidney of the corrupting influence of courts. In
1579 Estienne had shown his concern with the problems of a

new vernacular literature in his hastily written *Précellence du Langage François*, and he was doubtless aware of Sidney's own work and ambitions in England. Estienne's anxieties were ill-founded, for whatever Sidney's concern in the world of action might be, he could not lose his intellectual interests. Sidney's youthful friendship with the murdered Ramus had led, as de Banos remarked, to a continuing interest in the Ramist logic, though not to the exclusion of Aristotle. He recommended the study of the *Ethics* to his brother Robert, admired the *Politics*, knew the *Poetics* through and through (as may be seen from his *Apologie for Poetrie*), and translated the first two books of the *Rhetoric*.[1]

The Life of Ramus had been dedicated to Sidney by a Continental scholar : naturally therefore English Ramist works also had his patronage. Thus, in 1584 William Temple dedicated to him his *P. Rami Dialecticae Libri duo*, dated from Lincoln on February 4th in that year. Sidney acknowledged the dedication in the gracious and encouraging manner for which he was known, and since it is his only extant letter of this kind it may be quoted.

Good Mr Temple. I have receaved both yowr book and letter, and think my self greatly beholding unto yow for them. I greatly desyre to know yow better, I mean by sight, for els yowr wrytings make yow as well known as my knowledg ever reach unto, and this assure yourself Mr Temple that whyle I live yow shall have me reddy to make known by my best power that I bear yow good will, and greatly esteem those thinges I conceav in yow. When yow com to London or Court I prai yow let me see yow, mean whyle use me boldli : for I am beholding. God keep yow well. At Court this 23th of Mai 1584

Your loving frend

PHILIP SIDNEI

---

[1] These are now lost, but John Hoskyns remembered seeing a copy in the hands of Sir Henry Wotton.

Temple became Sidney's secretary, and held Sidney in his arms when he died at Arnhem. He received a legacy of £30 under Sidney's will, and contributed elegies on him to the Cambridge memorial volume, in which he alludes to the *Arcadia*, to *Astrophel and Stella*, and even to the *Apologie for Poetrie*. Of this last he wrote a minute and still un-published analysis. He had a distinguished career and became Provost of Trinity College, Dublin. His more famous grandson, Sir William Temple, continued the family's loyalty to Sidney, whom (he says) 'I esteem, both the greatest Poet and the noblest genius of any that have left Writings behind them, and published in ours, or any other modern Language'.

Another English Ramist, Abraham Fraunce, owed his education at Cambridge to Sidney's generosity. He matricu-lated on May 26th, 1576, at St. John's — an odd choice for a future Ramist, since it was the centre of the anti-Ramists ; but probably it was Sidney's influence that led him, like Gabriel Harvey, to study the critic of Aristotle. Fraunce dedicated his first work to Sidney ; as he says, it was then that he 'first came in the presence of that right noble and most renowned knight sir Philip Sidney, with a general discourse concerning the right use of Logike, and a contracted compari-son betweene this of Ramus and that of Aristotle'. This comparison still exists in manuscript, with a dedication 'to ye ryght Worshipful his verye good Mr and Patron Mr. P. Sidney'. As Sidney was knighted on January 9th, 1583, this must have been written before then, and Fraunce's own statement suggests 1581 as the year. In the same manuscript is another work of Fraunce's called '*The Shepheardes Logike*' which is a summary of Ramus's logical precepts, illustrated with examples from the *Shepheardes Calender* and dedicated to Edward Dyer. This was an early version of a book that was published in 1588 under the title of *The Lawiers Logike*. To the examples from Spenser's poems and elsewhere he had now added others from the Common Law. Thus Fraunce shifted his dedications only among the members of Sidney's most intimate circle of friends.

Fraunce also catered for other interests of Sidney's. There is in the Bodleian Library a manuscript of Fraunce's, in his own fine holograph, bound in vellum. On the front cover Fraunce has painted the scene from the third book of the *Aeneid* where Anchises rescues the castaway Achaemenides. On the back are some very ingenious Latin verses with a quadruple acrostic on VIVE VALE. Moore-Smith conjectured that the book was a farewell gift to Sidney on his leaving England, as these verses suggest: the most probable date seems to be February 1582, when Sidney was a member of the escort accompanying Anjou to the Netherlands. (Edward Dyer and Fulke Greville were also of this company.) The volume contains another philosophical essay, in which Fraunce professes his admiration for Plato and Aristotle above all others, and admits that he does not everywhere understand Ramus: however the implication is that Ramus is a worthy third to be associated with Plato and Aristotle. Of more interest than this is a series of forty *imprese* or devices drawn by Fraunce, with explanatory Latin verses below each. Most of them are the *imprese* of Italians: Lorenzo and Cosimo de' Medici, Francesco Sforza, the Duke of Urbino, Cardinals Hippolito and Alexander Farnese, Ariosto, Isabella d'Este, Vittoria Colonna.

Sidney's interest in these devices was well known in his own day and for long after.[1] He first learnt of them during his

---

[1] Samuel Daniel's translation of *The Worthy Tract of Paulus Jovius* gives what is probably the clearest and most concise account in English of the nature of *imprese*, and of the rules for their devising.

stay in Venice, where in Ruscelli's magnificent book he saw Sir Richard Shelley's device, 'a white Faulcon, with this Spanish Motto, Fe y Fidalguia'. *Id est* 'Faith and gentlenesse', as Camden says. This kind of ingenious and elegant fancy was sure to become fashionable in the court of Elizabeth, where 'at Justs, Turneis, Maskes, or at such like extravagant shewes' Sidney and his friends wore them, and rivalled each other in their invention. One of Fraunce's designs, of green boughs and flames, originally invented by Poliziano for Pietro de' Medici, is to be seen in a portrait of Sidney in the National Portrait Gallery. This had been reproduced in Symeoni's *Dialogo dell' Imprese*, from where Fraunce took his design. It is also mentioned by Daniel in his *Worthy Tract*. Camden describes many of Sidney's devices as of especial excellence, of which one example may be given. 'Sir Philip Sidney, to note that he persisted alwayes one, depainted out the Caspian sea surrounded with his shoares, which neither ebbeth nor floweth, and over it : "*Sine refluxu*".' But his favourite motto, sometimes inscribed under his arms, was *Vix ea nostra voco*, a very revealing quotation from Ovid's *Metamorphoses*, where the context is :

> Nam genus et proavos, et quae non fecimus ipsi
> Vix ea nostra voco.

(These words, from Ulysses' reply to Ajax in the contest for the arms of Achilles, are translated by Sandys :

> For Ancestors, divine originall,
> And deeds by us not done, we ours miscall.)

This motto was inscribed on Sidney's personal standard, which was borne in his funeral procession to St. Paul's. By it he proclaimed that proud as he was of the nobility of his descent he preferred to it the fame won by his own exertions. Long afterwards devices that had been worn at

tournaments were preserved in the Shield Gallery at Whitehall, where they seem to have survived until the Civil War :
there Henry Peacham saw many of Sidney's, and admired them
above all others. In March 1613 Shakespeare, who had used
a number of *imprese* in *Pericles*, helped Burbage to devise an
impresa for the Earl of Rutland, but it was of such tortuous
ingenuity that no one could understand it, thus breaking the
rules that they must not be 'too intricate in greate number, nor
so composed that they neede some Apollo to resolve them'.
But this was in the decadence of the tradition that had first been
established by Sidney and his friends.

The literary importance of these devices is slight, though
the closely related emblems greatly influenced writers of
the calibre of Spenser, Donne, and George Herbert. In the
Arcadia Sidney had further opportunities for exercising the
ingenuity which he often employed for himself, on behalf of
such characters as Phebilius. 'His armour and his attire was
of a Sea couler, his Impresa the fishe called Sepia, which being
in the nette castes a blacke inke about it selfe, that in the
darknesse thereof it may escape : his worde was, Not so.'
Such opportunities were necessarily limited, even in the
Arcadia. Yet these devices were thought worthy of serious
study by members of Sidney's literary circle, by Samuel
Daniel, whose first published work was the *Worthy Tract*
(which Sidney had read in the Italian), and by Abraham
Fraunce, who, besides the manuscript already described,
wrote two further treatises on the subject, one of which was
published in 1588, while the other, which he dedicated to
Robert Sidney, is still in manuscript.

Fraunce was an artist of some skill, and the painting of
the scene from the *Aeneid* is a very early example of its kind
in England. Sidney, as we should expect of a man who had
spent nearly a year in Venice, and who had sat to Veronese,

PHILIPPE du PLESSIS-MORNAY
Engraving by L. Gaultier

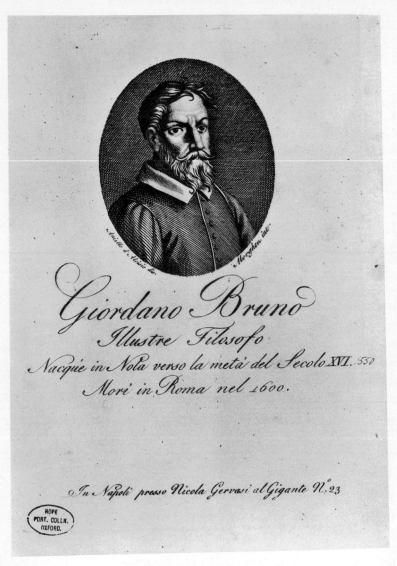

GIORDANO BRUNO
Engraving by Morghen after a portrait by Aniello d'Aloisio

had a lively interest in painting. In the *Arcadia* and elsewhere he makes frequent references which suggest that he is thinking of actual pictures.

Hard by was a hous of pleasure, built for a summer-retiring-place; whither Kalander leading him, he found a square room full of delightful pictures, made by the most excellent workman of Greece. There was Diana, when Acteon saw her bathing; in whose cheeks the Painter had set such color, as was mixt between shame and disdain, and one of her foolish Nymphs, who weeping, and withall lowring, one might see the workman meant to set forth tears of anger. In another table was Atalanta; the posture of whose lims was so lively expressed, that if the eies were onely judges, as they bee the onely seers, one would have sworn the very picture had run.

Sidney was frequently painted by English artists, or by visiting painters such as Gheeraerts. The authenticity of a number of portraits alleged to be of him is very doubtful, and some, most notably the famous miniature by Isaac Oliver, are certainly not of him. But he knew Nicholas Hilliard, and discussed painting with him, as Hilliard records in his *Treatise concerning the Arte of Limning*.

I would willingly give many observations tuching proportion fit to be knowne, but the bouck is great already, wherfor I omit them porposly, yet one would more in remembrance of an excelent man, namly Sr Philip Sidny, that noble and most valiant knight, that great scoller and excelent poet, great lover of all vertu and cuninge: he once demanded of me the question, whether it weare possible in one scantling, as in the lenght of six inches of a littel or short man, and also of a mighty bige and taulle man in the same scantling, and that one might well and apparently see which was the taule man, and which the littel, the picture being just of one lenght. I showed him that it was easely decerned if it weare cunningly drawne with true observations, for ower eye is cuninge, and is learned without rulle by long usse, as littel lads speake their vulgar tonge without gramour rulls. But I gave him rules and suficent reasons to noet and observe.

Even out of the chaos of Hilliard's prose we obtain a picture of Sidney eager as ever to learn how something was done, how an artist's skill and cunning could create the illusion of perspective. Perhaps the portrait Hilliard painted of Lady Rich was done for Sidney? It is no longer identifiable, and no authentic portrait remains to show the features of the most celebrated beauty of Queen Elizabeth's court.

Another interest of Sidney's, which he shared with many poets of his time, was in the translation of the Psalms. At the Reformation the Reformers wished to substitute the Psalms for the old hymns, and in Sidney's time the version known as 'Sternhold and Hopkins' was current, a dull and pedestrian affair which effectively destroyed their poetry. Those in whom piety had not entirely desiccated sensibility wished to have a translation that was dignified and valid, and at the same time easily arranged for singing. The history of the translation of the Psalms into English goes back to Saxon times, but this hardly concerns us here. Wyatt had translated the seven penitential Psalms, adapting them to his own circumstances, and so making partly personal poems out of them. In this he had been following Aretino, and perhaps Marot. Others came after in Wyatt's path, notably the Earl of Surrey and Sir Thomas Smith, whose translation was made while he was in the Tower, and refers to his own predicament. Princess Elizabeth made a version of fourteen Psalms when she was fourteen or fifteen years of age. Among Sidney's friends on the Continent there was a similar interest : Melissus made a German version to French chants of the first fifty Psalms, which was published at Heidelberg in 1572, and Scipio Gentili dedicated to Sidney his Latin versions *In XXV Davidis Psalmos Epicae Paraphrases*. This is an especially interesting dedication, for Gentili, while acknowledging that there are many reasons for admiring Sidney, confesses that his admiration is for the poet and patron of poets, and says that his versions of the Psalms are offered to Sidney in fulfilment of a promise. These 'epic paraphrases' of Scipio Gentili's are an attempt to adapt the Psalms to the classical metres, and thus to set them on the same level as literature with the masterpieces of Greece and Rome. Scipio Gentili's more famous brother Alberico was also interested in translations of the Psalms, as a letter that he wrote to Thomas Bodley on New Year's Day 1581 shows. He writes in Italian, and encloses the first twenty-five Psalms in a variety of Italian forms, ballata, capitolo, canzone, and sonnet. He says they are the work of an unnamed relative of his — not, presumably, his brother.

There were thus excellent precedents for Sidney to undertake a task in which his piety and his literary interests could be united, and he set himself to translate, into a great variety of metres, the whole of the Psalms. He had translated the first forty-three when he was killed, and his sister, who perhaps helped him from the beginning, completed the task. It has been suggested that the translation was made direct from the Hebrew, in which the Countess of Pembroke (if not Sidney himself) was assisted by her chaplain, Gervase Babington. Or they may have been translated from Tremellius' Latin Bible which Sidney knew : this seems to me the more probable, since there is no other evidence that Sidney ever studied Hebrew. For us the prose translations of the Prayer Book and the Authorized Version have an authority that almost excludes any estimate of the worth of Sidney's, or Wyatt's, or Milton's ; but Sidney's were well known in his own time and for long after, and are by no means without merit. Thus the nineteenth Psalm shows both Sidney's metrical skill and his sense of what is required for singing :

> Is not he blind that doth not find
> The Tabernacle builded
> There by his grace, for sunnes faire face,
> In beames of beuty guilded.

> Who foorth doth come, like a bridegroome
> From out his vailing places :
> As glad is hee, as giantes be
> To runne their mighty races.

And the twenty-fifth has a liturgical solemnity about it :

> To thee, O Lord most just,
> I lift my inward sight :
> My God, in thee I trust,
> Lett me not ruine quight :
> Let not those foes, that me annoy,
> On my complaint build up their joy.

Sidney uses stanzas of varying complexity and arrangement, some of them perhaps adapted to existing tunes or chants. He does not use classical metres, but translates one Psalm, the seventh, into *terʒa rima*. Lady Pembroke was rather more adventurous than her brother (admittedly she translated more than twice as many as he) : she turned the 150th into a sonnet, and in the 117th has the acrostic Prais The Lord.[1] There is a very Sidneian ingenuity in rhyming in the 66th Psalm, where only three rhymes are used throughout the seventy-two lines, which are divided into six stanzas rhyming *abc, cba, acb, bca*. Most readers have agreed that her Psalms surpass her brother's, and Psalm 44 makes a fine hymn :

> Lorde, our fathers true relation
> Often made, hath made us knowe
> How thy power, on each occasion,
> Thou of old, for them did showe.

English Puritans, like French Huguenots, could well have found inspiration in such hymns.

[1] See Plate 13, f.p. 225.

The Psalms were not printed until 1823, though they were widely known in manuscript in the sixteenth and seventeenth centuries. At least ten manuscripts remain, of which two are of special interest. One, now at Penshurst, is in the hand of John Davies of Hereford, the poet and calligrapher, who no doubt copied it for his patron, the Countess of Pembroke.[1] Aubrey knew that this manuscript had been in the library at Wilton, from where it was already lost in his day, perhaps at the time of the fire in 1647. It was bought at the Bright sale and, suitably enough, came to Penshurst. The other is in the Bodleian Library, and was transcribed by the Rev. Samuel Woodforde from a copy which seems to have had corrections in the hand of the translators. Woodforde noted on his transcript :

> The originall copy is by mee. Given me by my brother Mr John Woodford who bought it among other broken books to putt up coffee pouder, as I remember. But from this place (Psalms 131) to the end my copy is defective, the leaves being torn off. Ita testor Sam: Woodforde who for Sr Philip Sidnys sake, & to preserve such a remaine of him undertook the tiresome task of transcribing.

John Donne knew the translation, and wrote a rather poor poem on it, some time after the Countess of Pembroke's death, comparing it favourably with the Sternhold and Hopkins version which must have offended him in the churches. John Ruskin also much admired the Sidney Psalms, and even published a selection with the title of *Rock Honeycomb*.

The reputation which Sidney had won on the Continent led visiting scholars and Protestant refugees to seek his patronage when they came to England. Of his friendship with du Plessis-Mornay, whom he first met in England, and

---

[1] See Plate 13, f.p. 225.

of Charles de L'Ecluse's visit in 1581, I have already written. François Hotman, the distinguished author of the Huguenot tract *Franco-Gallia*, had met Sidney in Paris, and so when his son Jean Hotman, himself to become a famous lawyer, came to England in 1581, he wrote to introduce himself to Sidney. He had gone to Oxford, and Sidney wrote him a courteous letter in French, assuring him that he would be glad to help him in any way he could for the sake of his father. At the time of writing Sidney had not met Jean Hotman, but he met him not long after, and in the autumn of 1582 Hotman wrote to John Savile that he and Sidney had been talking much about him. Jean Hotman wrote to his father to ask him 'if he had one of his small works finished' to dedicate it to Sidney. (Apparently he had not.) He soon became friendly with Sidney; and others of his correspondents, among them Antony Corran, Melissus, and Alberico Gentili, asked him to pay their respects to Sidney. Melissus, writing while on a visit to England in 1586, is glad that Sidney has been pleased with some gift that he sent him early in the year, and regrets his absence from court. Gentili mentions that Hotman is highly thought of by both Sidney and Dyer, and expresses his greatest pleasure at this, for (as he had told Hotman in an earlier letter) he particularly valued the friendship of these two men.

The brothers Gentili left Italy with their father, Matteo, about 1578, having been converted to Protestantism, and Alberico, who is deservedly famous as a precursor of Grotius and the Father of International Law, arrived in England in 1579. He came to Oxford to lecture on law, and received stipends from Merton, where, no doubt, he met Bodley and Sir Henry Savile. He was also paid from the University Chest. He was introduced to Leicester by Tobie Mathew, at that time Vice-Chancellor and later Archbishop of York, and by the Queen's Italian master, Battista Castiglioni. He spent the rest of his life in England, except for an embassage to the Elector of Saxony in 1586, and through Walsingham's influence was appointed Regius Professor of Law at Oxford. In 1585 he published a treatise, *De Legationibus*, itself an important work in the history of International Law, which was based on lectures delivered in Oxford : he dedicated it to Sidney as being the very pattern of the ideal ambassador. He acknowledges the help that he had received from Sidney, both by letter and in person, since he first came to England, where his reception has been such that, like Bryskett, he finds himself using the first person of the English. 'Anglum me pro charitate facio, qua indies Angliae magis atque magis devincior.' In a long dedication Gentili records his devotion to all Sidney's family, and his special admiration for Sidney himself; but perhaps the most remarkable tribute of all is at the end of the treatise. There, in a long and eloquent peroration, Gentili defines the ideal ambassador, and completes his theorem with, as it were, a *Quod erat demonstrandum* in the words *Is est* PHILIPPUS SYDNEIUS.

Alberico Gentili was one of the most distinguished of the group of Italians who made their home in England for the sake of liberty of thought, when in Italy the intellectual rigour of the Counter-Reformation was paralyzing the humanism of the Renaissance. His brother, Scipio Gentili, also an eminent lawyer, spent most of his life in Germany, but yet dedicated several books to Sidney. I have already referred to his paraphrases of the Psalms which he dedicated to Sidney in 1584. In the same year he translated into Latin hexameters part of the fourth book of Tasso's *Gerusalemme Liberata* under the title of *Plutonis Concilium* and dedicated it to Sidney. (He had previously translated the first two books into Latin and published them in London and Venice. To us it seems a work of supererogation, but Gentili was an accomplished Latinist who would welcome the challenge of the great new heroic poem, of which the complete and authorized text had been published but three years before.) In 1585 Scipio Gentili addressed to Sidney on the birth of his daughter a Latin poem entitled *Nereus*, in which the sea-god Nereus, whom Hesiod had said was the most truthful of the gods, foretells the future of Elizabeth Sidney. These books of Gentili's were printed by John Wolfe, who had studied printing in Florence in 1576, and made something of a speciality of printing Italian books when he returned to London. His skill and care in this were praised by Petruccio Ubaldino, a Florentine who had been living in England since 1564. In one of his books Wolfe acknowledges Sidney's patronage of his work.

On his return from the embassage to the Emperor Rudolph Sidney seems to have wished to bring over to England an Italian scholar named Marcantonio Nifo, whom he had probably met at Padua, where Nifo was professor of medicine. He wrote to ask Languet to try to persuade Nifo, who was then in Vienna, to come to England, and though Languet was not very sanguine about it, Nifo did eventually visit England. He did not remain here, but for a time was at Leiden. He seems to have ended his days teaching geometry in Paris.

Among the Italians living in exile here were Lodowick Bryskett and John Florio, both of whom had been born in England. Bryskett, after his travels with Sidney, had returned to his work in Ireland, and may not have seen Sidney again. Florio was living in London, and had many connections with Sidney's circle. His father, Michel Agnolo Florio, who had fled to England to escape religious persecution, and who had been Italian tutor to Lady Jane Grey, dedicated his *Regole de la Lingua Thoscana* to Henry

Herbert, Earl of Pembroke, on August 21st, 1553. John Florio must have been acquainted with Sidney at least from the time of Mary Sidney's marriage in 1577. In 1578 he dedicated his first book to the Earl of Leicester. Oddly enough, he seems never to have dedicated a book to Sidney, though on November 12th, 1582, he dedicated to Edward Dyer his *Giardino di Recreatione*, a collection of Italian proverbs. In this dedication he refers to his teaching Italian at Oxford, from where he dates the book, and says : 'I know that the noble Italian language is no less welcome to you than are beautiful jewels to the ladies, or the finest and most perfect armour to soldiers'. There is, indeed, no doubt of this, since it was from Italy that the whole inspiration of the Renaissance had come, from the time when Torrigiano designed his superb tomb for King Henry VII to the time when Inigo Jones revealed in Whitehall the lessons he had learnt in the Veneto. The Earl of Surrey and Sir Thomas Wyatt

having travailed into Italie, and there tasted the sweete and stately measures and stile of the Italian Poesie as novices newly crept out of the schooles of Dante, Ariosto and Petrarch, greatly polished our rude and homely maner of vulgar Poesie, from that it had been before.

But it was left to Sidney and his companions to bring that pioneer work to success, and to enlarge English poetry till it could compass the *Faerie Queene* or Shakespeare's Sonnets. In this process John Florio is a man of high importance for many reasons — for his Italian Dictionary ; for his sensitive appreciation of English words and skill in their invention ; for the vigorous, quarrelsome, fantastic personality which is to be seen in the translation of Montaigne and, very possibly, in the character of Holofernes. Resolute John Florio (as he affected to sign himself) will force himself upon our attention later, but for the present he is to be observed conducting an even more fiery and voluble and brilliant Italian, Giordano Bruno, to Fulke Greville's house in London, there to dine in Sidney's company.

The scene is inimitably described by Bruno himself, but with such an accumulation of vituperative detail that I can here give only the gist. Bruno, very much on his dignity, had gone off in a huff when no one came to escort him, and on his return home found Florio with Matthew Gwinne, both much agitated, waiting for him. They bustled him off to the river, where they called out 'Oars' ('that is, gondolieri', says Bruno); and eventually a couple of ancient watermen came along in a creaking and ramshackle boat. During their leisurely progress on the river this February night Florio sings a stanza of Ariosto 'as if he were recounting his loves', and Bruno replies with another. After a time they are set ashore, only to lose their way in the foul and muddy streets, and to have insults flung at them by cockneys suspicious of foreigners. At last they arrived at Greville's house, where they were received upstairs, and made welcome with the passing of a loving cup — a strange and disgusting habit in Bruno's opinion. Though the lively ill temper with which Bruno records the events of this evening is characteristic enough of his response to English manners, he found England in many ways congenial.

Bruno came to England in the spring of 1583, preceded by a sharp note from the English Ambassador in Paris, Sir Henry Cobham, to Sir Francis Walsingham: 'Dr Jordano Bruno Nolano, a professor in philosophy, intendeth to pass into England whose religion I cannot commend'. He arrived with royal letters of recommendation to the French Ambassador in London, Michel de Castelnau, Marquis de Mauvissière, a man of notable humanity and liberal views. Florio was at the time living in Mauvissière's house as tutor to his daughter, and Bruno must have got to know him immediately. Probably Florio suggested the visit to Oxford, which took place in the early summer and resulted, almost inevitably, in Bruno's quarrelling with everyone in Oxford (except the Warden of New College, who quarrelled with all his colleagues), and in much abuse. Among the audience at one of his lectures was the scholarly and retiring Samuel Daniel. Bruno's turgid and vehement style may have persuaded Daniel of 'his Geny being more prone to easier and smoother studies, than in pecking and hewing at Logic'. Bruno probably met in Oxford Matthew Gwinne, who on that February night in 1584 accompanied Florio to his lodgings, for Gwinne had been lecturing on music in Oxford in 1583. Later he studied medicine and became a distinguished member of the Barber-Surgeons' Company. He was, as his name reveals, a Welshman, but with a keen interest in Italian studies, and for several of Florio's books wrote rather poor commendatory verses which he signed with an Italian translation of his name, Il Candido.

When at last Bruno arrived at Fulke Greville's dinner party he found Sidney also in the company, of whom, he says, he had already heard both in France and in Italy. He does not, unfortunately, tell us who had told him of Sidney, but to judge from the evidence of many writers of the time, in most of Western Europe if a cultivated or learned man were to mention that he intended to visit England someone would almost certainly advise him to make the acquaintance of Philip Sidney. This Bruno lost no time in doing, and he gratefully records that Sidney was both the first and the most consistent of his English friends. He admired Greville also, but said that someone later caused mischief between them — no very arduous task, for there can have been little compatibility of the cold and severe Englishman, with his spare and precise use of language, and the impatient, irritable Neapolitan who always had a torrent of words ready to pour forth in a dazzling tumult. For all that, it would have been difficult to find a third intellect at once as profound and as daring as Bruno's or Greville's in all Europe. There is nothing to show that the talk on this famous evening about the new Copernican astronomy much influenced Sidney. He had not thought it worth while to study astronomy while in Italy, and as he had written to Robert in 1580, 'I thinke you understand the sphere, if you doe, I care little for any more astronomy in yow'. But, unlike some of Bruno's hearers, he was at least capable of courteous and intelligent attention.

Bruno found the liberal intellectual atmosphere of England conducive to work, and wrote and published seven or more books in the two and a half years that he spent here. They include his finest work, and it is among Sidney's best rewards as a patron of learning that two of these books were dedicated to him. The first, *Spaccio de la Bestia Trionfante*, was published in London, but with the false imprint of Paris, in 1584. It contains three dialogues, and in the dedication Bruno explains his intention, which is to treat of moral philosophy in the light of the divine sun of the intellect. (An English version, *The Expulsion of the Triumphant Beast*, by W. Morehead, was published in 1713, so that the book may be read by those who are deterred by Bruno's Italian.) The work was adapted by Thomas Carew for the masque *Coelum Britannicum* danced by King Charles I and his court on Shrove Tuesday 1634, 'the noblest masque of my time to this day', in Sir Henry Herbert's opinion, 'the best poetrye, best scenes, and the best habitts'. Thomas Carew wrote the poetry and Inigo Jones designed the scenes and habits.

The second book which Bruno dedicated to Sidney is

much more to my purpose. This was *De gli Eroici Furori*, published in 1585 in London, again with the false Paris imprint. An English translation by L. Williams, *The Heroic Enthusiasts*, was published in 1887, but as this omits the long, instructive, and entertaining dedication I must here quote from it. The book, whose title might be better rendered *On Heroic Enthusiasms* (or *Heroycall Furies* as Florio calls it), is a discourse on the nature of true love, which, however much it may lack of Plato's humanity, matches his lofty idealism. Bruno begins his dedication with characteristic impetuosity.

Truly (most noble Knight) it is the mark of a low, beastly, and filthy mind to be always studying and gazing at and giving one's most careful thought to the beauty of a female body. Good God! what more vile and ignoble spectacle could be put before the eye of a man of true feeling than that of a man pondering, afflicted, tortured, sad, melancholy, now cold, now hot, now in a fervour, now all of a tremble, now pale, now flushed, now in the depths of perplexity, now active and resolute. . . . What a tragicomedy it is! What action (I say) more deserving of both pity and laughter can be represented in this theatre of the world, on this stage of our understanding, than this where such and so many actors are made thoughtful, contemplative, constant, stedfast, faithful lovers, cherishers, adorers, and slaves of a thing without faith, lacking any sort of constancy, destitute of any intelligence, empty of all merit, with neither gratefulness nor gratitude, and in which no more sense, intellect, or goodness is to be found than in a statue or a picture painted on a wall.

And so the tirade continues for page after page, twisting the very phrases of the sonneteers, Astrophel among them, into a mockery of the whole Petrarchan tradition, until suddenly at the end of the ninth page Bruno remembers that, after all, it is Astrophel whom he is addressing, and shamelessly concludes his anti-Petrarchist essay with a palinode. But of course (he says) everyone knows I never intended to include the ladies of your acquaintance in my condemnation, 'for they are not women, not ladies but (in the guise of these) they are nymphs, goddesses, of heavenly substance'. To complete his tergiversation he even goes so far as to end his dedication with a sonnet to the ladies of England, in which he repeats that they are not women but nymphs, goddesses, stars:

E siete in terra quel ch' in ciel le stelle.

Florio regarded this as a deliberate allusion to Sidney's Stella, and quoted the line in dedicating the second volume of his Montaigne to her and to Sidney's daughter. Florio must have known the truth of the matter.

Miss Yates considers that 'read in the light of the *Eroici Furori*, Sidney's sonnets are seen to be, like Bruno's, a spiritual autobiography, reflecting in terms of Petrarcan emblems, the moods of a soul seeking God'. I find this view difficult to accept. For, absurd as is Bruno's sudden recantation of his anti-Petrarchan passion, it could very well be prompted by his friendship for Sidney, and if he had believed in a spiritual interpretation of Sidney's sonnets he could have revealed it very differently. John Florio and Matthew Gwinne certainly did not regard *Astrophel and Stella* as a history of the soul's search for God; neither did Nashe, for whom 'the argument [was] cruell chastitie, the Prologue hope, the Epilogue despair'. No doubt Stella represents Virtue in many sonnets, as well as Beauty; but she also represents Penelope Devereux. For Sidney, as for Bruno, and as for so many men of the Renaissance, physical beauty was a guiding star to the world of spiritual and intellectual beauty. But Sidney was a poet, unwilling to kick away the ladder by which his apprehension mounted, and in this was like Spenser and other poets, rather than like Bruno, or Plato. Miss Yates very fairly quotes the warnings of both Bruno and Sidney against interpretations of their poetry through metaphor and allegory to please the reader's fancy:

> You that with Allegory's curious frame
> Of other's children changelings use to make,
> With me those pains, for God's sake, do not take.

Bruno certainly became intimate enough with Sidney to know some at least of his sonnets; and very possibly some of Fulke Greville's and Daniel's too, though verbal similarities between *Delia* and the *Eroici Furori* may be due to Daniel's reading of the book at a later date. Bruno's influence on the poets has not yet been thoroughly investigated, but the presence of so lively and stimulating a mind in London at that time must have had some effect, especially when he was well known to the leaders of the New Poetry. Whether or not Shakespeare drew Berowne from hearsay of Bruno we cannot certainly know; but it would be far more valuable to discover what Sidney and Greville, Spenser and Daniel learnt from Bruno, than to know that gossip about him formed a character in Shakespeare's imagination. Shakespeare could have imagined Berowne if he never heard of Bruno, and the only advantage he could hope to derive from the identification was a certain topicality. These matters have been studied at great length, and inconclusively: they are among the perennial delights of Shakespearean scholarship. It may therefore seem a trifling matter to record the mere facts of Bruno's acquaintance with Sidney and his friends, and to take note of views on poetry that he addressed to Sidney.

In the first dialogue of *De gli Eroici Furori* Bruno pours scorn on those who use the rules of Aristotle's *Poetics* as a yard-stick to measure poets by. There is an indefinite number of kinds of poets, and rules of criticism are to be derived from their practice, not otherwise. The arguments are put into the mouth of Tansillo, several of whose own sonnets are quoted; and he sums up in reply to his questioner Cicada.

TANSILLO.   You are quite right to conclude that poetry does not derive from rules, or only to a small extent, and by chance. The rules derive from the poetry, and there are as many kinds of true rules as there are kinds of true poets.

CICADA.   Then how are true poets to be recognized?

TANSILLO.   By the singing note in their verses; and besides, that by this singing they succeed either in delighting us, or in being useful, or in delighting and being useful at one and the same time.

CICADA.   To whom then are Aristotle's rules useful?

TANSILLO.   To the man who, unlike Homer, Hesiod, Orpheus and the rest, cannot sing without his rules, and who, for want of a Muse of his own, flirts with Homer's.

These opinions must have seemed very advanced at the time, when the New Poetry had not yet justified any confidence to stand free of classical rules and precedents. Sidney himself was dead a year later, but their boldness may well have encouraged Daniel in his independence. We may, if we wish, doubt whether Daniel ever met Bruno, though as brother-in-law to Florio he must have had excellent opportunities for doing so : we can hardly doubt that he knew the *Heroycall Furies*.

Presumably, in differentiating the music of the verse from the delight that poetry gives, Tansillo (or Bruno) intended to differentiate between the effects of metre and rhythm on the one hand and of rhetorical devices including metaphor, simile, and ornament on the other. He is willing to forgo these, as Greville generally does in his poems, while he observes metrical form with care and skill. Sidney's practice was somewhat different, as was his theory, for he refused to accept metre and verse as necessary ingredients in poetry. I do not wish to imply that Bruno influenced Greville in this matter, and not Sidney : their styles of writing were markedly different from the very beginning, several years before Bruno's visit, and if the unadorned style of Greville became more and more severe as he grew older, this is only what we should expect.

De gli Eroici Furori was the last book printed in England to be dedicated to Sidney. Bruno addressed Sidney not because he felt that a certain sensuousness was a flaw in Sidney's nature, nor in the hope of dissuading him from writing sonnets. He expressly disclaims any such intention, and says that he only wishes to insist that men should render unto Caesar the things that are Caesar's and unto God the things that are God's. 'I wish women to be honoured and loved, as women ought to be honoured and loved', — and not to be made the objects of an overweening idolatry. He dedicates his book to Sidney

because the Italian likes to talk with someone who can understand. The poetry in the book is under the criticism and protection of a poet ; the philosophy is nakedly revealed to so clear an intellect as yours ; and the heroic matters are directed to a heroic and noble mind, with which you have shown yourself to be endowed.

This tribute, coming from one who has many claims to be called the keenest intellect of his age, is a worthy summing-up of the gifts which had made Sidney the most famous contemporary patron of learning and of letters.

Bruno left England with Mauvissière only some two weeks before Sidney sailed for Flushing to take part in the campaign in which, eleven months later, he lost his life. In those last months in the Netherlands we may suppose that he had little opportunity for patronage, in spite of his having brought the use of learning into court and camp. But he knew some at least of the scholars who had gathered to the new University of Leiden, and one of them, Lipsius (as I have mentioned), dedicated to him a book on the correct pronunciation of Latin. This was in March 1586. A month later Lipsius wrote to Heinrich Rantzau, for many years stadt-holder of Schleswig-Holstein, and the owner of a considerable library, to say that Sidney and Leicester were with him at Leiden. Lipsius was a fine scholar but a man of weak and vacillating character who, in spite of writing a much-admired treatise on Constancy, shifted his religious position with little regard for that Stoic virtue. At this time he was (of necessity) Calvinist, but died, as he had been brought up, among the Jesuits. (He had also at one time been a Lutheran.) His name became a synonym for the turncoat, and it is hardly to be supposed that Sidney, any more than other contempo-raries, ever trusted him, though Lipsius seems to have been genuine in his admiration for Sidney.

More noble characters than Lipsius were the Dousas, father and son, both of whom Sidney knew. They were men of his own kind, aristocrats, scholars, and men of action: Charles Fitzgeffrey later complimented the younger Dousa as the Dutch Sidney. The elder, one of the heroes of the siege of Leiden, was Curator of the new University. He probably met Sidney for the first time while on a diplomatic mission in London, where he had many English friends. He was also much interested in the New Poetry in England, and on the movement that Sidney had done so much to encourage. He knew Mulcaster's work on the writing of English, and he had met Camden. He knew the work of the Pléiade, if we may judge from a poem addressed to him by a friend, and knew personally Ronsard, de Baïf, Sambuc, Estienne, and other French scholars and men of letters. Probably he and his son, like their friend Melissus in Germany, were eager to

introduce the culture of the Renaissance into the Netherlands as Sidney had done into England. The elder Dousa
addressed a poem to Sidney to accompany the gift of his
edition of Petronius, and his son wrote a poem to Sidney
while alive and four elegies on his death. He also knew
English, for he refers to the *Arcadia* in one of these poems,
and must therefore have seen it in manuscript ; and he translated a sonnet of Henry Constable's into Latin. This sonnet,

> Blame not my heart for flying up too high,

was addressed to Lady Rich, a fact that sets imagination
restlessly working, but to no conclusion. Why should
Constable address her, as he often does ? Was it at Sidney's
suggestion, when he himself had put off the part of Astrophel ?
Was Constable writing in England, and sending his poems
out to Sidney, or was he in the Netherlands, perhaps in Sidney's
train, for he knew Sidney ? The presence of the Roman
Catholic poet in such circumstances would be somewhat
surprising, but he was no fanatic, as his sonnets to the Princess
of Orange show. One of them was written 'upon occasion
of the murther of her father and husband' in the Massacre of
St. Bartholomew, an occasion which French poets like Ronsard
and de Baïf celebrated with horrible enthusiasm.

Geffrey Whitney, the emblem-writer, who was certainly
in the Netherlands at this time, wrote prefatory verses in
English to the elder Dousa's *Odarum Britannicarum Liber*,
and translated into English a poem to Leicester by the younger
Dousa. His book *A Choice of Emblems* was printed at Leiden
in 1586 with the long dedication to Leicester in which Whitney
discourses on the excellence of patronage. In one poem
Whitney celebrates, in bumpy Alexandrines, Sidney's achievement in bringing true poetry to England, both by his own
writings and by his criticism of others.

No haulting verse hee writes, but matcheth former times,
No Cherillus he can abide, nor Poetes patched rimes.
What volumes hath hee writte, that rest among his friendes,
Which needes no other praise at all, eche worke it selfe comendes.
So, that hee famous lives, at home, and farre, and neare ;
For those that live in other landes, of SIDNEY's giftes doe heare.
And suche as Muses serve, in darkenes meere doe dwell ;
If that they have not seene his workes, they doe so farre excell.

Certainly the Dutch were well aware of Sidney's fame as writer and as patron, and it is perhaps significant that the first language into which his *Apologie for Poetrie* was translated was Dutch. To his example they looked when they wished to create a vernacular literature, and the first to do so seem to have been the Dousas.

The Dutch also admired Sidney as a man of action and as a pattern of nobility. Arnold Eickius addressed a long poem in Horatian alcaics to Sidney to which he gave the sub-title *De vera nobilitate*, Of true Nobility : he dedicated it to his young son, holding up before him the image of Philip Sidney as the pattern of what he should strive to be.

William the Silent's widow, Louise de Coligny, whom Sidney may have known in Paris in 1572 (when she lost both her father and her first husband, Charles de Coligny, in the Massacre), was an intimate friend. She enjoyed Sidney's company and wrote to ask Jean Hotman to persuade him to visit her at Middelburg in April 1586. Later she was at Flushing, where she must have seen Sidney quite frequently, and in the postscript to a letter to Hotman from there, written on the eve of the fight at Zutphen, she alludes to the pleasure he and Sidney took in the company of fair ladies. Early in November she wrote to Leicester on hearing the news of Sidney's death, 'which I regret, and shall regret all my life, as if he had been my brother'. She adds that one of her chief pleasures since her widowhood had been in his conversation and friendship, the memory of which would help her to bear this new grief.

News of Sidney's death in battle was received with a shocked and uncomprehending sense of waste in an age when death by violence had not by its frequency made men callous. Sidney and Sir Richard Grenville were the only Englishmen of rank or fame to be killed in action in the reign of Elizabeth, for then famous victories might be won without the savage slaughter of millions or the stupid devastation of cities. We find it difficult, brought up to expect these things as part of our inheritance, to appreciate the sense of loss felt at the news of Sidney's death ; but the unparalleled magnificence of his funeral in St. Paul's, and the endless lamentation for him throughout the civilized world, may persuade us. In Holland the States of Zealand asked that they might have the honour of burying him, and undertook to erect as fine a monument as was ever erected to any Christian Prince, though it should cost them half a ton of gold. Even his country's enemies would not withhold their praise. Mendoza managed to combine praise of Sidney with derision of England, saying that 'he could not but lament to see Christendom deprived of so rare a light in these cloudy times, and bewail poor widow England, that having been many years in breeding one eminent spirit, was in a moment bereaved of him'. And in Spain that morose fanatic Philip II could pause in his plans for haling England back to Popery to remember that Philip Sidney was his godson. His friends were inconsolable, as their letters show. Fulke Greville wrote to the Scottish Ambassador :

My Lord, — I go no whither, therefore I beseech you pardon me that I visit you not. The only question I now study is whether weeping sorrow, or speaking sorrow, may most honour his memory, that I think death is sorry for. What he was to God, his friends and country, fame hath told, though his expectation went beyond her good. My Lord, give me leave to join with you in praising and lamenting him, the name of whose friendship carried me above my own worth, and I fear hath left me to play an ill poet in my own part. Well, my Lord, divide me not from him, but love his memory, and me in it. I shall not see your lordship so oft as I would do if you were yourself. It is enough I wish you honour and love you. From my lodge this night. Your lordship's friend,

FOULK GREVILLE.

P.S.—I was but gone to take air in the park when it pleased you to call.

Du Plessis-Mornay wrote to Walsingham that in all the trials and troubles which he had endured nothing had so deeply touched him as this loss. 'Henceforth I am resolved either to love no one, or to hate myself.' Jean Hotman wrote to Lipsius on hearing the news, begging him and Dousa, as friends who had been with Sidney in the last months of his life, to write to him in consolation. 'Everyone here', says Hotman, 'regrets that he threw away his life as he did.' And he adds as fine a compliment to Sidney's character as any among the hundreds that were written. 'I have noted one thing above all others in his life : that, although he had in him the highest virtues, he was untouched by any man's envy or detraction, so that he might deservedly be called the darling of the human race.'

CHAPTER 6

The Countess of Pembroke

THE death of Sir Philip Sidney brought dismay to the learned world even more than to the statesmen who saw in him a future leader and successor. The two Universities produced volumes of elegies in his memory, mostly written in Latin, but with a few poems in Greek, Hebrew, and Italian — the earliest of such collections to be made in England. The Cambridge volume, which contained verses in English by King James VI and other Scottish admirers of Sidney, was the first to be printed ; and William Gager of Christ Church found it necessary to apologize to the Earl of Leicester for the delay in the production of the Oxford volume which he edited. At Oxford a second collection of elegies was published, written by twenty-nine members of New College. Sidney himself had no connection with the College, but his father and the Herberts were all of New College : the volume was dedicated to his brother-in-law, the Earl of Pembroke. At Leiden another collection, edited by George Benedicti, was composed in his memory, and countless elegies and epitaphs were written in his honour at home and abroad. Spenser's *Astrophel*, though not published till some years later, is probably the most famous of these poems, together with the poems that accompanied it, by the Countess of Pembroke, Fulke Greville, Sir Walter Ralegh, Matthew Roydon, and Lodowick Bryskett. Some poets of an older generation, Thomas Churchyard, George

Whetstone, and Nicholas Breton among them, wrote elegies on his death, and so did younger poets who had never known him. Those who wrote in his memory include Thomas Watson, Samuel Daniel, Henry Constable, and Robert Peele, Ben Jonson, Michael Drayton, Richard Barnfield, Edward Herbert (Lord Herbert of Cherbury), and William Basse. Sir Arthur Gorges wrote two poems on his death, one of them a sonnet on the favourite theme of his equal distinction in the arts of war and peace :

> Mars and the Muses weare att mortall stryfe.

Sir William Herbert wrote a poem called *Baripenthes*, which has not survived. Thomas Moffett, who was later to win fame as an entomologist, but who was at this time family physician to the Earl of Pembroke at Wilton, wrote an elegy in Latin verse as well as a prose life, both of which remained in manuscript until our own day. The Epigrammatists John Owen and Thomas Bastard (who had both contributed to the New College *Peplus*), John Stradling, Charles Fitzgeffrey, Thomas Campion, Thomas Bancroft, and others all wrote his epitaph. In France de Lisle Groslot, who had known Sidney in the Netherlands, wrote a *Tumbeau*. In Holland the younger Dousa wrote four Latin poems to his memory. Even in Italy someone — I do not know who — wrote a poem on Sidney's death in Italian, from which a few lines are quoted before the Italian translation of the *Arcadia*. Byrd's settings of two poems on his death have already been mentioned ; there were popular ballads in his memory, all now lost, but entered in the Stationers' Register at various dates in 1587. Thomas Lant, Portcullis Pursuivant, produced a pictorial record of the funeral, with engravings by de Brij, a huge and handsome roll which John Aubrey remembered seeing in an alderman's house in Gloucester. 'He had contrived it to be turned upon two pinnes, that turning one of them made the figures march all in order.' In addition to all these celebrations of Sidney, formal, or intimate, or popular, there were many prose lives written of him, but since these, to a greater or less extent, have already been used in this study it is scarcely necessary to list them here. Best known of them, but (at least for my purposes) rather disappointing, is Fulke Greville's *Life*, which is not the biography of an intimate friend that would have been so welcome, but a dissertation on political wisdom based on Sidney's example.

Needless to say, a majority of the elegies on Sidney are pedestrian copies of verses equally lacking in literary merit and biographical information. The quantity of them is remarkable, and the quality, more often than not, despicable : it is a weary task to plod through acres of muddy bucolics, to look out across oceans of tears that, unlike those of Crashaw's Magdalene, are neither portable nor compendious, or to flick over the pages of a classical dictionary in a vain attempt to detect some point in yet another comparison. But when the task is done, a few scraps of information remain, so that it is possible from these memorial poems, and from other references to Sidney scattered about the poetry of the succeeding years, to discover something of what the poets believed that they owed to his work.

Of his patronage of the poets, naturally enough, these elegists most often write. So in the best of the poems in the Oxford *Exequiae* Richard Latewar, 'a most ingenious Latin poet' in Antony Wood's opinion, says that Sidney had taught him to try to win fame of the capricious Muses, and to attempt a lofty style. He had written three tragedies, on Croesus, Philotas, and the house of Pelops, none of which survive ; but his choice of Philotas is noteworthy, for (some years later) Daniel wrote a tragedy on this unusual theme.

Latewar, who must have been about twenty-four at this time, knew Sidney and Greville personally and was, as he says, familiar with Sidney's own poetry, both *Astrophel and Stella* — he calls his elegy *Stellati Pastoris* ΕΙΔΤΛΛΙΟΝ — and the *Arcadia*. He retained his connection with this circle of friends, becoming chaplain to Charles Blount, Lord Mountjoy, in whose service he was killed in Ireland in 1601. (To Mountjoy Daniel dedicated his *Philotas*.) Another contributor who had known Sidney personally was Matthew Gwinne, who urges Fulke Greville, Sidney's Patroclus, to write of him. Richard Eedes, who recollects that the last poem he wrote for Sidney was to celebrate his marriage, calls him 'first author of my writing poetry'. Other Oxford writers who had known him are Laurence Humfrey, President of Magdalen, 'a great and general scholar, an able linguist, a deep divine' of the Calvinist persuasion, and Francis Mason. Mason was a poor boy from Durham who came to Oxford in 1583 and three years later was elected probationer fellow of Merton. He became known for his controversial writings (which are composed without the savage scurrility usual among religious polemics) as *Vindex Ecclesiae Anglicanae*. It is a little surprising to find that such as he already knew not only the *Arcadia*, but presumably *Astrophel and Stella* too, for he describes Sidney's shield, in Homeric terms, as *Stellatus clypeus*, and gives other hints of his knowledge. Perhaps he was introduced to Sidney, or to Sidney's works, through colleagues at Merton, such as Savile, Bodley, or George Carleton, who had been a fellow of Merton since 1580. Carleton was a friend of Camden and Bodley, and married the daughter of Sir Henry Killigrew, whom Sidney knew. Like several others, he quotes Sidney's motto *Vix ea nostra voco*; but he is alone among the many readers of the *Arcadia* to mention that it was written at Wilton,

Pembrochia in aula. Whether or not this argues a special intimacy with Sidney, certainly Carleton seems to have had access to an eyewitness of the fight at Zutphen, for he gives a most vivid and circumstantial account of Sidney's exploit in rescuing Lord Willoughby de Eresby, which was the occasion — of his fatal wound. But for all that, Carleton chooses to write his warmest praise, not of Sidney's military prowess, but of his gifts as a poet and patron of poets. So it is with them all : for to these cultivated and civilized men war seemed a detestable and barbarous business, not at all worth the sacrifice of a life such as Sidney's. They even blame him for wasting his life, and for not leaving to others of less outstanding gifts the degrading tasks of a soldier. They are very far indeed from thinking of Sidney as the heroic soldier who had also written a romance and a number of sonnets, which is perhaps customary with us. For them he was a fine poet and a generous patron :

> Unum adeo, per quas animantur saecula, Musae
> Delitias nostri generis memorasse feruntur.

And they felt that he was irreplaceable. His achievement and his inspiration were unique, and he, above all men, should have lived into old age. So John Gifford, contributing a pastoral elegy called *Lycidas* to the New College volume, laments for him :

> Nunc igitur dolor est, non longos vivere in annos,
> Qui faciles praebent pastorum cantibus aures.

His whole poem (which is an admirable one) is devoted to the theme of Sidney's patronage of the poets.

Where men like the Earl of Oxford sought only to imitate Renaissance fashions, Sidney taught men to emulate Renaissance achievement. Lord Oxford set writers of the calibre of Anthony Munday translating Romances of Chivalry from

French, Italian, and Spanish, and encouraged others to waste their time in translations of French and Italian poems into Latin. Sidney set Spenser to write the *Faerie Queene*. Who would continue his work? What would become of the Muses, now their champion is dead? asks Richard Eedes. William Camden repeats this anxious question and answers it with an assurance that through Sidney the Muses now live, as he will live through them. But it was a real problem, not merely a phrase of compliment to a dead man : how were they to discover a patron as enlightened to take his place. Probably Camden was right, and Sidney had done enough already to ensure that the Muses would continue to flourish in England. But the matter was never put to the test, for the new patron who should continue his work was perfectly qualified to do so, the 'most deare, and most worthy to be most deare Lady', whose name had been the last word on his lips as he died, his sister Mary, Countess of Pembroke.

First among her tasks was to oversee the printing of her brother's works, for when he died nothing of his had been published. In manuscript the *Arcadia* and many of the poems were known, and had passed, somehow, beyond Sidney's closest friends, so that poor young scholars in Oxford, or statesmen concerned in the Dutch wars, had read and admired them. In the year after his death his translation of du Plessis-Mornay's tract, completed by Golding, was published, and though this was an influential work, several times reprinted, it scarcely concerns the development of English literature. The *Arcadia, Astrophel and Stella,* and the *Apologie for Poetrie* are Sidney's chief contributions to that development, and the Countess of Pembroke had her own views on their correct presentation.

The task that had devolved upon her was not altogether simple. The *Arcadia* existed in many manuscripts, and

since copyists are by no means infallible, a choice must be
made between the different copies. Further, the *Arcadia*
existed in two versions, an early, simpler version, which was
first published by Feuillerat in 1926, and a revised, more
sophisticated and complex version, which was left incomplete
by Sidney. The London publishers were eager to get hold of
a copy of a book that was much praised, and whose author's
fame was certain to assure success. Already in November
1586, within a month of Sidney's death, the booksellers were
vying with each other in their attempts to secure the rights of
publication, as we can see in a letter from Greville to Walsingham.

> Sr this day, one Ponsonby, a booke bynder in Poles Church
> yard, came to me and told me that ther was one in hand to print Sr
> Philip Sydneys old Arcadia, asking me yf it were done with your
> honors consent, or any other of his frendes? I told him, to my
> knowledge, no: then he advised me to give warninge of it, either
> to the archbishope or doctor Cosen, who have, as he says, a copy
> to peruse to that end.
> Sr I am loth to renew his memory unto you, but yeat in this I
> must presume; for I have sent my lady, your daughter, at her
> request, a correction of that old one, done 4 or 5 years sinse, which
> he left in trust with me, wherof ther is no more copies, and fitter
> to be printed then the first, which is so common : notwithstanding
> even that to be amended by a direction sett downe under his own
> hand, how and why ; so as in many respects, especially the care of
> printing of it, is to be don with more deliberation.

From this letter we learn that Greville possessed, perhaps
through Sidney's bequest of his books, the only copy of the
revised *Arcadia* then existing. The attempted piracy was
prevented, and on August 23rd, 1588, licence was granted to
Ponsonby to print the work. From Greville's manuscript
the first edition of the *Arcadia* was printed in quarto for
Ponsonby in 1590, arranged by its editor into chapters with

summary 'arguments', and with the poems inserted at his discretion. This he was scrupulous to point out in a note added after Sidney's dedication.

> The division and summing of the Chapters was not of Sir Philip Sidnei's doing, but adventured by the over-seer of the print, for the more ease of the Readers. He therefore submits himselfe to their judgment, and if his labour answere not the worthines of the booke, desireth pardon for it. As also if any defect be found in the Eclogues, which although they were of Sir Philip Sidnei's writing, yet were they not perused by him, but left till the worke had bene finished, that then choise should have bene made, which should have bene taken, and in what manner brought in. At this time they have bene chosen and disposed as the over-seer thought best.

The note is unsigned and it has generally been assumed that Greville was the sole 'overseer' of this first *Arcadia*. However, Miss Yates has suggested with great plausibility that John Florio also had a hand in the task as Greville's assistant, and she sees in the style of the chapter summaries evidence of his work. Certainly the style is very unlike Greville's. Florio attacked the editor of the 1593 edition of the *Arcadia*, Hugh Sanford, with much vehemence, in revenge (as it seems) for Sanford's strictures in his preface on 'the disfigured face' of the first edition. The violence of Florio's abuse implies that he had suffered a personal affront, and he returns to the attack more than once. I think that we can accept Miss Yates' suggestion, that the first *Arcadia* was edited by Florio from Greville's manuscript, and under Greville's supervision. Even as late as 1596 Thomas Wilson, in dedicating to Greville a translation from the *Diana* of Montemayor, said that it was by his 'noble vertue the world so hapily enioyes' the *Arcadia*. It was on the whole a cautious and scholarly piece of work, and the editors were at pains to make clear how much they had departed from the manuscript. The only fault that can legitimately be charged against them

MARIA
SIDNEY COM
PEMBROK

THE COUNTESS OF PEMBROKE
Engraving from Livio Alessandri's translation:
L'Arcadia della Contessa di Pembrok, 1659.

THE CIVILE WARES
betweene the Howses of Lancaster
and Yorke corrected and continued
by Samuel Daniel one of the Groomes
of hir Maiesties most honorable.
Priuie Chamber,

Ætas prima canat veneres
postrema tumultus.

PRINTED
AT LONDON
by Simon Waterſonne,
1609;

Cocksonus.

SAMUEL DANIEL
Title-page to *The Civile Wares*, 1609
Engraved by T. Cockson

is inadequate care in reading proofs. Some critics of the present day, like John Florio (who was probably an interested party), prefer the first quarto to the 1593 folio which superseded it. Such a judgment seems to me naïve.

This new edition was prepared at the instigation of the Countess of Pembroke, by her husband's secretary Hugh Sanford, whose initials sign the preface to the Reader which so much annoyed Florio. (That they are Sanford's initials is clear from John Hoskyns' reference to the 1590 edition as 'the first edition in quarto without Samford's Additions', as well as from Aubrey's express statement.) Sanford removed the chapter summaries, and instead of leaving the revised version unfinished as Sidney and his first editors had left it, completed the book from the old, unrevised *Arcadia*. Sanford carried out the Countess of Pembroke's wishes conscientiously, and his statement of what he had achieved is fair : the readers, he says,

shall for their better satisfaction understand, that though they find not here what might be expected, they may find neverthelesse as much as was intended, the conclusion, not the perfection of Arcadia, and that no further than the Author's owne writings or knowne determinations could direct.

Florio's criticism, that 'this end wee see of it . . . is not answerable to the precedents', is also true, for Sanford's edition is something of a hybrid : the parts added, though of Sidney's writing, are incongruous with the first part, since the revision had been so extensive as to make of the *Arcadia* a new book.

None the less this edition was continually reprinted, and became the most famous work of fiction in the English language throughout the seventeenth century. In the edition of 1621 the third book, in which the revised version had broken off, was supplemented by Sir William Alexander, perhaps with the consent of the Countess of Pembroke, whom he knew; and three years later a sixth book was added by R. Beling. There have been few more popular books in the whole history of our literature, and if its immediate success owed something to the fame of the author, since it was 'the silver image of his gentle wit and the golden pillar of his noble courage', its continuing popularity derived from its intrinsic excellence. Even Milton, when not concerned to vilify King Charles for taking pleasure in 'a vain, amatorious poem', could acknowledge that it was 'a book of worth and wit'; and less prejudiced readers did not conceal their delight in it. With the ladies, especially, it was always a favourite, to the distress of Puritans like Thomas Powell for whom the feminine ideal was the *hausfrau*:

Let them learne plaine workes of all kind, so they take heed of too open seaming. In stead of song and Musicke, let them learne cookery and Laundrie. And in stead of reading Sir Philip Sidney's Arcadia, let them read the grounds of good huswifery. I like not the female poetresse at any hand.

But the book continued to be read, and even in the eighteenth century it had its admirers, Cowper and Dr. Johnson among them; while Romantic taste owed not a little to the greatest of English romances. 'The Arcadia is about Vernditch and Wilton,' says Aubrey, 'and these romancy plaines and boscages did, no doubt, conduce to the heightening of Sir Philip Sydney's phancie.'

There are indeed Romantic hints and precedents scattered throughout Sidney's work : in his *Apologie for Poetrie*, where he insists on the divine nature of the gift of poetry, 'For poesie, must not be drawne by the eares, it must bee gently led, or, rather, it must lead'. Or, as Keats says, 'If Poetry comes not as naturally as the Leaves to a tree, it had better not come at all'. And again, in *Astrophel and Stella*, in the first sonnet of the series, when study of other men's verses but clogged his own invention, he found the remedy in the Romantic recipe :

Fool, said my Muse to mee, look in thy heart and write.

The whole of Sidney's work for English poetry had been based on the conviction that both inspiration and study were needed ; that the poet was both *vates*, seer, and ποιητής, maker. Nowhere does he show this better than in his *Astrophel and Stella*, the first and greatest of English sonnet sequences.

When he died these sonnets were known, like the *Arcadia*, in manuscript copies passed among friends. As with the *Arcadia*, the booksellers were eager to obtain copies to print from, and on this occasion Thomas Newman, a less scrupulous publisher than Ponsonby, succeeded in getting hold of a bad copy, which he printed with great carelessness in 1591. Astrophel was here revealed biting his tongue as well as his pen in his desperate search for inspiration ; lamenting the mean face with which the moon climbed the skies ; and being concerned (as well he might be) at Stella's vermilion eyes. Sidney's friends succeeded in getting this preposterous edition suppressed, and it has been left to the pedantry of a French scholar of the twentieth century to reprint it. (Even the piratical printer repented enough to remove three hundred and fifty misreadings and misprints in a new edition that he brought out later in the year : not so Professor Feuillerat.) For the first edition Nashe, presumably at Newman's invitation, wrote a characteristic preface, in which, with that Elizabethan genius for founding a felicitous phrase on a pun, he says that 'the tragicomedy of love is played out by starlight'. This preface, whose flattery of the Countess of Pembroke could not, apparently, compensate for its impudence, was suppressed in Newman's corrected edition. But neither of these editions was satisfactory, and it was not until 1598, when an edition of *Astrophel and Stella* prepared under the supervision of Lady

Pembroke was printed in folio with the *Arcadia*, that the authorized text was available.

A comparison of Newman's corrected text with this edition shows something of the tradition of circulating poems in manuscript that was then current. We may suppose that Newman obtained his copy from someone who was not an intimate friend of Sidney's, since no friend would have risked his good name with such a shoddy production. From Newman's copy certain poems, or parts of poems, were omitted, and these all have one thing in common : an intimacy of self-revelation which, we may well believe, Sidney would have kept from all except his closest friends. These passages are the thirty-seventh sonnet, with its scurrilous punning on the name of Stella's husband, Lord Rich ; parts of the eighth and tenth songs, and the eleventh song. In these the most passionate moments of the whole sequence are reached, and we can understand Sidney's wish to keep the exquisitely tender verses of Stella's reply to Astrophel in the eighth song, or the duet with her in the tenth, unsullied by the eyes of the profane. But this shows that there were two versions of *Astrophel and Stella* in circulation : one for Sidney's friends who knew Stella's identity and another for those who did not, and who could read the poems without discovering any secret passion by which Stella might be compromised. From this expurgated text for a wider public Newman printed his quartos ; but the Countess of Pembroke, twelve years after Sidney's death, and when Lady Rich's liaison with Lord Mountjoy was common knowledge, saw no reason for any further reticence. Possibly this offended both Lady Rich and Sidney's own daughter, the Countess of Rutland : Florio would otherwise hardly have chosen a dedication to these two ladies as the place where he might make unfavourable criticisms of the 1593 *Arcadia*, for which Lady Pembroke had been responsible, if there had not been at least what Sidney calls 'the ordinarie mislike betweene sisters in law'.[1]

However that may be, Lady Pembroke's edition of *Astrophel and Stella* is superior to Newman's in other ways than by the inclusion of a few private poems. She restored the songs, which Newman had printed at the end of the sonnets, to their proper places in the sequence : a very valuable change, for they mark pauses in the dramatic development of the story, and sum up with most consummate skill the mood of the moment that has been reached. Sidney's songs in *Astrophel and Stella* serve the same purpose as do Shakespeare's in his plays. This interspersing of songs and poems in other forms among the sonnets of a sequence was in the Italian tradition ; but, owing to Newman's unauthorized publication of *Astrophel and Stella*, where the songs were separated from the sonnets, it became usual in English for a sonnet sequence to consist of sonnets alone.

The publication of *Astrophel and Stella* in 1591 began the craze for sonneteering that is so characteristic of the 1590s. Newman had printed with Sidney's poems sonnets by Samuel Daniel as well as poems by Campion, the Earl of Oxford, and others. In the following year Daniel published his sonnet sequence *Delia*, disclaiming any responsibility for the previous association of his poems with Sidney's. He had for some years now been living at Wilton as tutor to the young Herberts, and he dedicated his sonnets to the Countess of Pembroke.

> I desire [he says] onely to bee graced by the countenance of your protection : whome the fortune of our time hath made the happie and iudiciall Patronesse of the Muses (a glory hereditary to your house) to preserve them from those hidious Beestes, Oblivioun and Barbarisme.

[1] It may be significant that this phrase does not occur in the 'old' *Arcadia*.

Daniel had probably begun writing sonnets in the later 1580s, and we may believe that Spenser (who had translated sonnets as a schoolboy in the 1560s) had been writing sonnets for some time. Others of Sidney's circle, Greville, Dyer, and Constable among them, had written sonnets before he died. Thomas Watson had published his ʽΕκατομπαθία in 1582, but his 'Passionate Centurie of Love' contains no sonnets except among the commendatory poems. None of these collections, nor the memory of sonnets by Wyatt and Surrey, was the source of the astonishing flood of sonnets that followed the publication of *Astrophel and Stella*.

Here I may mention Miss Wilson's attractive conjecture that Shakespeare wrote his fifty-fifth sonnet as a prefatory sonnet to *Astrophel and Stella*. There seems little doubt that it was written (as J. M. Robertson long ago suggested) in commendation of some collection of love-poetry : it would be more appropriate to *Astrophel and Stella* than to any other. 'The gilded monuments of princes' recalls the Dutch offer of a most sumptuous monument to him. The reference to wasteful war, and the Ovidian 'Nor Mars his sword nor war's quick fire shall burn' (as Miss Wilson points out), are suitable enough to a poet killed in the war-torn Netherlands ; and (I would add) hardly suitable to any other contemporary of Sidney's. It is pleasant to think of Shakespeare, whose admiration of Sidney's poetry and character is often apparent, writing this sonnet to accompany a copy, whether in manuscript or printed, of *Astrophel and Stella*. We cannot prove that he did.

To the Countess of Pembroke and Fulke Greville and others of Sidney's friends the publication of his writings, though an obvious means of continuing the work he had begun, was not the only means. They were not content with this complex act of piety, but knew that they must encourage the poets whom Sidney had helped, and discover other younger poets to carry on the new tradition. Already in her brother's lifetime Lady Pembroke had begun to gather about her at Wilton poets and men of learning. Thomas Howell had for some years before her marriage been in her husband's service, and Hugh Sanford, whom Aubrey calls 'a good scholar and poet', was certainly at Wilton in the early 1580s.

After Sanford's death there was published at Amsterdam in 1611 a Puritan tract of his writing, *De Descensu Domini Nostri Jesu Christi ad Inferos*. This combination of an interest in Puritan theology with a taste for poetry was quite usual, as will be seen, among those who enjoyed the patronage of Lady Pembroke. So too was the inventing of devices, the fashion for which Sidney had introduced from Italy. Sanford, like Howell, took pleasure in these. The device of a pig smelling at a bush of marjoram, with the motto '*Non tibi spiro*', which appeared on the title-page of his edition of the *Arcadia*, was of his own invention. Nashe and Florio mocked him for it, and others besides them seem not to have approved Sanford's taste in devices. Rowland Whyte in a letter to Sir Robert Sidney of September 26th, 1600, is anxious lest Sanford should foist some ridiculous device on the young William Herbert in his first tournament.

My Lord Harbert resolves this yeare, to shew hymself a Man at Armes, and prepares for yt; and because it is his first Tyme of runninge, yt were good he came in with some excellent Devise; I make yt known to your Lordship, that if you please to honor my Lord Harbert with your advice; my feare is, that Mr Sanford will in his Humor, persuade my Lord to some pedantike Invention.

Sanford had been tutor to Lord Herbert, the elder of Lady Pembroke's two sons, since 1586, and according to Robert Parker, writing in 1611, he had done his work so well that

William Herbert, by then third Earl of Pembroke, had no equal for learning among all the peers of England. Both Herbert brothers most ably continued in their generation the patronage of the arts which they had learnt at Wilton.

Whether Daniel succeeded Sanford as tutor to the young Herberts, or whether he came to Wilton to assist Sanford, we cannot say. More probably Daniel shared the work with Sanford, for there seems to have been no jealousy or rivalry between them, even though Daniel's brother-in-law John Florio was at daggers drawn with Sanford. Daniel was a peaceful, modest, retiring man, a good scholar and historian, who loved books and hated the bustle and agitation of town life. When, in King James's time, he became one of the Grooms of the Privy Chamber to the Queen, he still preferred his own company to the court, and, so Fuller says, 'As the tortoise burieth himself all the winter under the ground, so Mr Daniel would lye at his garden-house in Old Street, nigh London, for some months together (the more retiredly to enjoy the company of the Muses)'. Daniel came to Wilton in a happy day for a man of his tastes and temperament. He had been at Oxford in 1583, when he heard Bruno lecture there, and shortly after this had travelled on the Continent with Sir Edward Dymoke, the Queen's Champion. In Italy they met Battista Guarini, the famous Italian poet of *Il Pastor Fido*, whose haughty assumption that English was a language incapable of poetry must have put Daniel on his mettle. At least the remark was still rankling nearly twenty years later, when another Dymoke published the first English translation of *Il Pastor Fido* ; and a quiet conviction that English poetry could rival that of 'declined Italy' appears time and again in Daniel's work. In Italy Daniel came across Paolo Giovio's work on *imprese*, which Sir Edward Dymoke invited him to translate into English. This, his first book, is remarkable for the direct simplicity of style that was to distinguish all Daniel's writing in prose or verse, and indeed N. W. in his letter of commendation mentions 'the nakednes of your stile'.

Daniel was perhaps introduced by Florio to the Countess of Pembroke, who would have been interested in this translation of a work on devices which her brother knew in Italian. Her quick intelligence would at once have recognized in the translator, especially in Daniel's own preface to the book, a writer of uncommon ability; and not long after its publication Daniel came to Wilton. Probably Daniel never met Sidney, who left England in November 1585, for his many references to him do not suggest any personal acquaintance. But he saw very clearly that Lady Pembroke had set herself to continue his work for English poetry, and learnt by his own experience how she did so. She did not try to revive the use of classical metre in English, but preferred the rhymed accentual verse which she herself wrote with skill and grace. So Daniel, in addressing to William Herbert his *Defence of Ryme* against Campion's plea for a return to quantitative measures, refers to his own use of rhyme:

Having been first encourag'd and fram'd thereunto by your most worthy and honourable Mother, and received the first Notion for the formal ordering of those Compositions at Wilton, which I must ever acknowledge to have been my best School, and thereof always am to hold a feeling and grateful Memory.

At Wilton, therefore, he began to write poetry, under the guidance and encouragement of the Countess of Pembroke. His earliest poems were the sonnets whose unauthorized publication with *Astrophel and Stella* has been mentioned; and in the dedication of *Cleopatra* to the Countess he refers to his unambitious beginning, and to the harder task to which she had invited him.

> I, who (contented with an humble song,)
> Made musique to my selfe that pleasd me best,
> And onelie told of Delia, and her wrong,
> And praisd her eyes, and plaind mine owne unrest :
> (A text from whence my Muse had not digrest)
> Madam, had not thy well grac'd *Antony*
> (Who all alone, having remained long,)
> Requir'd his *Cleopatras* company.

For the moment I must leave aside consideration of these plays, to point out that the Countess of Pembroke was encouraging Daniel to larger attempts, just as her brother had set Spenser to the writing of the *Faerie Queene*.

Spenser made a similar appreciation of Daniel's abilities from reading the manuscript of his poems in Ireland, or when he came to England with Ralegh in 1590. (Ralegh was closely associated with the Countess of Pembroke, and his half-brother Adrian Gilbert had a chemical laboratory in her house at Wilton.) In *Colin Clouts Come Home Againe*, written in 1591 though not published till 1595, Spenser mentions Daniel, alone of contemporary poets, by his own name. He obviously admired Daniel's sonnets, and like the Countess of Pembroke, believed that he was capable of greater things.

> And there is a new shepheard late up sprong,
> The which doth all afore him far surpasse :
> Appearing well in that well tuned song,
> Which late he sung unto a scornefull lasse.
> Yet doth his trembling Muse but lowly flie,
> As daring not too rashly mount on hight,
> And doth her tender plumes as yet but trie,
> In loves soft laies and looser thoughts delight.
> Then rouze thy feathers quickly, Daniel,
> And to what course thou please thy selfe advance :
> But most me seemes, thy accent will excell
> In Tragick plaints and passionate mischance.

We can easily imagine the effect of this kindly and perspicacious criticism from the greatest of living poets upon the young Daniel, especially when it coincided with the advice of his admired patroness. Perhaps Spenser even prompted her advice, for nothing is more likely than that she would show to him the work which her new poet had been writing ; and we know from this same poem that while in England Spenser had been welcomed by her.

> They all (quoth he) me graced goodly well,
> That all I praise, but in the highest place,
> Urania, sister unto Astrophel.

Daniel refers to this advice which he had received from Spenser and the Countess of Pembroke in the motto from Propertius which he used on the title-page of *Delia* in 1592 :

> Aetas prima canat Veneres, postrema tumultus.[1]

That is to say, In youth I sing of loves soft laies and looser thoughts delight, and in maturity of Tragick plaints and passionate mischance. The volume included *The Complaint of Rosamund*, a tragic plaint of the kind made popular in *The Mirrour for Magistrates*, and perhaps the best of its kind. If I am right in thinking that Daniel's Latin motto to the book is intended as a reference to Spenser's advice, then not only must Spenser have seen Daniel's sonnets in manuscript, but Daniel must have seen Spenser's lines in manuscript also. This is very probable, when the two poets were so closely associated with the same patron : and the whole of this episode very well illustrates the influence that an intelligent patron could have on the poets.

In his sonnets Daniel differs from the practice of both Sidney and Spenser, and writes in the normal English form,

---

[1] He used it again in later works. See Plate 11, f.p. 181.

of three quatrains followed by a couplet. His was the first collection of these so-called Shakespearean sonnets, and Shakespeare was certainly much influenced by Daniel's example, both in form and diction. Daniel achieves a purity of style which Coleridge noted : his 'diction bears no mark of time, no distinction of age, which has been, and as long as our language shall last, will be so far the language of the today and forever, as that it is more intelligible to us, than the transitory fashions of our own particular age'.

With his sonnets, Daniel printed a short Ode, and a translation from the Italian of the canzone 'O happy, Golden Age!' which matches the famous *O bella età de l' oro!* from Tasso's *Aminta*. Many of the sonnets themselves were paraphrases from the French of Desportes, much improving on the feeble originals. He was always learning the business of a poet, from the poets of France or Italy or elsewhere, but learning in his own fashion and never surrendering his powers to those of any other. Thus Daniel was carrying on the Sidneian tradition of experiment, of exploring new possibilities for English poetry, instead of being content to follow the accepted examples of Sidney or Spenser. Sidney had never intended to create a 'school' of poetry, but rather to create the conditions which would enable poets to write as well as their own gifts would allow. Only later, when the first flowering of Renaissance poetry had begun to fade, did the lesser poets seek shelter in the shade of the great, and there were Spenserians, Metaphysicals, and those who sought to be sealed of the tribe of Ben. Daniel was perhaps closer to Greville than to any of the others in style, but with far more ease and elegance, and without the dark burden of philosophical speculation that at times overwhelms Greville's poetry. There is a broad-minded independence in these men who, while admiring each other's poetry, were yet not persuaded to imitation but could still develop their own individual styles without eccentricity. To Spenser, Daniel seemed to surpass all his predecessors; and to Daniel, Sidney and Spenser were the two great English poets who might be set up to rival the Italians.

The success of Daniel's *Complaint of Rosamund* prompted Thomas Churchyard to bring out again, after thirty years, a new edition of his poem *Shore's Wife*, 'not in any kind of emulation, but to make the world knowe his device in age was as ripe and reddie as his disposition and knowledge was in youth'. The old poet, who also had known the hospitality of Wilton, and who had been first in the field of all the elegists on Sidney with an *Epitaph of Sir Philip Sidney* published before the end of 1586, sought to attach himself to the group of new poets, knowing they had achieved something that had eluded him. Like the others, he had no doubt of the advantage they had enjoyed in the patronage of the Sidneys. In a work called *A Pleasant Conceite penned in Verse* which he presented to the Queen on New Year's Day 1593 he describes the Countess of Pembroke:

> Pembroke a pearle, that orient is of kind,
> > A Sidney right, shall not in silence sit;
> A gemme more worth, than all the gold of Ind,
> > For she enjoyes, the wise Minervaes wit,
> And sets to schoole, our poets everywhere:
> > That doth presume the lawrell crowne to weare.

But Churchyard was too old to change his style, and belongs still to the generation of Turberville and Gascoigne.

Abraham Fraunce continued after Sidney's death to belong to the Wilton circle. As a poet he never achieved anything of much importance: his most successful work was a translation of Thomas Watson's *Amintae Gaudia*, published in 1587 under the title of *The Lamentations of Amyntas for the Death of*

Phillis. This he dedicated to the Countess of Pembroke, with never a word to acknowledge that Watson was the author of the original. Watson made a mild protest about this when publishing his own English version of his poem *Meliboeus* on the death of Sir Francis Walsingham. 'I interpret my self, lest Melibaeus in speaking English by an other mans labour, should leese my name in his chaunge, as my *Amyntas* did.' This seems to have touched Fraunce's conscience, for when he reprinted his translation the following year, under the title of *The Countess of Pembrokes Yvychurch,* he admitted that he had 'somewhat altered S. Tassoes Italian, and M. Watsons Latine Amyntas, to make them both one English'. Fraunce's dedication of *The Lamentations of Amyntas* shows the hazards to which the custom of copying and recopying manuscripts subjected an author's works.

Amintas . . . being first prepared for one or two, was afterwards by the meanes of a few, made common to manie, and so pitifully disfigured by the boisterous handling of unskilful pen men, that he was like to have come abroad so unlike himselfe, as that his own Phillis would never have taken him for Amintas.

Fraunce continued to dedicate his works to the Countess of Pembroke : *The Arcadian Rhetorike* in 1588, *The Countesse of Pembrokes Emmanuell*, and *The Countesse of Pembrokes Yvychurch* in 1591. (Ivychurch was the name of a property of the Countess's near Salisbury.) In 1592 he published *The Third part of the Countesse of Pembrokes Yvychurch, entitled Amintas Dale. Wherein are the most conceited tales of the Pagan Gods in English Hexameters.* Fraunce, like Campion, was persisting in the attempt to write quantitative English verse long after wiser members of the group to which he belonged had abandoned it, and without Campion's excuse of writing for music. Other works, which he thought unsuitable for a feminine patron, Fraunce dedicated to other members of the Wilton company: the manuscript of *The Shepheardes Logike* he dedicated to Dyer; and when the book was published as *The Lawiers Logike* he dedicated it to the Earl of Pembroke. In the same year he dedicated to Robert Sidney a Latin work on devices. He outlived nearly all the gifted men and women who had encouraged him in his early years: so late as 1633 he wrote a masque for the marriage of Lady Magdalen Egerton, as he had written others for her sisters. For the last thirty or forty years of his life he seems to have been in the service of the Earl of Bridgewater, who was son-in-law to Spenser's Amaryllis, that Alice Spencer who acknowledged Spenser's kinship, and for whom Milton wrote *Arcades*. Had Fraunce not died in 1633 probably he, and not Milton, would have been asked to write the Masque performed in the following year at Ludlow Castle. As with Gabriel Harvey, the latter half of his life does not concern us, for the early promise which led Sidney to pay for his education at Cambridge sputtered out in a succession of trivial or pedantic works. Like Harvey, he must have lived on his memories of the days when he knew Philip and Mary Sidney, when he had been privileged to read the *Arcadia* and the *Faerie Queene* in manuscript, when he too (in Gabriel Harvey's words) had been 'commendably employed in enriching, and polishing [his] native tongue'. But in the learned and cultivated household of the Earl of Bridgewater he must have met many who would be glad to listen to his talk of those swiftly receding times, among them John Donne and John Milton.

Spenser, though far away in Ireland, maintained his connection with the Countess of Pembroke's circle. For the *Faerie Queene* he wrote no less than seventeen dedicatory sonnets to all the most powerful courtiers in England. He addressed only two ladies, his kinswoman Elizabeth Spencer

Lady Carey, and the Countess of Pembroke. In his sonnet
to her he recalls, as so often, how it had been her brother

> Who first my Muse, did lift out of the flore,

and comparing her to him, begs her to accept the dedication

> For his, and for your owne especial sake.

To her in the following year he dedicated *The Ruines of Time*,
in which he mourns both Sidney and the Earl of Leicester,
and acknowledges himself 'bounden by manie singular
favours and great graces' to her. When in England in 1590
he saw her once more, and in *Colin Clouts Come Home Againe*
he recalls the kindness with which she received him. In the
same volume with this poem Spenser again alludes, as in the
Faerie Queene sonnet, to the physical resemblance of Lady
Pembroke to her brother, and he designs his poem in memory
of Sidney as a prelude to hers, surely as fine a compliment
as it was in his power to pay.

From Dublin, on July 18th, 1586, Spenser dated his
sonnet to Gabriel Harvey, his friend from Cambridge days.
There is an unconscious irony in Spenser's reference to
Harvey's happiness, for only a few months before he had
signed himself 'Unhappy Harvey' in a letter to Lord Burghley
urging his claims to the Mastership of Trinity Hall, which he
had failed to obtain. But Spenser's tribute to one

> That, sitting like a looker-on
> Of this worldes stage, doest note, with critique pen,
> The sharpe dislikes of each condition,

was truly deserved. From this time on Harvey's career is a
gradual decline, accelerated by the controversy with Tom
Nashe, whose virtuosity in invective neither he nor anyone
else could match. Whether Harvey ever again met Spenser
we do not know, but he seems no longer to have played any

part in the development of English poetry, to which, in the early days, his sound scholarship and vigorous critical judgment had contributed not a little. Perhaps Spenser lent him a manuscript copy of Ralegh's *Book of the Ocean to Cynthia* which he praises in a note in his copy of Speght's Chaucer. He himself had written a similar poem at the suggestion of Philip Sidney, of which (for all its vast length, 'nigh as much in quantitie, as Ariosto') nothing remains. He became a country doctor, living in obscurity at Saffron Walden, and dabbling in astrology, but still, no doubt, making his sharp and perspicacious comments in the margins of such books as he could afford to keep. Appropriately enough, the latest printed book he is known to have possessed was the *Arcadia* of 1613. He seems not to have approved of the Countess of Pembroke's recension, for in his copy he divided the work into chapters, giving the contents of each, as had been done in the first edition.

Among the poets whom Harvey names in 1592 as 'among the deere Lovers of the Muses and namely the professed sonnes of the same' was Thomas Watson. He was a poet of considerable talents, and a competent scholar, who while at Oxford, according to Antony Wood 'did spend some time . . . not in logic and philosophy, as he ought to have done, but in the smooth and pleasant studies of poetry and romance, whereby he obtained an honourable name among the students of those faculties'. After going down he stayed some time in Paris, where he knew the Walsinghams. He was well read in the ancient classics, and in recent French and Italian poetry, but though he later wrote in English, his earliest work was in translating into Latin the *Antigone* of Sophocles and sonnets of Petrarch and other Italians, a futile occupation much encouraged at the time by the Earl of Oxford, who lacked Sidney's confidence in the English tongue. Yet to the Earl of Oxford in 1582 Watson dedicated his first collection of English poems, the Ἑκατομπαθία, often described as the first of English sonnet sequences, though it does not contain a single sonnet. In some prefatory Latin verses Watson refers to Sidney and Dyer in a manner that shows he knew of their experimental work ; and the elusive Matthew Roydon, who claimed Sidney's friendship in the title of his *Elegie*, wrote commendatory verses for the book. Watson reverted to writing in Latin, so that it was left to Abraham Fraunce, by his translation into English, to give currency to Watson's *Amintae Gaudia*. In the last year or two of his life Watson returned to publishing English work, by collaborating with William Byrd in *The First Sett of Italian Madrigalls Englished*. One of the madrigals 'How long with vaine complayning' is transformed into a lament for Sidney : in another, set by Luca Marenzio, his name is joined with Walsingham's, who had just died. Significantly, the volume was dedicated to the Earl of Essex, who was regarded as Sidney's successor among the English courtiers. In the autumn of 1592 Watson died, and shortly after his death his *Amintae Gaudia* was reprinted, with a dedication to the Countess of Pembroke, written in response to his dying request, and signed C. M. A year later true sonnets by Watson were published under the title of *The Tears of Fancie*, but by this time *Astrophel and Stella* had set the fashion. This record of Watson's frustrated career as a poet confirms the value of Sidneian patronage. He was the only poet of ability writing in the 1580s who, in spite of his acquaintance with the Walsinghams, never came directly under the influence of the Sidneys ; so that he wrote in English poems which he kept to himself, and published only the Latin works which his patrons supposed would survive. Thus his real gifts were obscured through Oxford's cautious preference for Latin, while the far less talented Fraunce, encouraged by the Sidneys to write in English, won the fame that should have been Watson's.

The friend of Watson's who dedicated *Amintae Gaudia* to the Countess of Pembroke was almost certainly Christopher Marlowe. If this is so, it is the only evidence we have of his acquaintance with her, though it is very probable, since she knew several of his friends, Matthew Roydon, Thomas Kyd, and Sir Walter Ralegh, who may well have introduced him to her. Marlowe refers to the Countess of Pembroke's fame at home and abroad, and addresses her as the Muse of the poets of our time. With an allusion to Daniel's newly published sonnets he calls her Delia, and, with a phrase that again suggests one of Daniel's, he describes her as the refuge where virtue can shelter from the onset of gross barbarism and ignorance.

There is, however, no reason to suppose that Marlowe himself ever benefited from her patronage. She had little interest, so far as we can judge, in the London stage, and when she patronized the dramatists it was for the writing of Senecan plays on the French model. She herself began the fashion with a translation of Robert Garnier's *Marc Antoine*, first published in 1592 under the title of *Antonius*, and again in 1595 as *The Tragedie of Antonie*. Her translation is dated 'At Ramsbury, 26 of November, 1590', and is remarkable because she uses blank verse with considerable skill in the very year in which *Tamburlaine* was first printed. But probably Kyd rather than Marlowe suggested that she should turn the rhymed Alexandrines into blank verse. In the choruses, which she translates more freely, she shows that same supple inventiveness as in her Psalms, and is more successful than in the literal translation of the dialogue. At her suggestion Daniel wrote his *Cleopatra* to be a companion piece to her *Antonie*, as he tells us himself in dedicating it to her.

She briefly diverted Thomas Kyd from his true vocation as a writer for the popular stage by persuading him, about 1594, to translate another play of Garnier's, *Cornélie*. Other members of her circle continued to write this chamber-drama : Daniel's *Philotas* was published in 1605 and got him into trouble for a supposed sympathetic reference to the Essex rebellion. Fulke Greville wrote *Mustapha* and *Alaham*, and a play on *Antony and Cleopatra* which, lest it should involve him also in the rebellion, he burnt. But Greville, unlike Daniel, did not intend his plays for presentation on the stage 'for them, against whom so many good, and great spirits have already written'. Later, Sir William Alexander carried on the tradition of Senecan plays, from which in the course of time the Heroic plays of the Restoration developed. We may wonder why the Countess of Pembroke should have encouraged the writing of these somewhat lifeless works, but her reason is, partly, at least, to be found in her brother's *Apologie for Poetrie*. There he had made some comments on the plays of his own time which were then sensible and relevant, but which in the 1590s became out of date through the rapid development of the romantic drama in the hands of Marlowe and Shakespeare. Some critics of Sidney seem to blame him for his inability to forecast the work of these two dramatists, neither of whom had written a play when he died. The classicism of his taste, in the early 1580s, was perfectly sound : he had acted in classical plays at school ; he had seen plays in France and Italy, and, as always, wished to bring English literature the lessons he had learnt abroad. We ought not to blame him for failing to foresee *Hamlet* : we ought rather to note the sureness of taste which led him to pick out *Gorboduc* as the one play of some merit which, as far as he knew, had been produced in England in his time. He is just, sensible, and circumspect.

Our Tragedies, and Comedies (not without cause cried out against) observing rules neyther of honest civilitie nor of skilfull Poetrie, excepting *Gorboduck* (againe, I say, of those that I have seene,) which notwithstanding, as it is full of stately speeches and well sounding Phrases, clyming to the height of Seneca his stile, and as full of notable moralitie, which it doth most delightfully teach, and so obtayne the very end of poesie ; yet in troth it is very defectious in the circumstances : which greeveth mee, because it might not remaine as an exact model of all Tragedies.

It is very easy for us to be wise after the event, and to discover antecedents of Shakespeare in some neglected poetaster, but which of us, writing about 1580, could have made a fairer judgment? But then, the Countess of Pembroke should have understood that the English drama would follow a native, not a classical, tradition, and should not have slavishly followed her brother's advice. This may be so, but when she was translating Garnier she could have seen *Gorboduc*, *Jocasta*, *The Misfortunes of Arthur*, and *Tamburlaine*. Whether she did see them is another question : but even if she had seen them all, was this enough to convince her that English drama would so soon and so far surpass the drama of Garnier? She was never so submissive to her brother's taste as to close her mind to new ideas, and though the story of Shakespeare's visit to Wilton in 1603 cannot now be substantiated, we may recall that Heminge and Condell dedicated the First Folio of his plays to her sons.

When in 1595 the third and last of Sidney's principal works, the *Apologie for Poetrie*, was published, only his treatment of the drama was out of date. In everything else he stated what was by now, thanks to him, the accepted critical position. Long known in manuscript, though not to so wide an audience as had read with delight the *Arcadia* and *Astrophel and Stella*, his essay was less an influence itself than a record of those influences which had shaped the New Poetry of England.

Here he summed up the whole Renaissance tradition of criticism, more concisely, more persuasively, with a more urbane elegance than any similar work in any language. Reading it we can understand how the astonishing development of English literature, in those twelve or fifteen years that had passed since Sidney returned from his embassage to the Imperial Court, had been brought about.

No wonder, then, that the poets to whom Sidney had given the freedom of the Renaissance counted it a reproach if they did not celebrate him in their verse. His prestige was unrivalled, and even the editors of the miscellanies felt that they were failing their readers if they did not set in the front of their collections some new poem of Sidney's as yet unpublished, or at least an elegy in his honour. That dishonest Welshman, Richard Jones, who in 1591 called his anthology *Brittons Bowre of Delights* without Breton's consent or knowledge, printed as the first poem in his book Breton's '*Amoris Lachrimae. A most singular and sweete Discourse of the life and death of S. P. S. Knight.*' The unidentified R. S. began his delightful anthology *The Phoenix Nest* with three elegies on Sidney, by Roydon, Sir Walter Ralegh, and Fulke Greville, which were reprinted two years later with Spenser's *Astrophel*. (Even the title alludes to Sidney, as Sir Edmund Gosse long ago pointed out. 'The idea of the compilers of this anthology was, in my opinion, that although the Phoenix, Poetry, had blazed on the funeral pyre of Sidney, it was reincarnated in the lyrical work of the young men who had taken heart of grace to pursue their art since their hero's death.') The Phoenix, it may be added, was often used by the poets as a symbol for Sidney himself; but it was also used for others, for Queen Elizabeth, the Countess of Pembroke, the Countess of Bedford, even for Stella. The next miscellany, *Englands Helicon*, appeared in 1600 with the fourth song from *Astrophel and Stella* in pride of place, and many other poems of Sidney's throughout the book. Lastly came Francis Davison's *A Poetical Rhapsody*, with 'Two Pastoralls, made by Sir Philip Sidney, never yet published', to whet the appetite of any prospective buyer. It was all very well for Davison to write in his preface : 'If any except against the mixing (both at the beginning and ende of this booke) of diverse thinges written by great and learned Personages, with our meane and worthless scriblings, I utterly disclaime it, as being done by the Printer, either to grace the forefront with Sir Ph. Sidney's and other names, or to make the booke grow to a competent volume'. But every anthologist since Sidney's death had found it worth while 'to grace the forefront with Sir Ph. Sidney's name', and Davison, who, through his mother, was connected with the Sidneys, had at least as much right to do so as the rest.

Such, then, during these last years of the Queen's reign, was the prestige of Sidney's name in the world of letters. Those who had been troubled, on hearing of his death, lest all his work should come to nothing, need not have feared. His friends of those early days at Wilton, Dyer and Greville and Spenser and, more than any of them, the devoted sister in whose house they met, had seen to that. With them were others who continued the loyal assistance already given, Abraham Fraunce, Thomas Howell, Hugh Sanford. Younger poets had been discovered to share in creating the New Poetry, Samuel Daniel and Henry Constable, Thomas Kyd for a brief moment when he was in distress, even the irreverent Tom Nashe, and perhaps the unstable, reckless Marlowe. Old Thomas Churchyard felt belated stirrings of his poetical sinews when Daniel showed what a new poet could make of an old kind of poem ; Barnabe Barnes, incompetent whether as poisoner or poet, in a trashy sonnet offered his 'first-born fruit' to Lady Pembroke 'of right'; and Michael Drayton scarcely ventured into print before paying an extravagant tribute to the Sidneys. But the catalogue would comprise all the poets writing in England in those days. And besides the poets, there were the nobles and courtiers vying with one another as they strove to emulate the Sidneys as poets or patrons of poetry : the Earl of Essex, the Earl of Southampton, Lord Mountjoy, the Countess of Bedford, the Countess of Cumberland, Sir Walter Ralegh, Sir Henry Goodere.

Sidney had raised a standard for the patrons as well as for the poets which had set the English Renaissance on its way, and would guide it for the future.

This I doe the more confidently affirm [says Fulke Greville] because it will be confessed by all men, that this one mans example, and personall respect, did not onely encourage Learning and Honour in the schools, but brought the affection, and true use thereof both into the Court, and Camp. Nay more, even many Gentlemen excellently learned amongst us will not deny but that they effected to row, and steer their course in his wake.

To these I must now turn.

CHAPTER 7

Many Gentlemen Excellently Learned

SIDNEY would have left his purpose but half accomplished if he had taught only the poets the new ideals of the Renaissance. He had to set an example also to men of his own class : to inform the taste of those for whom the poets would write. He could not deliberately instruct his contemporaries, but must hope that others would be attracted as he had been by the conception of a new English poetry. The irresistible charm of his personality persuaded the English courtiers to imitate him in this, as in everything else : for seeing in him the ideal of the courtier they accepted his literary tastes as they admired his diplomatic skill or his courage in battle.

On the field of Zutphen there had been with Sidney many famous men, among them the Earl of Essex, son of Sidney's old friend and brother of Stella, now, at the age of twenty, taking part in his first campaign. To him, in a codicil added to his will on the day of his death, Sidney bequeathed his best sword. Lacking the finest qualities that distinguished Sidney's mind and character, Essex was yet the man who seemed his nearest successor. Already in 1587 John Philip -dedicated to him as to the man most worthy to receive it his *Life and Death of Sir Philip Sidney*, a long poem which seems to have been intended to accompany Lant's engraved roll of the funeral. For many months after Sidney's death, we are told, 'it was a sin for any gentleman of quality . . . to appear at Court or City in any light or gaudy apparel'; and in Robert Peele's *Polyhymnia* there is a vivid picture of Essex as he appeared at a tournament at this time.

> Then proudly shocks amid the martial throng
> Of lusty lanciers, all in sable sad,
> Drawn on with coal-black steeds of dusky hue,
> In stately chariot full of deep device,
> Where gloomy Time sat whipping on the team,
> Just back to back with this great champion, —
> Young Essex, that thrice-honourable Earl:
> Y-clad in mighty arms of mourner's dye,
> And plume as black as is a raven's wing,
> That from his armour borrow'd such a light
> As boughs of yew receive from shady stream:
> His staves were such, or of such hue at least,
> As are those banner-staves that mourners beat;
> And all his company in funeral black;
> As if he mourn'd to think of him he miss'd,
> Sweet Sidney, fairest shepherd of our green,
> Well-letter'd warrior, whose successor he
> In love and arms, had ever vow'd to be:
> In love and arms, O, may he so succeed
> As his deserts, as his desires would speed!

Essex's martial adventures do not here concern us, but in love he succeeded Sidney, as the second husband of Frances Walsingham, that gentle and affectionate lady who, married in turn to the two most admired courtiers of her age, but stirs as a pale shadow scarcely to be noticed in the dazzle of these men and their brilliant sisters.

In 1592 Robert Dallington published his translation of the long famous work of Francesco Colonna, *Hypnerotomachia. The strife of Love in a Dreame*, with a dedication 'To the thrise honourable and ever lyving vertues of Sir Phillip Sydney Knight; and to the right honorable and others whatsoever, who living loved him, and being dead give him his due'. Dallington added a more orthodox dedication to Essex, in which he implies that he saw in Essex the true successor of Sidney, the man to whom a book dedicated in Sidney's memory could most properly be addressed. So too Thomas Moffett, in his life of Sidney, describes Essex as a kindred spirit who strives to emulate Sidney's way of life. Three years later William Jones dedicated to Essex a book which would almost certainly have been dedicated to Sidney had he been alive. This was his translation of an Italian courtesy book, *Nennio or a Treatise of Nobility*, in which the author (as is usual with Italians) maintains that true nobility derives not from high birth, but from noble conduct. Jones' translation is remembered now because three famous poets, Spenser, Daniel, and Chapman, all commended it : but it is somewhat strange to find Spenser here accepting Nenna's 'democratic' view of nobility, since in the sixth book of the *Faerie Queene*, which he must have been writing about the same time, noble birth is shown to be the foundation of nobility. Spenser always quietly insisted on his own connection with the noble family of the Spencers, a connection which they did not deny ; but Sidney had proclaimed his acceptance of Nenna's, or Castiglione's, or Dante's view, in his favourite motto, and probably Essex followed him. This is one of many reasons why it is futile to argue whether Sir Calidore portrays Sidney or Essex. Sir Calidore portrays them both, and portrays neither. Spenser knew and admired both men, but he is the poet of an imagined ideal, not the writer of a gossip column. The lines in which Spenser first describes Sir Calidore deliberately recall the lines in which he describes Sidney in *Astrophel*, and no contemporary reader could fail to be reminded of Sidney when he read the *Faerie Queene*. At the same time, in his dedicatory sonnet to Essex, Spenser had promised that in the later parts of the poem he would

> make more famous memory
> Of thine Heroicke parts ;

and the friends of Essex would certainly discover his memorial in Sir Calidore.

Essex must have met Spenser when he came to England with Ralegh in 1590, and he succeeded Sidney as a friend and patron of the greatest poet of the age. Spenser had little to learn from Essex, whose few surviving poems are of small merit, but he was glad to have his powerful favour ; and, as we may see from several allusions, he admired the man. Thus in the *Prothalamion*, written shortly after Essex's return from the capture of Cadiz, he celebrates England's new hero :

> Great Englands glory and the Worlds wide wonder,
> Whose dreadfull name, late through all Spaine did thunder,
> And Hercules two pillors standing neere,
> Did make to quake and feare :
> Faire branch of Honor, flower of Chevalrie,
> That fillest England with thy triumphes fame
> Ioy have thou of thy noble victorie,
> And endlesse happinesse of thine owne name
> That promiseth the same.

And in his *Vewe of the Presente State of Ireland* Spenser, turning, with an ease that is characteristic of the age, from the lofty idealisms of poetry to practical politics, recommends that Essex should be appointed Lord-Lieutenant of Ireland.

There is no reason to believe the tale told by Ben Jonson of Spenser's refusing a gift of money from Essex as he lay dying of starvation. He had received £8 only a fortnight before and John Chamberlain, mentioning his death in a letter written but four days after it took place, makes no reference to his being in need. The story is absurd, for men do not die of neglect in a fortnight, and within a few minutes' walk of their friends. Whether Essex saw Spenser in these last days of his life we do not know, but Essex decided that he should be buried in Westminster Abbey, near to his master Chaucer. Then, as all the world knows, his hearse was 'attended by poets, and mourneful elegies and poems, with the pens that wrote them, thrown into his tomb'.

Spenser's insertion of praise of Essex into the *Prothalamion*, written for the betrothal of the two daughters of the Earl of Worcester, was justified by the fact that the ceremony took place in Essex House. In this splendid house, set well back from the river behind elaborate knots, or formal gardens, Essex gathered some of the most gifted men of his time. Here lived Francis Bacon while he was writing the *Advancement of Learning*, and thinking out the new philosophy which won for him the title of the herald of the new age, the father of scientific method. Here too stayed Fulke Greville who, with a mind more questioning and sceptical than Bacon's, demanded how we could be assured that the knowledge we so laboriously attain is knowledge of any ultimate reality. The unrelenting force of his intellect was recognized by his contemporaries : as Naunton says, his 'health was distempered by the restless working of his own thoughts'. He agrees with Bacon in rejecting the traditional metaphysics and scholasticism, and also that the sciences are essentially practical and utilitarian. But he denies that the corrupt human mind can reach pure truth. His *Treatie of Humane Learning* must have been intended as a reply to Bacon, and was probably written at this time, during frequent intercourse with him. The plot of his play *Mustapha* may even derive from their talk together, for to the episode on which it is based (which took place in 1553) Bacon also refers in his essay *Of Empire*.

Bacon wrote in prose, but had all his more important work translated into Latin; Greville, still agreeing with Sidney that the poets are the best philosophers, used verse even for the most abstruse reasoning, and did not share Bacon's misgivings about the ephemeral nature of English. When Essex fell, Francis Bacon did not scruple to use his unequalled talents in the prosecution; but Fulke Greville remained always a loyal defender of his friend's character. Perhaps his remembrance of Bacon's conduct led Greville, when in his turn Bacon fell, to refuse him a trivial kindness.

Fulke Greville was coupled with Essex in *Polyhymnia* as his opponent in the lists:

> With this great lord must gallant Greville run,
> Fair man at arms, the Muses' favourer,
> Lover of learning and of chivalry,
> Sage in his saws, sound judge of poesy.

Peele's concise summing-up is admirable. We should have expected that the devoted friend of Sidney would strive in every way to continue the work they had begun together. In literature, as in everything else, Sidney's example being, as Greville says, 'ever in mine eyes, made me think it no small degree of honour to imitate, or tread in the steps of such a Leader'. His part in presenting the *Arcadia* to a wider audience has already been described; and I have quoted his enigmatic claim to have been Ben Jonson's and Shakespeare's master. Since we cannot discover precisely what he meant by this, it is idle to guess: I would only observe that he was not at all the man to make such a claim if it had no meaning. His love of learning and his judgment of poetry can be better illustrated by facts than by speculation. In his house the famous meeting with Bruno had taken place in 1584. He took into his service as a boy, and was (in Fuller's words) 'the rise and making' of the distinguished lawyer Sir John

Coke. He introduced to Queen Elizabeth the learned Dr.
John Overall, who was Regius Professor of Divinity at
Cambridge and one of Donne's predecessors as Dean of
St. Paul's. His undertaking the heavy task of restoring
Warwick Castle argues an interest in antiquarian matters and
in history of which there are many proofs. He had long
known Camden, through Sidney, when in 1597 he obtained
for him the post of Clarenceux King of Arms, an act of
patronage for which Camden in his will left Greville a piece
of plate. He helped the antiquarian and cartographer John
Speed. In about the last year of his life he founded the
first history lectureship at Cambridge, and appointed to it a
Dutchman Isaac Dorislaus, but soon removed him because
of the republican sentiments he professed when lecturing on
Tacitus. He had himself wished to write a history of the
reign of Queen Elizabeth, but was prevented by the jealousy
of Robert Cecil, who would not give him permission to see
the State papers that he needed to use.

Greville may have influenced Daniel towards too cautious
a respect for historical sources in his poem of *The Civile
Warres*, for which he was not unjustly criticized as 'too
much historian in verse'. Of all the poets whom Greville
knew at Wilton, Daniel was most in accord with his own
temperament and taste. So far as we know, Greville never
gave his patronage to Spenser, though he must have been
acquainted with him. The severity of his own style, his distrust of images of wit, the scepticism with which he observed
what he called 'an inchanted confusion imaged by the Poets',
must have made it difficult for him to sympathize with Spenser's
aims. Similarly Daniel, while admiring Spenser, avoids the
use of his Romantic trappings and archaisms :

> Let others sing of Knights and Palladines,
> In aged accents, and untimely words.

From the outset Daniel had shared Greville's literary tastes, and therefore, when he turned to write a poem setting forth his personal views on poetry, *Musophilus*, he dedicated it to Greville. This fine poem, 'containing' (as its sub-title affirms) 'a General Defence of Learning', may also be associated with those discussions in Essex House between Greville and Bacon, from which *The Advancement of Learning* and a *Treatie of Humane Learning* arose. In it Musophilus (Daniel) debates with the worldly Philistine, Philocosmus, about the value of poetry: in so doing he reveals much of what the poets of the time themselves felt about their art. As always when he is writing at his best (and he seldom writes below his best), Daniel expresses his meaning with much clarity. So he replies to the perennial Philistine question : Why write poetry which few care about or understand? with dignity and passion.

> And for my part, if onely one allow
> The care my labouring spirits take in this,
> He is to me a Theater large enow,
> And his applause onely sufficient is :
> All my respect is bent but to his brow,
> That is my All, and all I am, is his.
> And if some worthy spirits be pleased too,
> It shall more comfort breed, but not more will.
> But what if none ? I cannot yet undoo
> The love I beare unto his holy skill :
> This is the thing that I was borne to doo,
> This is my Scene, this part must I fulfill.

In his preface to *A Defence of Ryme* Daniel mentions a private letter on this subject which he had written 'to a learned Gentleman, a great friend of mine, then in Court', who may or may not have been Greville.

All his life Greville continued his interest in poetry. The dull and pious Henry Lok addressed a sonnet to him :

Who can of learning treat, and you forget ?

and claimed personal acquaintance. John Davies of Hereford wrote an epigram 'To the immortal memory, and deserved honor of the Writer of the Tragedy of *Mustapha*, (as it is written not Printed)', for it had been printed in 1609 without Greville's permission. Davies must therefore have seen the play in manuscript, which is likely enough, for he had for some time been a member of the Countess of Pembroke's circle. Young William Davenant was a page in Greville's house, where he learnt to admire Daniel's poetry and criticism, and thus became one of the principal channels by which the influence of the Sidneys was carried forward to the Restoration. Davenant criticized Greville's careful revision of his poems in later life, and must therefore have known them well long before they appeared in print. Richard Corbet in his *Iter Boreale* describes Greville's courteous welcome of him and his friends when they went to look over Warwick Castle.

> The phrase and wellcome of this knight did make
> The seat more elegant ; every word he spake
> Was wine and musick, which he did expose
> To us, if all our art could censure those.

With this picture of the stern old Calvinist welcoming to his magnificent house the gay and witty Dean of Christ Church, who detested the Puritans, we may leave the most intellectual, most successful, and most devoted of Sidney's friends, Fulke Greville, Lord Brooke.

There is a discreet silence, in the writings of Sidney's friends, on the subject of Lady Rich. We do not know what Greville, or Dyer, or Lady Pembroke thought of her : whether or not they considered her worthy of Sidney's best poetry, whether they too, like most of her contemporaries, condoned her continuing adultery with Charles Blount, Lord

Mountjoy. Sidney's Stella, the sister of Essex, was privileged to conduct her life as were few women of her age; and her handsome and gallant lover, one of the best soldiers of his time, was in no way injured by the liaison. There was an occasion when Essex quarrelled with him, but that was because of jealousy that the Queen had shown her admiration of Mountjoy. She had given him a chessman which he bound upon his sleeve: 'Now I see that every fool must have his favour', said Essex. In the duel that followed Essex was worsted, to the Queen's delight; but thereafter Essex and Mountjoy were very good friends.

Mountjoy was a soldier, but, like Christopher Carleile and other Elizabethan soldiers, he was also a man of learning. When, after Lady Rich's divorce, he was rash enough to marry her and thereby to bring down upon his head the execration which adultery had never provoked, he defended himself at length in a paper which largely relies on the tedious authority of innumerable Early Fathers. But though this suggests that his habitual reading was more arduous than in the poetry of his own day, and though his appreciation of Sidney's sonnets may have been a little perplexed by the fact that the lady was his mistress and bore him several illegitimate children, he probably relished the compliment of being compared to Sidney. So, in dedicating to him in 1589 *The Anatomy of Absurdity*, Nashe recalls a conversation he had with some companions about the qualities required by Castiglione in his ideal courtier. 'This was the upshot, that England never saw anything more singuler than Sir Philip Sidney, of whom it might truely be saide, *Arma virumque cano*. In this heate of opinions, many hopes of Nobility were brought in question, but nothing so generally applauded in every mans comparisons as your worshippes most absolute perfections', and so forth. Here Sir Charles Blount (as he then was) is set up as a candidate for the succession to Sir Philip Sidney. Some years later he was still regarded as one of the patterns of courtesy, when John Kepers dedicated to him his translation of an Italian courtesy book, *The Courtiers Academie* ; and Gervaise Markham could as fitly dedicate to the famous soldier his *Most Honorable Tragedie of Sir Richard Grinvile, Knight*, a poem celebrating the heroic last fight of the *Revenge*.

The poet whom Mountjoy most favoured, and who knew him best, was Samuel Daniel. To him Daniel addresses some lines at the beginning of his poem of *The Civile Warres*, in which he says that Mountjoy

> cheerd'st me on, these measures to record
> In graver tones then I had us'd before ;
> Beholde : my gratitude makes good my word
> Ingag'd to thee, (although thou be no more)
> That I, who heretofore have liv'd by thee,
> Doo give thee now a roome to live with me.

Mountjoy, so Gabriel Harvey tells us, recommended Daniel's poem to his friends at court, a service which we may suppose noble patrons usually performed for the poets under their protection. (In the same note Harvey says that 'The Earle of Essex much commendes [Warner's] *Albion's England*'.) Daniel repaid the debt when Mountjoy, created Earl of Devonshire in 1605, died the following year, erecting his best memorial in a *Funerall Poeme* which he then wrote. It is the finest contemporary portrait of any Elizabethan, an unaffected, candid, and vivid picture of the man's personality. Daniel tells us what Devonshire looked like ; tells us about his temper and disposition, his quiet, modest manner, concealing deep wisdom and learning. He tells us of his library at Wanstead, in the formation of which he had had the advice of the famous bibliophile, Sir Robert Cotton, and doubtless of

Daniel too; he mentions Devonshire's custom of making notes in the margins of his books. Then, after describing Devonshire in his private life at home, Daniel turns to give an account of his self-controlled, well-governed character that inevitably reminds the reader of Shakespeare's King Henry V, just as, later in the poem, Daniel's account of Devonshire's behaviour at the siege of Kinsale reminds us of Henry V at Harfleur. He passes on to Devonshire's attitude to death, since to Daniel, as to every Elizabethan,

> This action of our death especially
> Shewes all a man. Here only he is found.

Devonshire, like Grenville, or Sidney, or Essex, or Ralegh, accepts death with dignity and no impatience.

> And as for death, said he, I do not wey,
> I am resolv'd and ready in this case.
> It cannot come t'affright me any way,
> Let it looke never with so grim a face
> And I will meete it smiling : for I know
> How vaine a thing all this worlds glory is.
> And herein did he keepe his word.

In contrast with Daniel's noble elegy on a man whom he knew and loved was another elegy by a poet who confesses in his dedication to the Countess of Devonshire that he is 'a mere stranger, altogether unknown unto you'. The ill-scanned, tortuous twaddle of *Fame's Memorial* gives small promise indeed that its author, John Ford, would be remembered as one of the finest dramatic poets of the age.

Ford was not alone in dedicating his poem to the Countess of Devonshire, though most of the poets seem to have avoided celebrating her beauty, perhaps out of deference to Astrophel, perhaps from mere discretion. Even in the hundreds of elegies on Sidney she is seldom granted more than a casual brief allusion. Spenser in his *Astrophel* very oddly applies the name of Stella to Sidney's widow, transferring the sonnets to her. This is in keeping with the views of love and marriage to which Spenser devoted some of his finest poetry, as in the *Epithalamion* and in the third book of the *Faerie Queene*, and shows, presumably, how little importance he attached to a biographical interpretation of *Astrophel and Stella*. John Florio, in one of the fantastic dedications to his *Montaigne*, coupled Lady Rich with Sidney's daughter, Elizabeth, Countess of Rutland ; and Matthew Gwinne in a sonnet appended to Florio's prose identifies her with Stella. Thomas Campion also did not hesitate to make this identification, in his Latin poem *Umbra*, and he even mentions Mountjoy's love for her, as does Ford in his elegy. There is also a curious sonnet by John Davies of Hereford addressed to Lady Rich, where he alludes to her unhappy marriage :

> To descant on thy name as many doe
> (Sith it is fit t' expresse thine excellence)
> I should (deere Lady) but allude unto
> That, which with it compar'd, is indigence.

Florio and Gwinne had known Sidney personally : Campion and Davies knew the Countess of Pembroke and others of Sidney's circle. Richard Barnfield seems not to have had any discoverable reason for dedicating to Lady Rich the *Affectionate Shepherd*, the first of his books, except that she was a celebrated lady who might be assumed to have some taste for poetry. One poet alone, Henry Constable, dared to risk comparison with Sidney by addressing a number of sonnets to her : to judge from these he must have known her well. A manuscript in the British Museum describes a collection of them as 'Mr. Henry Constable's sonets to the Lady Ritche 1589' ; and in the previous year he wrote one on the birth of a daughter to her. He also addressed a sonnet, one of his best, 'to Mr. Hilliard, upon occasion of a picture he made of my

Ladie Riche', in which, after referring to both Michelangelo and Raphael, he contrives an elaborate compliment alike to painter and sitter. Constable included some of Sidney's sonnets among his own in *Diana*; and to Olney's printing of the *Apologie for Poetrie* his *Four Sonnets to Sir Philip Sidney's Soule* were added. But neither Constable, in any of his poems to Lady Rich or in memory of Sidney, nor Daniel, in his memorial of the Earl of Devonshire, makes any reference to the famous story of *Astrophel and Stella*. Thus the poets, who were ever ready to acknowledge their debt to Sidney, and who accepted the model of his sonnets, were confederate in silence upon the love of Philip Sidney and Penelope Devereux. Tact so ubiquitous is scarcely within the scope of human frailty: we ought therefore to conclude that these men recognized in *Astrophel and Stella* not mere self-revelation but (as its dramatic perfection shows) the work of a highly cultivated imagination.

Here brief mention may be made of a strange poem entitled *The Lamentation of Troy for the Death of Hector* by a poet of little talent who not unnaturally prefers the anonymity of initials I. O. The book is dedicated to Lord Willoughby of Eresby, the brave and dashing soldier in whose rescue Sidney received his mortal wound; but the poet seems never quite to have made up his mind whether he was writing about Hector or about Sidney. The allegory is confused and inconsistent: thus in at least one passage Astrophel and Stella are contrasted with Hector and Helen, but elsewhere Hector is identified with Sidney and Helen with Stella. (Further identifications of Paris with Mountjoy and of Menelaus, appropriately enough, with Lord Rich seem to be intended.) The most interesting part of a feeble poem is in I. O.'s repeated request to Spenser, 'the only Homer living', to write of Sidney; but it is hardly likely that I. O. was one of those friends who had upbraided Spenser for his neglect of this duty.

Among these friends of Spenser's Sir Walter Ralegh was surely one. He had probably known Sidney since their Oxford days, though he was never a member of Sidney's most intimate group of friends. They had many interests in common, in literature, in politics, in exploration, in plans for colonizing the New World. Ralegh was the more daring, more opinionated, more intolerant, but much admired the gentle Sidney, and wrote a noble epitaph upon his friend. With Ralegh, Spenser came to England in 1590 to oversee the printing of the first part of the *Faerie Queene*, and to him Spenser addressed his prefatory letter, as well as a sonnet of dedication. In this Spenser compares his poem, to its disadvantage, with Ralegh's poem to the Queen, and compliments Ralegh with the suggestion that the *Faerie Queene* is a stop-gap to be superseded when the *Book of the Ocean to Cynthia* shall be published. But Ralegh was not to be deluded by any such flattery, and though his own style is utterly unlike Spenser's, and has much of the tense and concentrated power of Greville's, he was very well able to appreciate the *Faerie Queene*, as his two sonnets in its commendation show. In the more famous of these Ralegh devises a magnificent and welcome compliment to a great poet ; in the other he makes a bantering reply to Spenser's sonnet to him. In the letter dedicating to Ralegh *Colin Clouts Come Home Againe* Spenser in turn shows the easy affection of their friendship. 'Sir, that you may see that I am not alwaies ydle as yee thinke, though not greatly well occupied, nor altogether undutifull, though not precisely officious, I make you present of this simple pastorall', and so on : the levity of that is very different from the formality of most dedications. This same tone is preserved in the poem itself when Spenser is recounting their recent visit to court; and it is easy to imagine the hilarity with which Ralegh, the courageous pioneer of colonization, would have read Spenser's account of the voyage to England. Then the sly Colin, returned home eager to impress his friends with his own courage in facing so great an adventure as a crossing of the Irish Sea, tells Coridon of the sea :

> So to the Sea we came ; the Sea? that is
> A world of waters heaped up on hie,
> Rolling like mountaines in wide wildernesse,
> Horrible, hideous, roaring with hoarse crie.

Coridon, open-mouthed at this description, asks for more.

> And is the sea (quoth Coridon) so fearfull?

Needless to say, this is exactly what Colin had hoped for, and he piles on the horror of it all still further.

> Fearful much more (quoth he) then hart can fear :
> Thousand wyld beasts with deep mouthes gaping direfull
> Therin still wait poore passengers to teare.
> Who life doth loath, and longs death to behold,
> Before he die, alreadie dead with feare,
> And yet would live with heart halfe stonie cold,
> Let him to sea, and he shall see it there.

And then, after a few more lines, comes the final, most delightful touch of all in the description of the ship that carried them across this monster-haunted flood :

> Yet was it but a wooden frame and fraile,
> Glewed togither with some subtile matter.

So Spenser entertains Ralegh with his awed, land-lubberly account of their journey and of the ship — a thing of sticks and glue. The passage is a good illustration of the advantage enjoyed by the Elizabethan poet in knowing for whom he was writing, for, if we did not know that Spenser was addressing Ralegh, the conversation of Colin and Coridon would lose all its delicate irony. As W. R. Lethaby very properly observed, 'Every real work of art looks as if it was made by one person for another'. Most of them were.

Ralegh was Sidney's contemporary, and already too mature and independent to wish to be considered as his successor, in the way that Essex did. The two men were rivals for the Queen's favour in the last decade of the century, and though they shared together in one famous enterprise, the Cadiz expedition of 1596, for the most part they went their own ways. Ralegh, who was at least as good a soldier as Essex, had a subtler intellect, a more comprehensive imagination. Like Sidney, he was interested in the new thought of the Renaissance, but unlike Sidney, had a more speculative mind, or a faith less securely based in Christianity. Much has been written about his intellectual, as about his imperial adventures, and there is no need here to add to this. Still less do I intend to discuss 'The School of Night', founded as it is upon a questionable interpretation of a dubious reading in a work of fiction.

Ralegh was at one with Essex in his patronage of Spenser and of other poets. His connection with Marlowe is suggested by his disenchanted reply to Marlowe's 'Come live with me and be my love'; and we can suppose that no contemporary could better have taught Marlowe the splendours and dangers of an aspiring mind than Sir Walter Ralegh. According to the informer Richard Baines, Richard Cholmley told him that Marlowe 'hath read the Atheist lecture to Sir Walter Ralegh and others'. Ralegh knew Marlowe then, well enough perhaps for them to write a pair of poems together, and to discuss the sceptical ways of thought which their less advanced contemporaries stigmatized as atheism; but to speak of his patronage of Marlowe would be extravagant. With

George Chapman, Ralegh's influence seems to have been more pervasive, though by no means always easy to detect in the contorted and allusive style of Chapman's poems. Chapman may have been especially attracted by Ralegh's thought, but he had an Elizabethan admiration also for the man of action :

> Give me a spirit that on this life's rough sea
> Loves t' have his sails fill'd with a lusty wind
> Even till his sail-yards tremble, his masts crack,
> And his rapt ship run on her side so low
> That she drinks water, and her keel ploughs air.

He praised Ralegh's South American enterprise in *De Guiana Carmen Epicum*, one of the few poems written about those enterprises overseas which we should have supposed so well worthy the writing. But it conveys very little of the excitement of it all — far less than Ralegh's own account of *The Discoverie of the Large and Bewtiful Empire of Guiana*.

For all his power and fascination, for all his marvellous gifts as a writer, whether of poetry or of prose, Ralegh was never one of the principal patrons of literature. Whatever he did, he did with the air of greatness, but concealed an inner uncertainty with the mask of a superb, disdainful self-confidence. He was a man who, like Byron, must work on his own. His individuality was too strong for him to be able to lead others to develop the best in themselves : though he had no wish to do so, he was bound to dominate other men. He could not, like Sidney, encourage and inspire others, and it was only with an established poet, whose genius was commensurate with his own, with Spenser, that he was able to achieve an easy and valuable friendship. Even so, Byron and Shelley could, and did, profit by each other's company, though they differed from each other quite as much as Ralegh and Spenser. But in the end even Shelley felt that he had 'lived too long near Lord Byron, and the sun has extinguished the glow-worm'. The impatience of an individuality so intense and vivid as Ralegh's or Byron's could only inhibit the shy, or deferential, or hesitant. Thus few books were dedicated to him, and scarcely any poet took his poetry as a model. We may seek his portrayal if we will in characters drawn by contemporary poets, in Spenser's Timias, or Shakespeare's Armado ; but the truth is less precise. Ralegh's memorial is rather in the enrichment which his legendary personality gave to the imagination of the poets of his time.

From this brief examination of the way in which four of the leading courtiers in England steered their course in Sidney's wake in the years after his death, we may pass on to consider the patronage which a less eminent friend of his extended to one of the chief poets of the age. Sir Henry Goodere, a Warwickshire squire whose father had bought some monastic property there, 'a gentleman much accomplished, and of eminent note in this Countie', had been on service in the Netherlands at the time of Sidney's death. He was captain of Leicester's guard at Zutphen, and was with Sidney when he lay dying, for he witnessed both the will and the final codicil, by which he was to receive a ring. By another clause Sidney bequeaths to Queen Elizabeth 'one Jewell, worth one hundred Pounds, which I pray Sir Henry Goodier, my good cousin and Friend, to present to her Royal Highness, as a Remembrance of my most loyal and bounden Duty to her Majesty'. It is clear from this that Sidney must have known Goodere, a man twenty years his senior, rather well. Some time about 1573, it seems, Sir Henry Goodere had taken into service as page in his house at Polesworth the son of a butcher or tanner from the neighbouring village of Hartshill, a ten-year-old child named Michael Drayton. The little boy very early had ambitions to be a poet, as he tells us himself with a charming lack of self-consciousness.

In my small selfe I greatly marvel'd then,
Amongst all other, what strange kind of men
These Poets were ; And pleased with the name,
To my milde Tutor merrily I came,
(For I was then a proper goodly page,
Much like a Pigmy, scarse ten years of age)
Clasping my slender armes about his thigh.
O my deare master ! cannot you (quoth I)
Make me a Poet, doe it ; if you can,
And you shall see, Ile quickly bee a man.

His kindly schoolmaster did not laugh at him, but promised that, if Michael would stick to his lessons, he would read him some poetry. The schoolmaster, who would have been chosen for him by Sir Henry Goodere (to whom Drayton acknowledged that he owed most of his education), no doubt told Sir Henry of the boy's ambition and of his promise ; and we may imagine the interest with which Goodere (who had himself written a copy or two of verses in his time) would note his progress. Drayton remained at Polesworth, except for a brief interval, until Sir Henry died in 1595, and all his life long continued to be the devoted friend of Anne Goodere, later Lady Rainsford, to whom he addressed poems for forty years. He used to visit her every summer at her charming house at Clifford Chambers, where if they were ill they were attended by Shakespeare's son-in-law, John Hall. But Sir Henry Goodere, thinking that the poet whom he had brought up in his house needed a more distinguished patron than his own daughter, a little before he died bequeathed Michael Drayton to the lady who, in his judgment, was most likely to help him.

This was Lucy Harington, whose father was a neighbour of the Gooderes at Combe Abbey. Either Sir Henry's perspicacity, or Drayton's good fortune, was remarkable ; for when Drayton inscribed his first dedication to her she was

THE COUNTESS OF BEDFORD
Drawing by Mathys van den Bergh after miniature by Peter Oliver

Laudate Dominum.
Psal: 117.

P raise him that ay
R emaines the same :
A ll tongues display
I ehouas fame.
S ing all y^t share
T his earthly ball :
H his mercies are
E xpos'd to all .
L ike as the word
O nce he doth giue .
R old in record
D oth time outlyue ..

PSALM 117 TRANSLATED BY MARY SIDNEY
From John Davies of Hereford's transcript at Penshurst

only thirteen years old, but she lived to be, after the
Countess of Pembroke and her son, the most famous patron
of poets in her time. Drayton himself tells us that to her
service

I was first bequeathed, by that learned and accomplished Gentleman, Sir Henry Goodere (not long since deceased,) whose I was
whilst he was : . . . the first cherisher of my Muse, which had
been by his death left a poore Orphane to the worlde, had hee not
before bequeathed it to that Lady whom he so dearly loved.

It seems to us a rather odd transaction, but to Drayton, who
was a man of sturdy independence, it can have implied no
loss of dignity : he regarded it, very sensibly, as an act
of generous and practical forethought. We have only to
consider what would have been Drayton's career if this
bequest had not been made. He was in his early twenties,
born and brought up in an out-of-the-way corner of the
Midlands, with no powerful connections, no University
education or reputation. He could have gone up to London
and lived the hand-to-mouth existence of men like Greene,
for which by nature he was very ill-equipped ; being 'very
temperate in his life, slow of speech, and inoffensive in company' ; he could have tried to write for the stage, as he did,
unsuccessfully, for a year or so later on ; or he must have
abandoned poetry altogether. After a time he seems to have
been cast off by Lucy Harington, but by then, thanks to her
and to Sir Henry Goodere's forethought, he was established,
and was able to continue writing till his death.

Drayton's *Matilda* was not the first book dedicated to
Lucy Harington. When she was but three years old Claud
Holyband, a French Huguenot schoolmaster whose name
before it was anglicized had been Desainliens, dedicated to
her his *Campo de Fior*, a language manual, and probably
both he and Drayton took some part in her education. A

little before her fourteenth birthday, Lucy Harington married Edward Russell, Earl of Bedford — a marriage which prompted some good-humoured merriment on the part of Sir John Harington of Kelston at the expense of his prosperous and ambitious cousin, her father. 'He hath married his daughter to one, that for a grandfather, for a father, for two uncles, and three or foure aunts, may compare with most men in England.' In the year after her marriage Drayton dedicated to her his graceful poem on a classical theme, *Endimion and Phoebe*, which he had perhaps written for that occasion. Already he addresses the young girl as 'Great Ladie, essence of my cheefest good', and thanks her for her generous gifts to him. In the following year Drayton published two books, *Robert, Duke of Normandy* and *Mortimeriados*, both of which he dedicated to her : in the second of these he calls her the heir of Sidney's virtues. His excuse, if he needed an excuse, was that Lucy Harington was Philip Sidney's first cousin once removed ; but kinship was of less importance than example, and she, who very soon became the centre of a brilliant group of writers, would have been flattered by the reference, even if she had been unable to boast of any Sidney blood.

Coming from Drayton, the compliment was quite sincere, for though he was, apparently, never patronized by the Pembrokes, his admiration for Sidney and the Countess of Pembroke equalled that of poets who owed everything to them. Like the others, he was in no doubt that the New Poetry derived from Sidney's work, and of the many references to him as poet and patron, this, from the *Elegie to Henry Reynolds*, is the most explicit. Drayton has been writing of Spenser, with whom he naturally joins Sidney.

> The noble Sidney, with this last arose,
> That Heroe for numbers, and for Prose.

That throughly pac'd our language as to show,
The plenteous English hand in hand might goe
With Greeke and Latine, and did first reduce
Our tongue from Lillies writing then in use.

Drayton also recognized that the Countess of Pembroke
— Pandora, the giver of all good gifts, as he calls her — had
inherited Sidney's task.

Sister, sometime she to that shepheard was,
That yet for piping never had his peere,
Elphin, that did all other swaines surpasse,
To whom she was of living things most deare,
And on his Death-bed by his latest will,
To her bequeath'd the secrets of his skill.

This acceptance by the disinterested Drayton of the Sidney
tradition is good evidence of its validity. He had nothing
to gain by alleging that the New Poetry owed its origin and
continuance to the patronage of the Sidneys, and if it had
not been universally admitted, he might have risked offending
his own patrons by his frequent insistence. But they, and he,
knew it for the truth, and so he provoked no jealousy.

The Countess of Bedford, a sweet and courteous lady,
Ben Jonson says, 'hating that solemne vice of greatnesse,
pride', seems to have been in no way jealous of her cousin's
fame as a patroness, and did not think of herself as a com-
petitor of the Countess of Pembroke. Her kinsman, Sir John
Harington of Kelston, the witty and ribald translator of
Ariosto, sent her a copy of three of the Psalms in the Countess
of Pembroke's translation, on December 29th, 1600. In his
accompanying letter he compares Lady Bedford to Lady
Pembroke, and says, 'I suppose none comes more neere
hir, then yourself in those, now rare, and admirable guifts
of the mynde, that clothe Nobilitie with vertue'. Samuel
Daniel enjoyed the patronage of both, and there is nothing

to suggest that he regarded them as rivals : it would have been quite foreign to his character to transfer his loyalty in such a cause. Patronage was not an exclusive right, and the poet who wrote Senecan plays for the Countess of Pembroke was not thereby precluded from writing masques at the invitation of the Countess of Bedford. At the time of Essex's rebellion the Earl of Bedford abandoned Essex as soon as he was proclaimed traitor, and those who favoured Essex jeered at him for a coward. In this execration 'his fine dancing Dame' had some share, especially as it was by her influence with Cecil that his fine was reduced by half. The Bedfords must have waited for the old Queen's death with some impatience, for all their hopes, after the Essex fiasco, were set on winning the favour of the new King. So, when the Queen died, the Countess of Bedford with her mother and some other ladies went privately to Scotland to escort Queen Anne into England, forestalling the official deputation that had been appointed by the Council. It is an episode of little dignity and much shrewdness, and the Countess of Bedford thereby, among other things of more consequence to herself, was enabled to introduce her poets to Royal favour. First among them was Daniel whose *Panegyrick Congratulatory* was composed to welcome the King on his way south, when he stopped at Burley Hill, Lady Bedford's father's house in Rutland. When the poem was published Daniel printed with it his epistle to the Countess of Bedford, written on the same occasion, in which, in his most stately and solemn manner, he praises her for her learning and her interest in serious studies. Daniel's poem, which he probably declaimed himself before the King, must have been a success, for he was commissioned to write the first of the long series of masques with which the extravagant Anne of Denmark delighted to amuse her court. The *Vision of Twelve Goddesses* was produced on January 8th, 1604, at Hampton Court, probably with designs by Inigo Jones, who had just returned from a visit to the court of Christian IV of Denmark, brother of the Queen. This may have been the occasion when Ben Jonson behaved himself so badly that he had to be thrown out : if so, Daniel was 'Lucy's better verser' of whom Jonson grumbled to the Countess of Rutland. He need not have been so absurdly jealous of Daniel, whom he soon superseded as masque-writer to the court. When the printed account of this masque was published later in the year, Daniel gratefully dedicated it to the Countess of Bedford, and though he gave up the perhaps uncongenial writing of masques, he wrote a pastoral tragi-comedy, *The Queen's Arcadia*, for presentation before her at Christ Church in August 1605. He long continued to profit by Lady Bedford's introduction to the Queen, for she appointed him, together with John Florio, to be a Groom of her Privy Chamber.

Ben Jonson also probably owed his introduction at the new court to the Countess of Bedford. He had known her at least as early as 1601, when he had a leaf carrying a verse of dedication to her specially inserted in a copy of his *Cynthia's Revels*. In the same year he refers to her, again in terms which suggest a certain familiarity, in the Ode ἐνθουσιαστική, which he contributed to *Poeticall Essaies . . . in the Phoenix and Turtle* in Chester's *Love's Martyr*. (These *Essaies* contain poems by Shakespeare, Chapman, Marston, and others, as well as by Jonson, and it may be, as B. H. Newdigate suggested, that all refer to the Countess of Bedford. But her fame as a patron is securely established on the facts, without adding these probabilities.) Jonson addressed three of his epigrams to Lady Bedford, in one of them thanking her for the gift of a buck, and in another commending Donne's Satires, of which he was sending her a copy. Jonson delighted to pun on the meaning of Lucy's name with lucent or bright, and so he begins this epigram :

> Lucy, you brightnesse of our sphere, who are,
>   Life of the Muses day, their morning-starre !
> If workes (not th' authors) their owne grace should looke,
>   Whose poemes would not wish to be your booke?

The pun permitted Jonson to address the Countess of Bedford as Lucy in his poems : we are not to conclude that he did so when they met in person.

She had asked Jonson to obtain a copy of Donne's Satires for her, which suggests that she knew of the poems before she knew the poet. When she first met Donne I cannot say. He may have contributed to the *Phoenix and Turtle*, but his authorship and the reference to the Countess of Bedford are alike uncertain. She may not have met him till 1607 or 1608, but when they met he was at once attracted by the charming and cultivated lady whose very name suggested radiance, and he addressed many poems to her. These include some of the most far-fetched and obscure that he ever wrote, but we need not suppose that Lady Bedford especially enjoyed being perplexed with nice speculations of philosophy. Donne was a well-known poet when she first knew him, and could not change his manner to suit her taste. What she made of the *Nocturnall upon S. Lucies Day*, or *Twicknam Garden*, both of which are likely to have been written for her, is hard to guess. Even by the verse letters to her she may have been as much bewildered as flattered. But when at her invitation Donne wrote an elegy on Mistress Cecilia Boulstred, who died in her house at Twickenham on August 4th, 1609, he produced a poem so tasteless and unmoving, that Lady Bedford herself (so it appears) wrote an elegy which deliberately challenges Donne's verses. Donne, unlike most Elizabethans, was often at his worst when faced by the fact of death : it stirred in his mind the murkiest sediments of his mediaeval learning, and in his poetry (though not in his sermons) he wrote of the dead without dignity and without compassion. So it was with another elegy written for Lady Bedford, on the death of her only brother Lord Harington. She can hardly have been consoled in her loss by the tedious wit of Donne's poem, and even Donne was inclined to be ashamed of it.

I am almost sorry [he wrote to Goodere] that an Elegy should have been able to move her to so much compassion heretofore, as to offer to pay my debts ; and my greater wants now, and for so good a purpose, as to come disengaged into that profession, being plainly laid open to her, should work no farther but that she sent me £30.

'That profession' refers to Donne's resolve to enter Holy Orders. Before doing so he wrote to a number of his wealthy friends to ask them to pay his debts, so that he might 'come disingaged' into his new way of life, and, as this letter shows, Lady Bedford, whose piety was as sincere as her charity was generous, was one who helped him, though not, apparently, as much as he had hoped. It is unfortunate that Donne and Lady Bedford were not earlier acquainted, for he might then have addressed to her poems as fine as some he wrote for Magdalen Herbert. As it was, he came to know her only when the wearisome virtuosity of the scholar had, for a time, worn down the acute perception of the poet : she can hardly have found such pleasure in his poems as in those which Drayton, Jonson, and Daniel wrote for her.

The Countess of Bedford did not restrict her patronage to the poets, any more than did the Sidneys. As early as 1598 John Florio joined her name with the Earls of Southampton and Rutland in the dedication of his Italian Dictionary *A World of Words*. Lady Bedford's patronage was of much importance to Florio for, after he had translated one of Montaigne's essays at the request of Sidney's old friend Sir

Edward Wotton, she urged him to complete the work, which he had begun in her house. She encouraged him in his labours, as he says in a dedication to her : 'You often cryed *Coraggio*, and called çà çà, and applauded as I past'. He needed and received much help in the task, the kindly hospitality and cheering interest of the great ladies to whom he dedicated the *Essays*, the gifts of money from the Earl of Bedford and others, the scholarship of his good friends Matthew Gwinne and Theodore Diodati. Gwinne, Florio says, 'did undertake what Latine prose ; Greeke, Latine, Italian or French poesie should crosse my way (which as Bugge-beares affrighted my unacquaintance with them) to ridde them all afore mee, and for the most parte drawne them from their dennes', which presumably means that Gwinne identified and translated Montaigne's numerous quotations. Diodati, another Italian Protestant living in England, and like Gwinne a doctor of medicine, helped Florio with the more difficult passages 'like Ariadne's thread in the inextricable labyrinth, or the guide-fish which the whale follows through the rocky rough ocean'. (The diminutive, irascible Florio's comparison of himself to a whale is, as he would have said, amusing.) Finally Daniel wrote a long poem in commendation of his brother-in-law's translation, that strange and marvellous mine of words which Shakespeare knew, and by which John Florio is remembered.

In the theatre the Countess of Bedford's taste was for the sumptuous masques in which she so often took part, shows that owed at least as much to the costumes, décor and complicated stage-machinery, and to the intermezzi of music and dancing, as to poetry. She loved these things, as well she might, for the genius of Inigo Jones ensured that their lavishness did not degenerate into vulgarity ; and the age was rich in musicians. One of these, John Dowland, dedicated to her, in

1600, his *Second Book of Songs or Airs* : patronage of the poets who wrote the masques must have implied patronage of the musicians who composed the music, since the two worked together. Besides all this the Countess of Bedford sat to many painters, among them Peter Oliver and Cornelius Jansen, and in her time the nucleus of the great collection of paintings at Woburn was formed. She died in 1627, before Drayton, or Donne, or Jonson, though she was younger than any of them; within six years of the only other lady of her time who could compare with her as a patron of the arts, Mary, Countess of Pembroke.

As long as Lady Pembroke lived she was regarded by the poets as their best friend and protector : we hear no criticism, no complaint against her, such as Drayton made against Lady Bedford. To the Countess of Pembroke, said Drayton, 'all shepherds dedicate their lays', and there are indeed few poets of the time who, whether or not they ever received any favour from her, failed to insert some praise of her in their poems. Myra, Amaryllis, Urania, Clorinda, Miriam, Pandora, Pembrokiana, Poemenarcha — she is addressed by countless names, and addressed always as the living inspiration of the English Renaissance. Not only did she invite the poets to visit her at Wilton, but her household was staffed by them : Samuel Daniel was her sons' tutor, Hugh Sanford her husband's secretary, Thomas Howell had long been in his service, Thomas Moffett was the family doctor. He dedicated to her a curious and interesting poem on *The Silkewormes and their Flies*, 'for the great benefit and enriching of England'. In his verses to her he takes advantage of his official position to beg her to rest a while from all her literary labours.

> Let Petrarke sleep, give rest to Sacred Writte,
> Or bowe, or string will breake, if ever tied,
> Some little pawse aideth the quickest witte.

Even the children who were born in her house became poets, for when her husband's steward Arthur Massinger fathered a son in 1584, he named him (inevitably) Philip. Lady Pembroke herself did not, so far as we know, take much interest in that gifted dramatist, but both her sons, who had much more liking for the romantic drama than she had, did so.

There is a long and verbose description by Nicholas Breton of 'the courtlike house of a right worthy honourable Lady' which can hardly refer to any other house than Wilton, for Breton knew Lady Pembroke well and dedicated several of his books to her. His account is similar to Aubrey's, but has the advantage that he writes from personal knowledge. Her house, he says, was

in a maner a kinde of little Court . . . where first, God daily served, religion trulie preached, all quarrels avoyded, peace carefully preserved, swearing not heard of, where truth was easilie believed, a table fully furnished, a house richly garnished, honor kindly entertained, vertue highly esteemed, service well rewarded, and the poore blessedly relieved . . . let this suffice for the sum of my speech, that where the eye of honour, did set the rule of government, kindnesse was a companion in every corner of the house.

Breton goes on to give an example of the lady's kindness to 'a poore Gentleman in the ruine of his fortune' who was introduced to her. Some have supposed that here Breton was referring to himself: this seems to me unlikely, for when he wrote, in 1597, he had enjoyed Lady Pembroke's patronage for at least five years, and was to continue to enjoy it for some years to come, so that he would hardly have described himself as 'like a shadowe without substance, a purse without money, and a body without a spirit'. Breton, who was a stepson of the best of the older poets, George Gascoigne, had reached maturity before Sidney had begun his work for the New Poetry. He was a very prolific writer

whose facility is his chief defect : his poetry is usually melli-
fluous and pretty, but too much watered down. His reputation has suffered from the unscrupulous use of his name by
the piratical Richard Jones, who foisted two miscellanies
on him in the 1590s. That it was worth Jones's while to do so
suggests that Breton was a well-known and popular writer
at the time. At his best, as in the poems chosen by the discriminating editor of *England's Helicon,* he can stand comparison with all but the finest writers of song or pastoral, and he
was sensitive enough to adapt his style to the new taste, which
Churchyard failed to do. Like everyone else, he had written
an elegy on Sidney : this may have brought him to the notice
of Lady Pembroke. The elegy, *Amoris Lachrimae,* was
published by Jones in 1591, and in the following year Breton
addressed the first of his dedications to Lady Pembroke in *The
Pilgrimage to Paradise joyned with the Countesse of Penbrookes
Love.* For some reason or other he seems to have thought it
appropriate to dedicate to her only works of piety. The
others are *Auspicante Iehovah; Maries Exercise,* 1597, a collection of prayers ; *A Divine Poeme, divided into two Partes ;
The Ravisht Soule and the Blessed Weeper,* 1601 ; and *The
Countesse of Penbrookes Passion,* a poem on Christ's Passion
which was written before 1600, but which remained unpublished until 1853. Breton outlived the Countess of Pembroke,
but seems not to have dedicated any more of his works to
her. Pious lady though she was, she may have grown a little
bored at being addressed as if she were nothing else, especially
when she knew that Breton recognized her other qualities.

Another work of somewhat long-winded piety was dedicated to Lady Pembroke and ten other ladies in 1611 by
Aemilia Lanyer. This was a poem in two hundred and thirty
stanzas of *ottava rima,* entitled *Salve Deus Rex Judaeorum.* The
verse dedication to Lady Pembroke mentions the unpublished

translation which she and Sidney had made of the Psalms, and alleges that she

> In virtuous studies of Divinitie,
> Her pretious time continually doth spend.

Of 'Mistris Aemilia Lanyer, wife to Captaine Alfonso Lanyer, Servant to the King's Majestie', as she describes herself, I know nothing. Her Christian name, and her husband's, suggest that they may both have been Italian. There was an Italian musician named Nicholas Lanyer at the court about this time, who set two of Jonson's masques in the new *stylo recitativo,* and who may have been some relative of her husband.

A much more welcome dedication (we may suppose) was that which Lady Pembroke received on some New Year's Day in the 1590s from William Smith. He admits that he is unknown to Lady Pembroke but offers '*A New-yeares Guifte; made upon certen Flowers*'. The manuscript contains some introductory verses, followed by six stanzas on the flowers, and concludes with another headed *Time.* The flowers are The Primerose, Marygould, Rose, Gillyflower, Violett, and Cowslipp, each of which in turn is compared to Lady Pembroke. The poet offers her his charming posy purely for her pleasure, and it is not difficult to imagine her delight when she read this :

THE VIOLETT

> The violet doth growe in grove or feeldes,
> In hedges, or in gardens, or high waies,
> But whereso'ere it growes, it pleasure yeeldes :
> So : where I come, I allwaies finde yor praise,
> Your name, and vertue too, all people heare
> and touch with wounder, everie common care.

This must have seemed like a fresh breeze from the fields after all the elaborate and courtly compliment to which

Lady Pembroke was subjected. I should like to know more
of the poet who devised so elegant a fancy, and who was
capable of the fine simplicity of that last line.

The manuscript in which these flowers are contained is
beautifully written, perhaps by Smith himself, with each
flower on a separate sheet, surrounded by a border in pen
and ink. The graceful Italian hand, which Sidney himself
learnt, was used by many of his circle, by Harvey, Fraunce,
and Florio among others. Florio probably taught it to the
noble pupils whom he instructed in Italian, and did as much
as anyone to make it fashionable. In the new reign the young
Prince of Wales learnt this hand from John Davies of
Hereford,[1] a gay and witty writer, whose poetry, like so much
of the poetry of the period, is now more or less inaccessible.
He addressed a number of sonnets, epistles, and epigrams to
Lady Pembroke and other members of her family, whose
kindness to him he gladly acknowledged. He had known them
at least since 1601, for he wrote *A Dump upon the Death of the
most noble Henry late Earl of Pembroke*, who died that year, a
poem which was later set by Weelkes as *A Remembrance
of Thomas Morley*. In the following year he dedicated his
first book, *Mirum in Modum*, to 'my best beloved Lorde,
William Earle of Pembrooke', and to Sir Robert Sidney
and Edward Herbert of Montgomery (the poet), 'my most
honored and respected Friendes'. In 1612 Davies joined
Lady Pembroke's name in the dedication of *The Muses'
Sacrifice* with those of Lady Bedford and Elizabeth Lady
Carcy: further evidence, if any were needed, that there
was no jealousy between these ladies. Some time or other he
made a present of a book, probably his *Wits Bedlam*, to
Lady Pembroke, and wrote in it one of his more frivolous
epigrams :

[1] See Plate 13, f.p. 225.

Gods mee, how now? what Present have we here?
A Booke, that stood in perill of the presse :
But now its past those pikes ; and doth appeare
To keep the lookers on, from heavinesse.
What stuffe containes it ?   Fustian, perfect spruce ;
Wits Gallimalfrey, or Wit fride in steakes.
From whom came it, a God's name? from his Muse
(O do not tell) that still your favour seekes.
And who is that? faith that is I.   What I?
I per se I.   Great I, you would say.   No :
Great I (indeed) you well may say ; but I
Am little i, the least of all the Row.
You cannot choose but know me now : no do?
I am the least in Yours, and Worlds esteeme ;
I am the same : Madam, go to, go to,
You know me now (I know) though strange you seeme.
    Not yet? why then (great lady) I am hee
    That (maugre Fate) was, is, and still will bee
      The Triton of your praise
          I. D.

Davies' position as writing master to Prince Henry gave him a wide acquaintance at court, and he was a friend of many of the poets of his time. Michael Drayton seems to have had some writing lessons from him, and Davies obviously missed his company when he was engrossed in *Poly-Olbion*, if we may judge from his merry and irreverent epigram.

    Michael, where are thou?   What's become of thee?
    Have the nyne Wenches stolne thee from thy selfe? . . .

Another congenial friend was William Browne of Tavistock, for the second book of whose *Britannia's Pastorals* Davies wrote verses of commendation.

Browne was of the country gentry in Devon, and was educated at Exeter College, Oxford. He became a member of the Inner Temple when he was about twenty, and wrote a famous masque which was performed there on January 13th,

1614. He was twice married, on the second occasion to the daughter of Sir Thomas Eversfield of Horsham in Sussex. He lived the life of a cultivated country gentleman, and often enjoyed the hospitality of Wilton, where he must have felt much more at home than among the witty and scurrilous lawyers. We may believe that he was one of the most welcome guests there in the last years of Lady Pembroke's life, for she would have appreciated his sensitive observations of the countryside, which she much preferred to the city, and would have been delighted by the natural and unaffected admiration with which he regarded her. He was born after Sidney died, so that for him Lady Pembroke must have represented an almost legendary past : yet he writes of her not as a remote and alarming old lady, but as a gracious and kindly friend. And in the end Browne, by some miracle of understanding, wrote for her the perfect epitaph.

> Underneath this sable herse
> Lies the subject of all verse :
> Sidney's sister, Pembroke's mother :
> Death, ere thou hast slain another,
> Fair, and learn'd, and good as she,
> Time shall throw a dart at thee.

Her sons William Herbert, third Earl of Pembroke, and his brother Philip who succeeded him, continued the tradition of patronage in which they had been brought up. In their childhood Lady Pembroke had employed Samuel Daniel as their tutor, who, of all poets of the English Renaissance, had the loftiest ideal for the future of the language and its literature. To William Herbert he dedicated his *Defence of Ryme*, and this was surely not the first occasion on which the pupil heard the tutor's opinions.

Me thinkes we should not so soone yeeld our consents captive to the authoritie of Antiquitie, unlesse we saw more reason : all our understandings are not to be built by the square of Greece and Italie. We are the children of nature as well as they; we are not so placed out of the way of Judgement but that the same sunne of Discretion shineth upon us.

Spenser had heard similar things from his schoolmaster, Richard Mulcaster. Sidney had been no less certain of the excellence of the English language: 'For the uttering sweetly and properly the conceits of the minde, which is the end of speech, that hath it equally with any other tongue in the world'. So was the essential confidence in the quality of the language and its capacity for great literature passed on. The young William Herbert was, besides, a receptive pupil, and received from his mother some gift as a poet. Before his eyes she must ever have kept the example of his uncle, Sir Philip Sidney, but so discreetly and wisely that all his life he felt it an honour, never derogatory to his own dignity, to be known as 'the nephew of the great Philisides'. When he was twelve Thomas Moffett addressed to him an exemplary Life of Sidney, entitled *Nobilis*, which he ends with an exhortation to the young Herbert to model his life on Sidney. According to Moffett, this was also the advice of John Lloyd, who was William Herbert's tutor when he came up to New College a few months later.

Lloyd was a Welshman from Denbigh, highly thought of 'for his rare learning and excellent way of preaching', who had been a Fellow of the College since 1579. He edited, and dedicated to Herbert's father, the New College collection of elegies on Sidney's death. Why New College and not Christ Church should have produced this volume, is something of a mystery. There was a strong Wykehamical tradition of writing Latin epigrams, which may have led many members of the college to wish to show their ability on this occasion. Perhaps Lloyd was a protégé of Sir Henry Sidney's,

HIC TVVS ILLE COMES GENEROSA ESSEXIA NOSTRIS
QVEM QVAM GAVDEMVS REBVS ADESSE DVCEM

THE EARL OF ESSEX
Engraving by W. Kip

THE EARL OF PEMBROKE
Engraving by Simon van de Passe

who was of New College, and persuaded his colleagues to cooperate in the book out of piety towards him. His gifts of persuasion must have been quite exceptional.

William Herbert remained at New College for two years, before leaving to enter on the life of a courtier. Though at first he was 'very well thought of', he was soon in disgrace, for before he was of age he was father of an illegitimate child by Mary Fitton. He fell far short of Sidney in his moral character, and, as Clarendon says,

He indulged to himself the pleasures of all kinds, almost in all excesses whether out of his natural constitution, or for want of his domestic content and delight, (in which he was most unhappy, for he paid much too dear for his wife's fortune by taking her person into the bargain,) he was immoderately given up to women. But therein he likewise retained such a power and jurisdiction over his very appetite, that he was not so much transported with beauty and outward allurements, as with those advantages of the mind as manifested an extraordinary wit and spirit and knowledge, and administered great pleasure in the conversation.

Neither his private recreations nor his public career much concern us, but he won the reputation of being 'the greatest Maecenas to learned men of any peer of his time or since'. However reprehensible his relaxations may have been, this was the true and valuable work of his life, in which he showed the same discriminating taste and fine judgment as his uncle and mother. After he succeeded to the title, early in 1601, he seems more and more to have taken her place as a patron of letters, though many books were still dedicated to her, and the poets showed no inclination to forget or forsake her. She would have lived less constantly at Wilton than before, and had much business with the many estates in which her husband had left her a life interest, Ivychurch, Devizes Park, the borough and castle of Cardiff among them. She was on the Continent for her health's sake from 1614 to 1616, and, as she grew older, she would withdraw a little from the centre of the intellectual life of the country. (Yet even her absence at the Spa was lamented in verse, by William Basse.) Sometimes, as by John Davies of Hereford, by Daniel, or by Robert Newton in *The Countesse of Montgomerie's Eusebeia*, her name was joined with others of her family, and many a courteous reference to her was made in dedications to her sons. Francis Davison dedicated to William Earl of Pembroke his *Poetical Rhapsody*, addressing him as

> Thou Worthy Sonne, unto a peerlesse Mother,
> Thou Nephew to great Sidney of renowne.

His name was again coupled with his mother's in the opening paragraph of Daniel's *Defence of Ryme*.

Pembroke's interests were as varied as his mother's, or as Sidney's, and he was as perspicacious as either of them in discovering talented young men. In his taste for poetry and the drama he showed the same remarkable catholicity, for he was the patron of John Donne and William Browne and George Herbert, of Shakespeare and Jonson and Massinger. His vigorous and restless mind ranged over the whole life of his age. He was much addicted to tilting, and delighted in the invention of ingenious devices : 'he leapes, he dawnces, he singes, he gives counterbuffes, he makes his horse runne with more speede'. He was interested in the colonization of the New World, so that John Rolfe (he who married the Indian Princess Pocahontas) dedicated to him his *True Relation of the State of Virginia*. He sent Inigo Jones to Italy to collect pictures for him, and was as generous and distinguished a patron of painters as he was of poets. Learning, in the narrower sense in which we use the word, also attracted the attention of the man who 'had scarce an equal for learning among all the Peers of England' : he became Chancellor of the University of Oxford, and gave his name to the college which had been Broadgates Hall. He is fittingly commemorated in the Bodleian quadrangle by the fine bronze statue which Le Sueur made of him.

I need not list all the books which were dedicated to this remarkable man, for many of them were the work of obscure and negligible writers who presumed to address him as a means of self-advertisement. Besides, the number of writers of distinction who acknowledged his kindness or invited his help is long enough. John Florio asked a favour of him early in the new reign, and persuaded Pembroke to accept the dedication of the first book by one John Healey, which was published in 1609. This was a translation of Joseph Hall's satirical *Mundus Alter et Idem*, which Healey called *The Discovery of a New World*. The publisher asked Florio to get Pembroke's patronage also for Healey's next book, a translation from Epictetus. Florio may perhaps have taught Pembroke Italian, but there is no evidence to prove this, and the origin of the connection between the two men remains unknown. By his will, made shortly before his death in 1625, Florio bequeathed to the Earl of Pembroke

all my Italian French and Spanish bookes, as well printed as unprinted, being in number about three hundred and fortie, namely my new and perfect dictionary, as also my tenn dialogues in Italian and English, and my unbound volume of divers written collections and rapsodies,

to be put in the Earl's library either at Wilton or at Baynards Castle. He appoints the Earl to be his literary executor, to see that his revised dictionary and dialogues might be printed for the benefit of his widow. As a further bequest Florio left him 'the Corvine stone . . . wch Ferdinando, the great duke of Tuscanie, sent as a most precious gift . . . unto Queen Anne', who had presumably left it to Florio. In return for this magic stone, whose 'use and vertue' were 'written in two pieces of paper both in Italian and English being in the little box with the stone', Florio asked the Earl to look after his widow, and to help her to obtain the considerable arrears of his pension. The will of this lonely, quarrelsome Italian whose instinct for words had done so much to enrich the English language, is a pathetic document : it would be uncharitable to laugh at him for supposing that the Lord Chamberlain would find much use for the Corvine stone.[1] One of Florio's executors was Theophilus Field, Bishop of Llandaff, who was a friend of Lady Pembroke, but for some reason or other he and his co-executor renounced the execution. I see no reason to draw the conclusion, as does Miss Yates, that Lord Pembroke had refused the legacy and its obligations. We simply do not know either why Florio made the bequest (and it is difficult to believe that he would have made it without first sounding the Earl through Field) or whether it was accepted.

Florio, like Daniel, had long been known to the Pembroke family, and the third Earl would expect to continue old responsibilities in patronage. John Davies of Hereford, who addressed an epigram in *Wits Bedlam* to him, probably knew him through his mother ; but William Browne of Tavistock is more likely to have been first brought to Wilton by Lord Pembroke. To him Browne dedicated the second book of *Britannia's Pastorals* in 1616 in a sonnet which suggests that he was already on terms of warm friendship. He seems to have lived at Wilton for some time, perhaps, as Antony Wood says, in the later 1620s, though that cannot have been his first

---

[1] 'Corvia, a stone of many vertues, found in a ravens nest, and fetcht thither by the raven, with purpose that if in her absence a man have sodden her egs and laid them in the nest againe, she may make them raw againe'. J. Florio : *Queen Anna's New World of Words*, 1611.

visit. In addition to his elegy and epitaph on the Dowager Countess, Browne wrote another elegy and epitaph on a friend and servant of Lord Pembroke's named William Hopton; wrote an epitaph on his chaplain John Smyth; dedicated to Philip Herbert, Earl of Pembroke and Montgomery, his translation of *The History of Polexander*; and wrote elegies on his first wife, who died in 1629, and on their son Charles, Lord Herbert of Cardiff, who died in Florence in 1635. In this last poem he refers to his epitaph on the Dowager Countess of Pembroke :

> my weak and saddest verse
> Was worthy thought thy grandam's hearse.

He seems to have been regarded as elegist to the Pembroke family, a task he performed to admiration.

Lord Pembroke's own poetry was written for the amusement and pleasure of his friends. Witty and accomplished, it expresses the conversation of a gentleman, as Dryden said of Sir John Suckling's poetry. Like Sidney, Pembroke was a poet who enjoyed the company of poets, and though he did not have his uncle's gifts, nor the serious and determined purpose which created the New Poetry, there is no great divergence between their attitude. Sidney had always regarded his own poetry as an accomplishment befitting a gentleman, and enjoyed the poetic rivalry of his good friends Fulke Greville and Edward Dyer. Similarly Lord Pembroke delighted to exchange poems with his friends, especially with Sir Benjamin Rudyerd, whose poems were printed with his own. There were several contemporary poets of his name and kin : his mother; his cousin the Countess of Rutland; Edward Herbert, whose wit and urbanity have been too much obscured by the eventual piety of his brother George; and William Herbert, author of a poem called *A*

Prophesie of Cadwallader. Lord Pembroke certainly knew the two gifted sons of Magdalen Herbert of Montgomery Castle, and through his influence George Herbert was presented to the living of Bemerton. He probably also knew William Herbert of Glamorgan, who wrote commendatory verses to the second book of Browne's *Britannia's Pastorals*, in which he implies that he knew Lord Pembroke's liking for the poems. Other courtiers and gentlemen of the time who exchanged verses with their friends include Sir Henry Wotton, some of whose poems were printed with Lord Pembroke's, and the younger Sir Henry Goodere, nephew and son-in-law to Drayton's first patron. He collaborated with Donne in writing alternate verses of the poem which begins

> Since ev'ry Tree begins to blossom now.

Similarly Donne wrote his preposterous Elegy on Prince Henry, as he confessed, 'to match Sir Ed. Herbert in obscurenesse'. Much that is best in the poetry of the Renaissance was written, like Shakespeare's sonnets, for circulation in manuscript among private friends. And because the courtiers, following Sidney's example, regarded the art of writing poetry as a skill which any cultivated person should be able to acquire, many of them did acquire it. They thought of this private poetry as of interest only to their friends, and therefore ephemeral. They did not trouble to publish, and much of it is lost. But because these men were themselves poets they were such good judges of poetry, such excellent patrons of poets.

Lord Pembroke, much more than Sir Philip Sidney, was a man of the city and court. Sidney confessed that he loved to withdraw from the bustle and commotion of the court to read and discuss in the quiet company of a few friends. Lord Pembroke hated the rustic seclusion of Wilton : 'Undoubtedly

I shall turn clowne, for Justice of peace I can by no means frame unto, & one of the two a man in the cuntry must needs be'. So he wrote to Robert Cecil when in disgrace for the affair with Mary Fitton : we need not suppose that his love for the country increased as he grew older. Much of the poetry written by his friends has the hardness and glitter that we expect of poetry of the city. The poet must raise his voice to be heard — Donne nearly always seems to be cutting into a conversation in a crowded room. The wit is more sophisticated, the irony harsher, the metaphor more extravagant. There is the constant seeking after the newest fashion, simply because it is new ; and the iconoclasm that necessarily goes with this. The poetry is to give an immediate and momentary effect, before it is cast aside for something newer still. Men did not read and re-read Donne as they read and re-read Spenser : the poetry was not designed for a continuing growth the more we read it, but for a swift impact, a brief check while some private reference or far-fetched allusion is caught, and the thing is complete, done with, to be brushed off the table into the waste-paper basket.

> Stella, the only planet of my light . . .
> Go and catch a falling star . . .

There is the difference.

The shy, retiring poets who preferred the country houses, at Wilton, Penshurst, Clifford Chambers, Grace-dieu, went on writing. Lord Pembroke revealed his unrestricted pleasure in poetry by appointing William Browne as a kind of family laureate ; but the poets who could best thrive in the tumult of London came into their own in King James's time. Donne, the satirists, and the two principal dramatists of the age, had already established their names in the 1590s, when the young men just down from the Universities, and the lawyers of the

247

Inns of Court, were beginning to take an interest in the New Poetry. Not only the courtiers now, but the professional middle classes also were providing an audience, especially for the dramatists. For the new drama Lord Pembroke and his brother soon discovered a great liking, and to this 'incomparable pair of brethren' who 'prosequuted the author living with so much favor', the First Folio of Shakespeare's plays was dedicated. As Lord Chamberlain after 1615, Pembroke was officially much concerned with the players, and, in addition to Shakespeare, Jonson, Chapman, and Massinger, all enjoyed his favour. But patronage of the drama is, in the nature of things, altogether different from patronage of poetry, and is a subject which I do not intend to discuss. Neither will I enter the morass of controversy concerning the identity of Mr. W. H. to whom a piratical printer, not Shakespeare himself, dedicated the *Sonnets*. I prefer to end this brief account of Lord Pembroke's work as a patron of poets with indisputable fact. Perhaps because he still retained something of the classical taste in the drama in which he had been brought up, Lord Pembroke was especially generous to Ben Jonson. He used to send him £20 every New Year's Day to buy books, a considerable sum when £60 a year was considered an adequate salary for a Groom of the Privy Chamber. With this Jonson was able to build up a fine library, and though many of his books were lost in a fire in 1623, many still remain to bear witness alike to his learning and his patron's munificence. To Lord Pembroke Jonson dedicated in 1616 what he considered his best and most polished work, his *Epigrammes*. He disclaims any slanderous intention in the poems, or any wish to shelter behind Lord Pembroke's name; but 'I must expect, at your Lo: hand, the protection of truth, and libertie, while you are constant to your owne goodnesse'. It is a fine and fitting tribute to the man in whose house the patronage of learning seemed to be hereditary; who, following in the famous example of the Sidneys, had given liberty to many scholars and poets to seek truth, for 'truely, I thinke truely; that of all writers under the sunne, the Poet is the least lier'.

The death of the Earl of Pembroke in 1630 may end this narrative of the enlightened patronage that had given to England a literature fit to compare with the other great literatures of Europe. Soon the country was to be divided in civil war, and though the Cavaliers would continue to cherish the tradition of the Sidneys, and though a Puritan General would take into his house as his daughter's tutor the gentle and sensitive Marvell, the old relationship of poet and patron was breaking down. In the year of the Restoration of King Charles, the younger Donne edited, at the command of the Dowager Countess of Devonshire, who had preserved them, the poems of Lord Pembroke. The author's fame, he says, had 'lain asleep in all the noise of Drums and Trumpets, when all the Muses seemed to be fled, and to have left nothing behind them but a few lame Iambicks, canting at the corners of our desolate streets'. With those melancholy times we need have no concern.

CHAPTER 8

Epilogue

WILLIAM HERBERT, third Earl of Pembroke, died on his fiftieth birthday, as Hugh Sanford had prophesied at the time of his birth. In those fifty years the English language had developed from something that might be serviceable for giving practical instruction to those who knew no Latin, into the subtle and delicate medium in which Shakespeare could record the infinite variety of mankind. Already in 1598 Francis Meres had said 'that the Muses would speak with Shakespeares fine filed phrase if they would speak English'; but the Sidneys had taught the new language to the Muses. Dr. Johnson observed something of this when compiling his Dictionary.

I have fixed Sidney's work for the boundary, beyond which I make few excursions. . . . If the language of theology were extracted from Hooker and the translation of the Bible; the terms of natural knowledge from Bacon; the phrases of policy, war, and navigation from Raleigh; the dialect of poetry and fiction from Spenser and Sidney; and the diction of common life from Shakespeare, few ideas would be lost to mankind, for want of English words, in which they might be expressed.

In addition to their work in enlarging the vocabulary and establishing the diction of English poetry, the Sidneys had by their metrical ingenuity freed it from the clumsy shackles of Poulter's measure and fourteeners in which it had clanked through the middle years of the sixteenth century. They had shaped it to the graceful Italian rhythms, and with astonishing virtuosity poets and musicians had come to work together to create the incomparable songs which the Elizabethans delighted to sing. The new poets had attempted every kind of poetry from the epigram to the heroic poem, and had succeeded in every kind. Poetry from being an object of contempt had become the honoured accomplishment of any courtier who would claim to have a cultivated mind, so that there were few who failed to win their mistress' favour for lacking skill of a sonnet, or whose memory has died from the earth for want of an epitaph.

The historians of literature used to say that the Elizabethans were 'a nest of singing birds', that Shakespeare's 'untutored genius' was part of some unexplained miracle which brought about the golden age of English poetry. Or we were asked to believe that the national pride and vigour which led to Drake's voyage of circumnavigation, the defeat of the Armada, and the colonization of Virginia were also responsible, somehow, for the poetry and drama of the age. But the Italy in which Raphael and Michelangelo painted, and Boiardo and Ariosto wrote, was not famous for vigour and enterprise in practical affairs ; neither have the artistic achievements of the England that defied and defeated Hitler been remarkable. No : such arguments are sentimental and illusory. 'I doe finde', said Philip Sidney, 'the very true cause of our wanting estimation is want of desert : taking upon us to be poets in despight of Pallas. . . .' From that sensible premiss Sidney began, and by experiment, criticism, and encouragement led the English poets to deserve estimation. There was nothing fortuitous about their achievement : the *Faerie Queene* and *Hero and Leander*, Shakespeare's Sonnets and Campion's songs, were not written by accident. They were written by men of marvellous gifts, certainly, but intelligent and reasonable men who knew that the art of poetry was a craft about which there was much to learn, a skill which with humility and diligence they could develop.

For a man to write well [said Ben Jonson] there are required three Necessaries. To reade the best Authors, observe the best Speakers : and much exercise of his own style. . . . No matter how slow the style be at first, so it be labour'd and accurate : Seeke the best, and be not glad of the forward conceipts, or first words that offer themselves to us, but judge of what wee invent ; and order what wee approve.

I have tried to describe the creation of the New Poetry in England in the terms in which the men of the Renaissance described it. Like them, I have attributed the chief glory of its creation to the Sidneys : to Philip Sidney, in whose receptive mind the contrast between the culture of Englishmen and the culture of the friends with whom he had lived for three years on the Continent must have been startling ; and to Mary Sidney, who, after her brother's death, ensured that his work should continue. In the English Renaissance they played the part of the Medici in Florence. With their firm Puritan faith and their strong moral convictions they differed from the Italians, much as Daniel's poetry differs from the poetry of Poliziano, or the *Faerie Queene* from *Orlando Furioso*. These differences were, and are, intrinsic to the national character of the two peoples, but they did not prevent Englishmen learning all that they could from the poetry and criticism of the Italians. The personality of Philip Sidney shaped the literature of his countrymen, as it set an example for them to cherish. Because he was what he was, English poetry did not become academic, the pursuit of learned and sequestered persons troubled to settle *Hoti's* business, but not at all by the larger anxieties of man.

But the truth is his end was not writing, even while he wrote ; nor his knowledge moulded for tables, or schooles ; but both his wit and understanding bent upon his heart, to make himself, and others, not in words or opinion, but in life and affection, good and great.

In England, academies, which were innumerable in Italy and in France, never existed. The Areopagus was a joke. Poetry here was written by courtiers who accepted Sidney as their pattern, or by men occupied in various business. Donne wrote poems while on the Islands voyage; Whitney, while campaigning in the Netherlands; Sandys translated Ovid as he sailed across the Atlantic to take up his post as Treasurer in Virginia; Middleton completed his Welsh translation of the Psalms in the West Indies. Spenser was an administrator of proved capability in Ireland; Fulke Greville a distinguished public servant for fifty years; Sir John Davies a lawyer; Shakespeare an actor; Campion a physician; Sir Walter Ralegh, like the great Florentines, a man 'infinite in faculties', one who both by his pen and by his actions made history, a poet who mocked at the falsities of the court, a statesman who saw opening before his gaze a whole New World.

Had Sidney indulged his recurrent desire to withdraw from public life and devote himself to literary studies in the seclusion of Penshurst or Wilton, the poetry of the age would have been different, and far less splendid. He could have offered Spenser some retreat in England, and let him experiment with pastoral and sonnet, canzone and sestina: instead he sent him off to Ireland with Lord Grey, and told him to write a heroic poem. He himself could, certainly, have remained at home endlessly trying out new patterns of metre and rhyme; but he entered fully into the life of the day and, as Charles Lamb says, his sonnets are 'full, material and circumstantiated. Time and place appropriate every one of them.' Daniel, a modest man, who might well have preferred the seclusion of the country houses, found preferment at the court of Anne of Denmark. The concern of poets such as Sidney and Spenser with the moral value of poetry may have been confusedly expressed at a time when men still had to justify a taste for poetry written by ancient pagans. To the question 'Why write poetry?' these men could give only one answer that would satisfy their critics: 'Because it makes men better'. Shelley's insight into the problem of how this comes about was perhaps not yet possible; certainly it would not have been accepted as a convincing defence to say that imagination is the faculty by which we perceive moral good, and that poetry strengthens the imagination as exercise strengthens a limb. Yet however crudely they stated their criticism of poetry they were surely right to reject the plea of the aesthetes. Poetry is made with words, obviously — and no people has ever rejoiced in words more than Englishmen of the late sixteenth century; but words (in spite of Mallarmé) are not the equivalent of musical notes, they convey ideas and images. Therefore in the criticism of poetry two distinct judgments are required, of the technical skill with which the poet has communicated his thought, and of the value of the thought itself. Most of us would judge *Hamlet* to be a greater work of art than 'Never weather-beaten sail', but we might find it difficult to justify such a judgment merely on technical grounds. *Hamlet* is greater because it discovers to us infinitely more of human nature than Campion's song attempts to do. Its life-enhancing qualities (as Mr. Berenson would say) are far more. That certain refined pleasure which we derive from poetry cannot be divorced from our experience as men: even from ivory towers there is a view of some sort. The men of the Renaissance did not inhabit such remote and fragile structures: they lived and wrote, like Sidney, in court and camp.

Thus their poetry is never much concerned with the

tenuous pleasures of self-revelation, even when it is in that idiom. Fully and vigorously as they lived their lives, they were always capable of an ironical observation of themselves.

> I might ! Unhappy word — O me, I might,
> And then would not, or could not, see my bliss. . . .

Or,

> I wonder by my troth, what thou and I
> Did, till we lov'd ? were we not wean'd till then ? . . .

Here Sidney and Donne are at one. They could comprehend an audience not supposedly coextensive with the human species. Sidney did not impose his own taste on the age : he invited it to the enjoyment of poetry of any and every kind. He was not much taken with the Lancashire accent of some of Spenser's shepherds, but he saw that Spenser would become the chief poet of the time. 'Whosoever had any reall parts, in him found comfort, participation, and protection to the uttermost of his power ; like *Zephyrus* he giving life where he blew.'

This inspiration from Sidney set the English Renaissance on its course. Within a few years there had been created in the inadequate language that foreigners disdained to learn, a body of poetry to rival the achievement of centuries in Greece and Italy. In the process the language itself had been enriched in an astonishing way, so that years before the first English colony was founded in the New World, Daniel could foresee the eventual triumph of English.

> And who, in time, knowes whither we may vent
> The treasure of our tongue, to what strange shores
> This gaine of our best glory shall be sent,
> T'inrich unknowing Nations with our stores ?
> What worlds in th' yet unformed Occident
> May come refin'd with th' accents that are ours ?

How preposterous this would have seemed a mere twenty years before, when Spenser dedicated to Sidney the first great work of the New Poetry.

From those first beginnings, after Sidney came home from the Continent, English poetry had flowed on, disjunct yet continuous as a river, so that it is possible to follow the broad flood of poetry that existed by 1630 back to a common source. So the poets themselves saw their work. My purpose has been to see with their eyes, and thereby to restore perspective to the scene of the English Renaissance.

NOTES AND REFERENCES

ALL who study the life of Sir Philip Sidney must rely on the work of their predecessors, Collins, Zouch, Fox-Bourne, Wilson, and above all Wallace whose admirable biography I have used constantly and have been able to supplement in only a few details. For the Countess of Pembroke the pioneer work was excellently done by Frances Berkeley Young in her biography, published in 1912. I have not here given references for facts recorded by Wallace or Young, since any who wish to study the lives of Philip and Mary Sidney must use these works. Neither have I given references to all the biographies of persons mentioned in this book, whether these are articles in the appropriate Dictionaries of National Biography, or monographs such as Miss Yates' fascinating study of Florio or F. W. T. Hunger's fine book on Charles de L'Ecluse, though I have mentioned particular points from some of these. In order to save space I have omitted references to Sidney's letters, printed by Feuillerat, and to Languet's letters to Sidney (*Epistolae*) which I have used constantly.

For all translations I am myself responsible, though I have used Pears wherever possible for translations from the correspondence of Sidney and Languet. I should point out that, quite apart from omissions, Pears is by no means always reliable.

I have used the following abbreviations :

AP. *An Apologie for Poetrie*, ed. E. S. Shuckburgh.

A & S. *Astrophel and Stella*, ed. M. Wilson, 1931.

Epistolae. *Huberti Langueti . . . Epistolae . . . ad Philippum Sydnaeum*, ed. Lord Dalrymple, 1776.

FQ. *The Faerie Queene*, ed. J. C. Smith and E. de Selincourt.

Feuillerat. *The Complete Works of Sir Philip Sidney*, ed. A. Feuillerat, 1912–26.

Life. Fulke Greville, *The Life of the Renowned Sir Philip Sidney*, 1652 (ed. Nowell Smith, 1907).

SC. *The Shepheardes Calender*, ed. J. C. Smith and E. de Selincourt.

CHAPTER I

P.   1. Robinson's dedication : B.M. Royal MS. 18A. lxvi. *Robinson's Eupolemia.* Robinson describes the book as 'The Reverend D.

Philip Melanthon his prayers translated oute of Latin into English with the prayers of other learned Germaynes. 1579.' This apparently no longer exists.

P. 2. Prior: *A Satire upon the Poets.*
Crashaw: *Wishes. To his (supposed) Mistresse.* This stanza was first printed in 1646.

3. Martial: VIII. 56. 5.

4. Moral thunder: J. H. Reynolds, preface to his *Peter Bell*, 1819. Artificial: e.g. 'The manner of singing that Bidon useth, which is so artificiall etc. that the spirites of the hearers move all and are inflamed'. Sir T. Hoby's translation of *The Courtier*, 1561. 'The Madrigall is next unto the Motet the most artificiall and to men of understanding the most delightfull.' T. Morley, *A Plaine and Easie Introduction to Practicall Musicke*, 1597.

5. tournament: *A & S*, XLI.

6. Lamb: On some Sonnets of Sir Philip Sydney, in *Last Essays of Elia*.
Cokayne: *A Chain of Golden Poems embellish'd with Wit, Mirth and Eloquence*, 1658. The poems are to Isabel Manifold of the *Black Swan*, Ashbourne; to John Young of the *Bear*, and Henry Right of the *Cock*, both at Polesworth.

7. Harington and Vignola: J. Collinson, *History of Somersetshire*, 1791, I. 128.
Harington's fountain: J. Nichols, *Progresses of Queen Elizabeth*. Harington's translation of Ariosto's description is in his *Orlando Furioso*, 1591, XLII. 71-3.

8. 'To overgo Ariosto': G. Harvey, *Three proper and wittie familiar Letters*, 1580.
Jonson: *Discoveries.*
Lucretius: *De Rerum Natura*, I. 832 and III. 260.
Pope: preface to *Works*, 1717.

9. Lorenzo de' Medici: *Comento sopra alcuni de' suoi sonetti.*
Waller: *Of English Verse.*

10. Mulcaster: *First Part of the Elementarie*, 1582.

11. Drayton: preface to *The Barons Warres*, 1609.
Daniel: *Defence of Ryme*, 1602.

12. Spenser: dedication to *The Ruines of Time*, 1591.
Daniel: *op. cit.*
a general *Maecenas*: *Life.*
Planting our roses: Daniel, dedication of *Cleopatra*, 1594.
Nashe: preface to Greene's *Menaphon*, 1589.

13. Sonnet on Isabella Markham: *Nugae Antiquae*, ed. H. Harington, 1769.

Tusser : *Five hundreth points of good husbandry*, 1573, etc.

P. 14. Skelton pleased 'only the popular eare' : G. Puttenham, *The Arte of English Poesie*, 1589.

15. Spenser's grave : W. Camden, *Historie . . . of Princesse Elizabeth*, 1630.

Milton told Dryden : preface to the *Fables*, 1700.

17. *Piers*, I have pyped erst : *SC, October*.

18. Spenser as our Virgil : e.g. Nashe, *Strange Newes*, 1592 ; C. Fitzgeffrey : *Affaniae*, 1601.

20. Ascham detested the Italian influence : *The Scholemaster*, 1570.

J. E. Spingarn : *Literary Criticism in the Renaissance*, 1899.

21. N. Drake : *Shakespeare and his Times*, 1817.

My drift I fear : *The Prelude*, 1850, V. 293-4. (Corrected from 'My drift hath scarcely, I fear, been obvious'. 1805, V. 291-2.)

Keats : e.g. *Endymion*, I. 340-43 ; II. 757-8 ; III. 477-9 ; *Lamia*, I. 59-65 ; 330-32.

Horace : *De Arte Poetica*, 360.

Tasso : *Gerusalemme Liberata*, I. 3.

Spenser : *Letter to Raleigh*.

palpable designs : Keats, letter to J. H. Reynolds, February 3rd, 1818.

22. writing for mankind : Wordsworth, preface to *Lyrical Ballads*, 1802.

Bliss was it : *Prelude*, 1805, X. 693-4.

unprecedented in literary history : *Letters*, I. 186.

23. Upon this *Urn* : I. Walton, *Life of Dr. Donne*.

Shakespeare's sonnets among his private friends : F. Meres, *Palladis Tamia*, 1598.

24. Donne deplored : letter to Sir Henry Goodere, December 20th, 1614.

Drayton : Address to the Reader in *Poly-Olbion*, 1612.

26. Wordsworth's uncle : quoted from *St. John's College in Wordsworth's Time*, in *Wordsworth at Cambridge*, 1950.

Jonson told Donne : *Conversations with William Drummond*.

27. Jonson on Sidney : *op. cit.*

29. Sidney asked that the *Arcadia* should be destroyed : J. Owen, *Epigrammatum Libri Tres*, 1607, II. 67, seems to be the first to say so. Cf. Edward Leigh, *A Treatise of Religion and Learning*, 1656, p. 324. The fact is also mentioned in the preface to the Italian translation, 1659, and no doubt elsewhere.

fragments : The notable exceptions are Marlowe's *Hero and Leander*, and the *Faerie Queene*, both unfinished at the poets' deaths. Even so, Chapman completed Marlowe's poem. And the *Arcadia*, whose revision was incomplete at Sidney's death, was completed by Sir William Alexander and R. Beling. Such was the age's dislike of untidy fragments. The only true fragment that was published unfinished though the author still lived seems to have been Davies's *Orchestra*, 1596.

Breton : dedication of *The Pilgrimage to Paradise*, 1592.

Byron : *Beppo*, LXXV.

P. 30. Where breath most breathes : Shakespeare, Sonnet 81.

31. Greville as Shakespeare's master : D. Lloyd, *Statesmen and Favourites of England since the Reformation*, 1665.

CHAPTER 2

P. 33. Gower : *Confessio Amantis. Prologus*, 22-56.

Drant : *On the Right Honorable and most noble Lorde, the Lord Robert Dudley, Erle of Leicester*, in *A Medicinable Morall*, 1566.

34. Daniel : dedication of *Cleopatra*, 1594.

35. A sweet attractive kind of grace : Matthew Roydon, *An Elegie or friends passion for his Astrophill*.

neither knew English : of those mentioned, only Charles de L'Ecluse seems to have known English. Bruno refused to learn English during his two years in England because 'all Englishmen of rank know that their own tongue is only used in their own island, and would think themselves barbarians if they could not speak in Latin, French, Spanish and Italian'. *La Cena de le Ceneri*.

36. grace : the term used by Hoby to translate Castiglione's *gratia*. E.g. 'If I doe well bear in minde, me thinke [Count Lewis] you have this night often times repeated, that the Courtier ought to accompany all his doings, gestures, demeaners : finally all his motions with a grace'.

Bryskett : *Discourse of Civil Life*, 1606. Cf. Languet, *Epistolae*, XXXIX, where, urging Sidney to overcome his dislike of Pibrac, he says : 'Ego soleo de hominibus aliter judicare quam plurimi faciant, nisi sint plane scelerati : nam talium vitia non puto esse dissimulanda. Decerpo virtutes, si quae sint ; et si qua in re vel errore, vel animi imbecillitate peccant, illud tego quantum in me est.'

37. *Hamlet*, III. i. 154-7. I do not wish to assert that Shakespeare was thinking of Sidney when he wrote these lines — he was thinking of Hamlet. But if Sidney had not lived he would not have thought of Hamlet in this way.

Holinshed : *The Third Volume of Chronicles*, etc., 1587, pp. 1553-
1555.

neglect of correspondence : Languet's first complaint was in
his second letter, written when Sidney had left for Italy : 'You
might at least have sent a note to say "Arrived safely" '.

because Sir W. Pelham was without his : *Life*.

sonnet *A & S*, LIV.

P. 39. epitaph on Thornton's tomb : 'Ubiq ; pauperibus bonae spei
adulescentulis literarum studiosis certum dum vixit refugium ;
ab omni largitione semper intactus fidei suae comissum sive in
electionibus puerorum, sive in collationibus Beneficiorum nihil
unquam preci vel pretio indulsit ; Iuventutis lectissimae, et
inter alios Philippi Sidnaei equitis Nobilissimi Academicae
educationi Praepositus fuit'.

my darling master Philip : Sir William Cecil to Sir Henry
Sidney, August 10th, 1568. *C.S.P. Ireland, Eliz.* XXV.

41. Carew remembered a great occasion : in 1569. *Survey of
Cornwall*, 1602, p. 102.

The Excellency of the English Tongue : first printed by Camden,
Remaines concerning Britaine, 1614.

42. Nashe : *Strange Newes*, 1592.

43. to the evidence assembled by Wallace about Sidney's residence
at Cambridge (pp. 105-7) add Gabriel Harvey's statement in
one of the poems addressed to Sidney in *Gratulationes Valdinenses*, 1578 : 'Utrunque Lycaeum Delitias inter foveat'.

the light of his family : 'Which eminence, by nature and industry, made his worthy Father stile Sir Philip in my hearing
(though I unseen) Lumen familiae suae' : *Life*.

Licence to travel : Collins, I. 98.

44. Bryskett thinking of himself as an Englishman : 'For although
our English tongue have not that copiousnesse and sweetnes
that both the Greeke and the Latine have above all others', etc.
Discourse.

two poems of Bernardo Tasso's : W. P. Mustard, *Am. J. Philol.*,
1914, XXXV. 192 *sqq.*

Leicester to Walsingham : quoted by Wallace, p. 115.

45. He was so admired : Bryskett, *op. cit.*

Théophile de Banos : so he signed his name, or, when writing
Latin, Theophilus Banosius. Quotations from Banosius, *De
Vita P. Rami*, prefixed to *Petri Rami Commentariorum de
Religione Christiana Libri Quatuor*, 1576.

46. Abraham Fraunce : the evidence for Sidney's paying for his
education is in BM. Harl. MSS. 6995, f. 35.

Harvey: *Ciceronianus*, 1577. *Rhetor*, 1577. Cf. E. K.'s reference
to Harvey's *Rameidos* in a gloss to *SC, September*.

Temple : P. *Rami Dialecticae Libri Duo scholiis G. Tempelii
Cantabrigiensis illustrati*, (?) 1584.

de Banos' letters to Sidney : BM. Adds. 15914 ff. 21, 27, 28 ;
17520 f. 8 ; 18675 ff. 4, 6, 7, 8. (Four in Latin, four in French.)
I have not discovered a dedication to Sidney in any of Ramus's
numerous posthumous works, but I may not have seen them
all.

P. 48. Languet knew Tasso in Paris : Henri Chevreul, *Hubert Languet*,
1852, p. 106.

Du Bartas : quotation from Joshua Sylvester's translation of
Bartas his Divine Weekes & Workes, 1605.

Swan-like tunes : the common pun Sidney-Cynge. Cf. Frontis-
piece.

Sidney's translation : mentioned by Sylvester, *op. cit.* B2 ;
entered to Ponsonby August 23rd, 1588.

49. Ramus's phonetic reforms : F. P. Graves, *Peter Ramus and the
Educational Reformation of the 16th Century*, 1912, ch. vi.

J. E. Spingarn : *Literary Criticism in the Renaissance*, 1899.
Two other very Commendable Letters, 1580. Cf. Harvey's reply.
J. Hall, *Virgidemiarum*, 1598, VI. 255-8.

50. Languet to Elector of Saxony : *Huberti Langueti Epistolae ad
Joachimum Camerarium etc. editae quondam a Ludovico Camera-
rio nepote, nunc recusae & quibusdam epistolis ad Augustum
Sax. Electorem auctae*, 1685, XVIII.

the house of Andreas Wechel : *Life.*

as Wechel acknowledged : in dedicating to Languet his edition
of Krantz, *Wandalia sive Historia de Wandalorum vera origine*,
1575.

51. Camerarius compares this correspondence : *op. cit.*, dedication.
Languet had known Buchanan : *Georgii Buchanani Scoti ad viros
sui saeculi clarissimos, eorumque ad eundem, Epistolae*, 1711.

52. Languet, the shepheard best swift Ister knew : *Arcadia*, III.
Henry of Navarre : *Life.*

It is not, perhaps, beyond question that Sidney met Michel de
L'Hôpital, though his praise of him, *AP*, p. 48, suggests personal
acquaintance. M. du Fay, son of M. de L'Hôpital, seems to have
been a friend of Sidney's in the Netherlands. Letter of the
Princess of Orange to Hotman, April 28th, 1586, in *Correspondance de Louise de Coligny*, ed. P. Marchegay, 1887, No. XX.

54. defence of the Massacre : *Ornatissimi cuiusdam viri de rebus
Gallicis ad Stanislaum Elvidium Epistola*, 1573.

P. 55. and even to many strangers : Timothy Bright, dedication of
An Abridgement of the Actes and Monuments, 1589.
Timothy Bright : *In Physicam Gulielmi Adolphi Scribonii . . .
Animadversiones*, 1584.

57. Spenser : *Astrophel*, 21-2.

58. three lines adapted from an epistle of Horace's :

> Quid Sidneius agit ? monitus multumque monendus
> Ut partas tueatur opes, & perdere vitet
> Dona palatino puero quae infudit Apollo.

Cf. Horace, *Ep.* I. 3. 15-17.

59. Hoby : *A booke of the travaile and lief of me Thomas Hoby*, ed.
E. Powell, *Camden Miscellany*, X. 1902, p. 4.
Sidney at Basle : letter of d'Argenlieu to Sidney. BM. Adds.
15914 ; cf. letter of Claudius Auberius Triuncurianus to Sidney
in same collection. A mystery has been made of Sidney's visit
to Basle, quite unnecessarily. Languet mentions de la Val
'whom you saw at Basle', quem vidisti Basileae, in *Epistolae*,
XCVI, but this seems to have been overlooked by Sidney's
biographers.
de Banos : *op. cit.*

60. Hakluyt : quoted (without reference) article 'Tulip' in R.H.S.
Dictionary of Gardening, 1951, IV. 2161.
de L'Ecluse's correspondence : there is a mass of it, of great
interest, and mostly unpublished, in the University Library at
Leiden, where I studied it. There was once a photograph there
of a letter from Sidney to de L'Ecluse, but the photograph, taken
in 1911, had not been fixed, and the sheet is now blank. The
original seems now also to have disappeared, which is most
unfortunate, since it has never been published.

61. Crato to Sidney : BM. Adds. 15914, f. 17.

62. drinking his health : BM. Adds. 15914, f. 31.
tall and comely : R. Ascham, *Report and Discourse of the affaires
and state of Germany*, 1552.

63. de L'Ecluse's letter : BM. Adds. 17520, f. 6. The reference may
be to another copy of the medallion (if it was a medallion) rather
than to another portrait.

CHAPTER 3

P. 64. Shelley : Letter to Peacock, April 1818.

66. Wotton : Letter to Earl of Salisbury, in L. Pearsall Smith, *Sir
Henry Wotton*, 1907, I. 400.

Pibrac reconstituted de Baïf's Academy : F. A. Yates, *French Academies of the Sixteenth Century*, 1947. Cf. A. Cabos, *Guy du Faur de Pibrac*, 1922.

P. 67. Camerarius owned Zindelini's letters : preface to *Viri Cl. Huberti Langueti Burgundi, ad Joachimum Camerarium etc. Epistolae*, 1646.

Melissus : *Schediasmata Poetica*, 1586.

Sidney's letter : XXXVIII. Feuillerat prints 'heare saie', which seems rather pointless. Five out of the eight MSS. collated by Feuillerat read 'heresie', which I prefer.

68. Sidney seems to have had more friends among the French and Germans. This may well be the chance result of the survival (or discovery) of their letters, and the disappearance of the Italians', for, as will be seen, in England more Italians than French or Germans came to him.

Carafa : Aldimari, *Storia della famiglia Carafa*, 1691.

it was said of him : G. B. Tafuri, *Istoria degli scrittori nati nel regno di Napoli*, 1754, III. iii. 189.

69. Bruno heard of Sidney : *La Cena de le Ceneri*, 1584.

G. M. Manelli : *Vita di Giulio Agricola*, 1585.

Sidney and Grimani : BM. Adds. 17520, f. 4.

licence to carry arms : in Venetian archives. (i) *Consiglio de Dieci*, No. 78, fol. 127 (wrongly dated and wrongly translated in *C.S.P. Venetian* VII). (ii) *Capi del Consiglio de Dieci : Lettere, filze* 75 (unpublished).

71. du Plessis-Mornay makes no mention of the portrait in his will, printed in *Archives curieuses de l'histoire de France. Sér. 1. Tome 15e*. 1837. His books, which were left to the Protestant Church in Saumur, were burnt in the Fronde. (I owe this last disappointing news to my former pupil R. J. Rickett, who kindly made some enquiries for me when in Saumur.)

72. knew the *Poetics* : *AP passim*.

Zabarella : Bayle, *General Dictionary*, 1734–41, X. 243 *sqq*.

studies of Venetian government : Contarini, *La Republica, e i Magistrati di Vinegia*, 1544; Donato Giannotti, *La Republica de Vinegia*, 1570.

collections of letters : *Lettere di Principi*, ed. G. Ruscelli, 1562. *Lettere di tredici huomini illustri*, ed. T. Porcacchi, 1565.

73. J. Lipsius : *De recta pronunciatione Latinae Linguae*, 1586.

74. Inscription on Lord Windsor's monument : 'Inscr. Odoardo Windesor Baroni Anglo. Ill. parentib. orto, qui dum religionis quadam abundantia vitae probitate, et suavitate morum omnib. carus clarusq. vitam degeret, immatura morte correpto, cele-

berrimis exequiis decorato, Georgius Lewhnor [*sic*] affinis, poni curavit, obit anno D. MDLXXXIII die mensis Januarii XXIIII aetatis suae XXXXII.' Cicogna has no notes on this inscription, not even in MS.

Carafa to Sidney : BM. Adds. 15914, f. 15.

P. 75. to hear him speake : Roydon's *Elegie*.

76. Edward Wotton : later Lord Wotton of Marley ; half-brother of Sir Henry Wotton.

77. sonnet : *A & S*, XLI.

78. an anonymous writer : *The Life of Sir Philip Sidney*, in *The Works of . . . Sr Philip Sidney, Kt.*, 1715.

letter to Augustus : *Huberti Langueti Epistolae*, etc., 1685, XVII. Ursinus's inscription is quoted by Dalrymple in his notes to *Epistolae*.

79. Drant's poem : *Praesul*, 1575, p. 45.

80. Lipsius observed : dedication to Earl of Warwick of G. Whetstone, *Sir Philip Sidney his honorable life, his valiant death and true vertues*, 1587.

the hope of all learned men : Spenser, dedication of *The Ruines of Time*, 1591.

the Queen at Kenilworth : Nichols, *Progresses*.

81. tragedy by Frangipani : *Tragedia* del S. Cl. Cornelio Frangipani, 1574.

Capitolo by Menechini : *Capitolo, nel qual, la Santiss. Religion Catholica è introdotta a' favellar co 'l Christianiss. Potentissimo, & Invittiss. Henrico III . . .* composto dall' eccellente Sig. Andrea Menechini, 1574.

triumphal arch. : *L' Historia della pubblica et famosa entrata in Vinegia del Serenissimo Henrico III . . .* composto nuovamente per Marsilio della Croce, 1574.

82. the Queen had invited Mary : letter to Sir Henry Sidney quoted by Young, pp. 27-8.

though young in years : *The Queenes Majesties Entertainment at Woodstock*.

83. de L'Ecluse wrote : BM. Adds. 17520, f. 6 ; 15914, ff. 29, 31. letter printed by E. Roze : *Charles de L'Escluse*, 1899.

Carafa wrote : BM. Adds. 17520, ff. 4-5 ; 15914, ff. 15, 25.

Moller : BM. Adds. 15914, ff. 19-20.

84. Juliet : *Romeo and Juliet*, I. iii. 69-73.

85. Addison : *Spectator*, 1711, Nos. 70, 74.

86. Monau : G. Vossius, *Commentarius de rebus . . . gestis F. à Dohna*, 1628.

88. Languet was in Sidney's company : *Huberti Langueti . . . ad*

Joachimum Camerarium Patrem, & Joachimum Camerarium Filium . . . Epistolae, 1646, XXX. (17 Ju : [*sic*] 1577.)
Nuremberg : Letter to the Camerarii. Feuillerat, IV. 402.
V. also A. P. McMahon, *Sir Philip Sidney's Letter to the Camerarii*, in *P.M.L.A.* XLII, 83-95.

P. 89. record of conversation : *The Living Librarie . . . written in Latin by P. Camerarius . . . and done into English by John Molle Esquire*, 1621, pp. 98-9.

93. du Plessis-Mornay : *Vindiciae contra Tyrannos.* For the arguments in favour of his authorship, rather than Languet's, *v.* H. J. Laski's introduction to his edition of the English translation, *A Defence of Liberty against Tyrants*, 1924.
Du Plessis-Mornay in England : *Mémoires et Correspondance de Duplessis-Mornay*, 1824, I. 117-18, etc.
Languet met Du Plessis-Mornay : Chevreul, *op. cit.*
her godfathers : *Mémoires*, I. 119.
Samson Lennard : *The Mysterie of Iniquitie : That is to say, The Historie of the Papacie*, 1612. Lennard became Bluemantle Pursuivant and died in 1633.

94. Languet asked Sidney : *Epistolae*, LXVI. The boy's name was Joannes Fridericus Bromius, whose father had assisted English Protestant exiles during the Marian persecutions.

CHAPTER 4

P. 95. Aubrey : *Brief Lives*, ed. A. Clark, 1898, I. 311.
like his cousins : *Autobiography* of Lord Herbert of Cherbury.
Lewis Glyn Cothi : *Gwaith*, 1837.
Guto 'r Glyn : *Gwaith*, ed. Sir I. Williams and J. Ll. Williams, 1939.
William Middleton's poem is printed in *MS. Gwyneddon 3*, ed. Sir I. Williams, 1931.

96. *Henry V* : IV. viii. 106.
Tasso : *Discorsi del Poema Eroico*, II.
Jonson : *Conversations.*
Milton's Arthuriad : *Mansus*, 78-84.
Cambro-Britons : e.g. *Letter* XII ; M. Drayton, '*To the Cambro-Britans and their harpe, his Ballad of Agincourt*'.

97. Another book : *Angliae regni florentissimi nova descriptio.*

98. Spenser had Irish poetry translated : *A Vewe of the presente state of Ireland.*
Sidney to Earl of Sussex : *Letter* XXXII, and *v.* Feuillerat's note, with which I agree.

P. 99. Moffett: *Nobilis*, ed. V. B. Heltzel and H. H. Hudson, 1940, pp. 27, 83. (The English translation which follows the Latin text is crude and unreliable. *Hospitium*, in the present context, does not mean 'inn'; cf. Languet's use of the word: 'Nondum mihi privatum hospitium conduxi'. *Epistolae*, LXXXI.)

he tells us himself: dedication of *Arcadia*; *Two Pastoralls*.

Southey: *Works*, X. 126. Mrs. Elizabeth Cooper in *The Muses' Library*, 1727, p. 216, had said much the same.

100. Sir Robert Naunton: *Fragmenta Regalia*, 1641.

101. as early as 1575: *The Song in the Oak* was sung to the Queen at Woodstock in that year.

Harvey called him: quoted by R. M. Sargent, *At the Court of Queen Elizabeth*, 1935, p. 167.

102. Sidney's will: Feuillerat, III.

105. Mrs. Humphry Ward: *English Poets*, 1880, I. Cf. J. M. Purcell, *Sidney's Astrophel and Stella and Greville's Caelica*. *P.M.L.A.* L. 413-22. But he overstates the case.

with her sitting by him: dedication to *Arcadia*.

as Miss Yates has pointed out: *T.L.S.* August 7th, 1937.

106. certainly Queen Elizabeth: e.g. *Caelica*, LXXXI.

Bacon: *Apophthegmes New and Old*, 1625.

Myraphill: *Caelica*, LXXII.

107. as, item, two lips: *Twelfth Night*, I. v. 255 *sqq.*

Caelica's hair a wig: *Caelica*, LVII.

109. happy, blessed trinity: in the first of the *Two Pastoralls*. Dyer's *Fancy* was also imitated by Robert Southwell, *Maister diers phansie turned to a sinners complaint*, BM. Harl. 6921.

Sargent, *op. cit.* p. 207; A. R. Bullough, *Poems and Dramas*, 1939.

110. pleasing sauce: *Treatie of Humane Learning*, 112.

Those words in every tongue are best: *op. cit.* 109.

113. Pattison: *Music and Poetry of the English Renaissance*, 1948.

114. Basset to Stradling: *Sidneiana*, ed. S. Butler, 1837.

115. Queen's College MS.: quoted by R. W. Zandvoort, *Sidney's Arcadia*, 1928.

116. Ascham: *The Scholemaster*, 1570.

Tolomei: *Versi e Regole della Nuova Poesia Toscana*, 1539.

117. Campion: *Observations in the Art of English Poesie*, 1602.

118. Spenser on dedications: 'Newe Bookes I heare of none, but only of one, that writing a certaine Booke, called The Schoole of Abuse, and dedicating it to Maister Sidney, was for hys labor scorned, if at leaste it be in the goodnesse of that nature to scorne. Such follie is it not to regard aforehand the inclination and

qualitie of him to whom wee dedicate our Bookes. Suche might I happily incurre, entituling my Slomber and the other Pamphlets unto his honor.' *Two . . . Letters.*

Spenser's account of the execution of O'Brien : *A Vewe of the presente state of Ireland.*

P. 119. Nashe : *Have with you to Saffron-Walden,* 1596.

120. Greville's Sapphics : *Caelica,* VI.

123. Petrarch : Mia benigna fortuna e 'l viver lieto.

124. Keats 'hoisted himself up, and looked burly and dominant, as he said, "What an image that is — *sea-shouldering whales* !" '
Cowden Clarke : *Recollections of Writers,* 1878.

126. T. Blount : *The Academie of Eloquence,* 1654.
J. Smith : *The Mysterie of Rhetorique Unvail'd,* 1657.

129. Spenser's sestina : *SC, August.*

131. W. L. : perhaps one William Lisle.

CHAPTER 5

P. 134. composition of *Arcadia* : dedication ; Aubrey, *Brief Lives,* II. 248.

Milton's scorn : *Eikonoklastes,* 1649.

Translations of Arcadia : Dutch, *D'Arcadia van de Gravinne van Pembrok,* voor Felix van Sambix de Jonghe. Delft, 1639, 1641 ; Amsterdam, 1659.

German : *Arcadia der Gräffin von Pembrock,* tr. by Martin Opitz ('Valentin Theocritus von Hirschberg'), 1629, 1630, 1638, 1642, 1643, 1646.

Italian : *L' Arcadia della Contessa di Pembrok.* Portata dal Francese dal Signor Livio Alessandri. Venice, 1659.

Marie de Médicis sent Baudoin : *v.* A. W. Osborn, *Sir Philip Sidney en France,* 1932. Baudoin's translation was published Paris 1624–5. Jean Loiseau de Tourval's unpublished translation *c.* 1605–11 is Bodleian MS. Rawl. D. 920. Other French translations by Mlle Geneviève Chappelain, Paris, 1624 ; and a Frankfort catalogue of 1623 mentions a translation by Theodore Jacquemot, which perhaps was never published.

135. Dousa : *Jani Dousae F. Poemata,* 1607.

Peiresc : his copy is now in the Bibliothèque Nationale.

135. Guarini to Daniel : Daniel's commendatory sonnet to the Dymoke translation of *Il Pastor Fido,* 1602.

an enthusiastic German : quoted (without reference) by Wilson, p. 142.

pious Cavalier children : Messrs. Sotheby's catalogue, June 22nd, 1953, item 137.

used as a cover story : *A Draught of Sir Philip Sidney's Arcadia*. Unpublished MS. in my possession.

imitated : e.g. Lady Mary Wroth's *The Countesse of Mountgomeries Urania*, 1621 ; Mlle de la Roche Guilhem, *Almanҳor and Almanҳaida*, 1678, 1690.

paraphrased into verse : e.g. Francis Quarles' *Argalus and Parthenia*, 1629.

dramatized : e.g. James Shirley's *A Pastorall called the Arcadia*, 1640 ; Antoine Mareschal, *La Cour Bergère*, 1640.

opera by Parisetti and Alveri : *Il Re Pastore, overo Il Basilio in Arcadia* ; F. C. Bressand, *Der königliche Schäfer oder Basilius in Arcadien*.

P. 136. Molyneux : in Holinshed, *Third Volume of Chronicles*, etc., 1587, p. 1554.

Howell's other books : *The Arbor of Amitie*, 1568. *Pleasant Sonnets and Prettie Pamphlets*, ? 1568.

137. Spenser observed : *Two . . . Letters.*

139. Vida : *De Arte Poetica*, 1527.

those that preface the *Aeneid* : the four lines beginning ' Ille ego qui quondam ', etc., which according to Donatus were excised by Varius.

140. his friends upbraided him : dedication to *The Ruines of Time.*

141. quotation from *Aeneid*, V. 344.

142. Ralegh : *The 11th and last booke of the Ocean to Scinthia*, l. 61. Drake sailed into Plymouth on September 26th, 1580.

de L'Ecluse and Drake : *v.* Hunger, *Charles de L'Escluse*, 1927, pp. 145-7. Cf. *C. Clusii Atreb. Aliquot Notae in Garciae Aromatum Historiam. Eiusdem Descriptiones nonnullarum Stirpium . . . quae a Generoso viro Francisco Drake . . . observatae sunt*, 1582.

143. dedication to Sidney and Dyer : *Simplicium Medicamentorum ex novo orbe delatorum . . . historiae liver tertius*, 1582.

subscriptions to Frobisher's voyages : *C.S.P. Colonial, E. Indies*, 1513–1616, p. 18.

144. prevented from sailing with Drake : *Life.*

as Aristotle saith : *AP*, p. 24, quoting *Ethics*, I. 1.

All thought exists for the sake of action : R. G. Collingwood, *Speculum Mentis*, 1924.

145. Daniel, *Musophilus*, 1599, ll. 198-200.

147. Temple's analysis of *AP* is among the *De L'Isle and Dudley MSS.* in the P.R.O.

Sir William Temple : *Essay on Poetry.*

he first came in the presence : preface to *The Lawiers Logike*, 1588.

This comparison : BM. Adds. 34361.

P. 148. Bodleian MS. Rawl. D. 345.

Aeneid, III. 590 *sqq.* Fraunce has given a wrong reference on the MS. as in spite of quoting 'Tollite me, Teucri', he has written 4° Aeneidos on the cover.

149. Camden : *Remaines.*

On the portrait of Sidney in N.P.G. *v.* E. M. Denkinger, *The Impresa Portrait of Sir Philip Sidney in the N.P.G. P.M.L.A.* XLVII. 17-45.

Ovid : *Metamorphoses*, XIII. 140-41.

150. H. Peacham : *The Compleat Gentleman*, 1634.

Shakespeare's *impresa* : *v.* E. K. Chambers, *William Shakespeare*, 1930, II. 153. Cf. *Pericles*, II. ii.

must not be too intricate : Daniel's preface to *The Worthy Tract*. Fraunce's MS. among the *De L'Isle and Dudley MSS.* in the P.R.O.

151. on the authenticity of portraits of Sidney *v.* esp. B. Siebeck : *Das Bild Sir Philip Sidneys in der Englischen Renaissance*, 1939.

152. Hilliard's portrait of Lady Rich : Henry Constable's sonnet *To Mr. Hilliard, upon Occasion of a picture he made of my Ladie Rich.*

no authentic portrait : the portrait called Lady Rich at Lambeth Palace cannot be of her.

translations of the Psalms : *v.* T. Riese, *Die englische Psalmenübersetzung im 16ten Jahrhundert.*

153. A. Gentili to Bodley : MS. Bodleian 13.

he had translated the first 43 : Greville, in his letter to Walsingham of November 1586, mentions 'about 40 of the psalms' among Sidney's literary remains. The number 43 is established by notes in three of the MSS. Bodleian Rawl. Poet. 25 (the Woodforde transcript) ; B.M. Adds. 12048 ; Queen's Coll. Oxford MS. 341.

direct from Hebrew : so Riese, *op. cit.*

Sidney refers to Tremellius : *AP.* This Bible was first published Frankfort 1575–80, and in England 1579–80.

155. Feuillerat lists nine MSS. There is a tenth, which belonged to Sir Kenelm Digby, in the Library of the University of Paris. Aubrey : *Brief Lives*, I. 311 ; *Memoires of Naturall Remarques in the County of Wilts.*, ed. J. Britton, 1847, p. 86.

156. Hotman to Savile : *Francisci et Joannis Hotomanorum patris ac filii, et clarorum virorum ad eos Epistolae . . .* 1700, No. 37.

Hotman to his father : quoted by A. W. Osborn, *op. cit.* ch. ii.

Corran to Hotman : *Hotomanorum Epistolae*, No. 64.

Melissus to Hotman : *op. cit.* No. 92.

Gentili to Hotman : *op. cit.* Nos. 78 and 79.

P. 158. Hesiod : *Theogony* 233.

Wolfe : in imprint of Jacobus Acontius's posthumous *Una essortatione al timor di Dio* he calls himself 'servitore de l' illustrissimo Filippo Sidnei'.

praised by Ubaldino : *La vita di Carlo Magno imperadore*, 1581.

Regole de la Lingua Thoscana : U.L.C. MS. Dd. xi. 46.

159. his first book : *Florio His firste Fruites*, 1578.

Giardino di recreatione : BM. Adds. 15214.

Surrey and Wyatt having travailed into Italie : Puttenham, *op. cit.*

Florio's Dictionary : *A Worlde of Wordes*, 1598 ; *Queen Anna's New World of Words*, 1611.

160. Bruno : *La Cena de le Ceneri*, 1584. Dialogo secondo.

161. the Warden of New College : Dr. Martin Culpepper. 'Dr Culpepper being warden of Newe Colledge in Oxon : and much disliked by the fellowes thereof : one Mr Payne dyinge generally beloved of all the society, and accordinge to ye use of scholars of ye howse clappinge verses about the wall of the colledge cloysters one amongst the rest to sheawe howe much beloved of them all, Mr Payne was & howe much dislyked Dr Culpepper was : sett up in the cloyster this one verse followinge

Poena potest tolli, Culpa perennis erit.'

Bodleian MS., Tanner 169 f. 76.

Daniel at Bruno's lectures: N. W. in preface to *The Worthy Tract*.

Daniel's Geny : Wood, *Athenae Oxonienses*.

Sidney, Greville, and Bruno : dedication of *Spaccio de la Bestia Trionfante*, 1584.

162. Herbert's opinion : quoted by R. Dunlap in his edition of Carew's *Poems*, 1949.

163. *Heroycall Furies* : dedication of *Montaigne*, 1603, to Countess of Rutland and Lady Rich.

164. Miss Yates : *The Emblematic Conceit in Giordano Bruno's De gli Eroici Furori and in the Elizabethan Sonnet Sequences*, in *England and the Mediterranean Tradition*, 1945.

165. You that with Allegory's curious frame : *A & S*, XXVIII.

168. Lipsius to Rantzau : *Hotomanorum Epistolae*, Ep. Misc. No. 5.

Fitzgeffrey : *Affaniae*, 1601.

he knew Mulcaster's work : *Odarum Britannicarum Liber*, 1586, V.

a poem addressed to him : by N. Clemens Mosellanus, in *Iusti Lipsi Aliorumque ad I. Dousam Carmina*, appended to *Iani Dousae a Noortwück Elegiarum Lib. II Epigrammatum Lib.*, 1586.

P. 169. poem to Sidney : *Odarum Britannicarum Liber*, IV.

his son wrote : *Iani Dousae Filii Britannicorum Carminum Silva* (appended to *Od. Brit.*), No. 7 ; and *Iani Dousae F. Poemata*.

Constable's sonnet : *op. cit.* p. 79. This translation was noted by Janet Scott in *M.L.R.* XX.

170. Dutch translation of *AP* : in *Eglentiers poetens Borst-weringh*, translation by T. Rodenburgh, 1619.

Eickius : *Elogium illustrissimi Principis Roberti, Comitis Leycestrii . . . cum Elogio Clarissimi viri, D. Philippi Sidnei . . . seu de vera Nobilitate*, 1586.

Louise de Coligny to Hotman : *Correspondance de Louise de Coligny*, Nos. XVII, XX ; to Leicester, No. XXIV.

171. the States of Zealand : *Life*.

Mendoza : *Life*.

Greville to Scottish Ambassador : Hist. MSS. C. Salisbury MSS. III.

172. du Plessis-Mornay to Walsingham : *Mémoires*, IV. 488-9.

Hotman to Lipsius : *Hotomannorum Epistolae*, No. 95.

CHAPTER 6

P. 173. University elegies : *Academiae Cantabrigiensis Lachrymae Tumulo Nobilissimi Equitis D. Philippi Sidneij Sacratae*, 1586 (i.e. 1587). *Exequiae Illustrissimi Equitis, D. Philippi Sidnaei, gratissimae memoriae ac nomini impensae*. Oxford, 1587. *Peplus. Illustrissimi viri D. Philippi Sidnaei supremis honoribus dicatus*. Oxford, 1587. *Epitaphia in Mortem Nobilissimi et Fortissimi Viri D. Philippi Sidneij Equitis . . .* Leiden, 1587.

174. Whetstone : *Sir Phillip Sidney, his honourable Life, his valiant Death and true Virtues*, 1587.

Breton : *Amoris Lachrymae*, in *Brittons Bowre of Delights*, 1591.

Watson : in *Meliboeus*, 1590 ; also in *The First Sett of Italian Madrigalls Englished*, 1590.

Daniel : *To the Angel Spirit of Sir Philip Sidney*.

Peele : in *An Eglogue Gratulatorie*, 1589.

Jonson : e.g. in *To Penshurst* ; *Epigrammes* LXXIX, CIII ; *Epistle to Elizabeth Countess of Rutland*, etc.

Drayton : *Sixt Eglog* of *Idea the Shepheards Garland*, 1593 ; *Eighth Eglogue* of *Pastorals*, 1606 ; *The Owle* ; *Elegie to Henery Reynolds*, etc.

Barnfield : *An Epitaph upon the Death of Sir Philip Sidney, Knight,* 1598.

Lord Herbert of Cherbury : *Epitaph on Sir Philip Sidney lying in St Paul's without a Monument.*

Basse : *Pastorals, Eglogue* VIII.

Gorges : *Poems,* ed. H. E. Sandison, 1953.

Baripenthes : licensed to John Windet, January 16th, 1587 ; mentioned by Thomas Lodington in *Exequiae.*

Moffett : *Nobilis* and *Lessus Lugubris.*

Owen : *Epigrammatum Libri tres,* 1607 (and subsequent editions).

Bastard : *Chrestoleros,* 1598.

Stradling : *Epigrammatum Libri IV,* 1607.

Fitzgeffrey : *Affaniae,* 1601.

Campion : *Epigrammatum Libri II,* 1619.

Bancroft : *Two Bookes of Epigrammes, and Epitaphs,* 1639. Cf. *The Heroical Lover,* 1658, p. 70.

others : these include two on Sidney (and a third 'upon the morning horse', Sidney's charger at his funeral), headed '*A Remembrance of Sir Ph. Sidneie Knight the 17th Nov 1586*', in BM. Adds 41499. The first is

> Tres fuimus fido coniun[c]ti foedere, quorum
> unus dum patriae, divaeq ; in principis armis
> occidit : h[a]ec nobis celebranda trophae[a] reliquit.

These lines must surely refer to Sidney's 'happy blessed trinity' and are presumably by Greville or Dyer.

de Lisle Groslot's Tumbeau : *Mémoires de Pierre de l'Estoile,* X. 42.

popular ballads : *A doleful dyttie of the death of Sir Philip Sidney,* entered February 22nd, 1587 ; *A Ballad of the buriall of Sir Philip Sidney,* entered February 27th, 1587 ; *A Mirrour of the life and death and vertues of Sir Philip Sidney,* entered June 15th, 1587.

Lant : *Sequitur celebritas et pompa funeris,* etc., 1587.

Aubrey : *Brief Lives,* II. 249-50.

P. 176. Eedes' *Epithalamion* seems to have vanished : presumably it was in Latin.

177. Munday's dedications to Oxford : *The Mirror of Mutability,* 1579 ; *Zelanto,* 1580 ; *Palmerin d'Oliva,* 1588 ; *Primaleon of Greece* (? date of lost first edition ; but in dedication of edition of 1619 Munday says it had been dedicated to Oxford).

178. whose name had been on his lips : John Owen in *Peplus.*

P. 179. Greville to Walsingham : *C.S.P. Dom. Eliz.* CXCV.
180. Thomas Wilson's translation of the Diana : B.M. Adds. 18638.
181. Hoskyns' reference : *Directions for Speech and Style.*
Aubrey : *Brief Lives*, I. 311.
Florio's criticism : dedication of *Montaigne.*
182. the silver image : G. Harvey, *Pierces Supererogation*, 1593.
Powell : *Tom of all Trades*, 1631.
Aubrey : *Natural History of Wiltshire*, 1847, p. 108.
Keats : letter to John Taylor, February 27th, 1818.
183. biting his tongue : I.
the mean face of the moon : XXXI.
vermilion eyes : CII.
185. the ordinarie mislike betweene sisters in lawe : *Arcadia*, I.
187. Whyte's letter : quoted by Yates, *Florio.*
188. travelled with Sir E. Dymoke : dedication of the *Worthy Tract.*
declined Italy : dedication of *Cleopatra.*
190. Adrian Gilbert's laboratory : Aubrey, *Brief Lives*, I. 262, 311.
191. Propertius : II. x. 7, where the Oxford text reads 'extrema' for Daniel's 'postrema'.
192. Coleridge : *Biographia Literaria*, 1817, ch. 22.
193. Sidney and Spenser the two great English poets : *Musophilus*, l. 441 ; dedication of *Cleopatra.*
195. Latin work on devices : *Insignium quae ab Italis Imprese nominantur, explicatio*, 1588.
masque for Lady Magdalen Egerton : Hunter's *Chorus Vatum.* B.M. Adds. 24488.
Harvey : *Foure Lettres*, 1592.
196. Unhappy Harvey : letter quoted by Moore-Smith.
197. Harvey's poem : letter to Sir R. Cecil, in *Works*, ed. A. Grosart, III. xxvii.
he knew the Walsinghams : he says so in *Meliboeus.*
199. C.M. as Marlowe : this identification is accepted by F. P. Wilson, *Marlowe and the Early Shakespeare*, 1953.
Ramsbury, Wilts., was a property of the Earl of Pembroke.
200. Daniel in trouble over *Philotas* : *v.* his letters printed by H. Sellers, *A Bibliography of the Works of Samuel Daniel*, 1585–1623, in *Oxford Bibl. Soc. Proc. and Papers*, II. i. 51-2.
Greville burnt *Antony and Cleopatra* : *Life.*
201. Shakespeare's visit to Wilton : *v.* E. K. Chambers, *William Shakespeare.*
202. Gosse : quoted (without reference) by H. E. Rollins in his introduction to *The Phoenix Nest*, 1931, p. xxxvii.

P. 203. Barnes' sonnet : in Arber's *English Garner*, 1895, V. 485. On Barnes' criminal activities *v.* M. Eccles in *Thomas Lodge and other Elizabethans*, ed. C. J. Sisson, 1933.

CHAPTER 7

P. 205. codicil : Feuillerat, III.
   206. Robert Dallington : so Douce conjectured, probably correctly.
   207. Moffett : *Nobilis*, p. 46. (The translation of the passage, p. 94, is a howler.)
   Spenser and the Spencers : e.g. *Prothalamion*, ll. 130-31 ; *Colin Clouts Come Home Againe*, ll. 539-40. Cf. Gibbon in his *Autobiography* : 'The nobility of the Spencers has been illustrated and enriched by the trophies of Marlborough ; but I exhort them to consider the Fairy Queen as the most precious jewel of their coronet'.
   Dante : *De Monarchia*, II. iii.
   description of Sir Calidore : *FQ*, VI. i. 2. Cf. *Astrophel*, ll. 19-22.
   208. Jonson : *Conversations*.
   209. attended by poets : Camden, *loc. cit.*
   Naunton : quoted by M. W. Croll, *Works of Fulke Greville*, 1903.
   210. Greville defended Essex : *Life*, chs. xiv, xv.
   Greville refused Bacon : Aubrey, *Brief Lives*, I. 67.
   211. Dr. Overall : *v.* J. Edmondson, *An Historical and Genealogical Account of the noble Family of Greville*, 1766, pp. 75 *sqq.*, for several of the details in this paragraph.
   too much historian in verse : Drayton, *Elegie to Henery Reynolds*, l. 126.
   Daniel : *Delia*, LII.
   213. Henry Lok : *Ecclesiastes*, 1597.
   Davies of Hereford's epigram : *The Scourge of Folly*, 1611.
   Davenant as page in Greville's house : Aubrey, *Brief Lives*, I. 205.
   his criticism of Greville : quoted in Croll, *op. cit.*
   214. Carleile was present in Bryskett's cottage on the occasion described in his *Discourse of Civil Life* ; so too were Thomas Norris, Warham St. Leger, and Nicholas Dawtrey.
   Devonshire's defence : B.M. Stowe 423, ff. 81-103.
   215. *The Courtiers Academie*, 1598, was translated from the Italian of Annibale Romei.
   Harvey : *Marginalia*.
   217. Davies of Hereford : *Microcosmos*, Oxford, 1603.
   Constable MS. B.M. Adds. 28635, f. 90.

P. 221. W. R. Lethaby : *T.L.S.*, April 17th, 1953.
   222. Give me a spirit, etc. : Chapman, *Byron's Conspiracy*, III. i.
      J. C. Stella : *Columbeidos libri priores duo*, 1585, was very suitably dedicated to Ralegh by the younger Castelvetro, then in London.
      Shelley : Letter to Horace Smith, May 1822.
   223. Goodere's ring : there is a reference to this in Owen, *Epigrammatum*, II. etc, which probably alludes to this occasion.
   224. In my small selfe, etc. : *Elegy to Henery Reynolds*, ll. 21-30.
   225. I was first bequeathed, etc. : dedication of *England's Heroical Epistles*, V. Cf. Lord Burgh to Sir Robert Cecil, February 24th, 1596 : 'The four boys, with all his instruments, were all by my worthy companion bequeathed me'. Hist. MSS. Comm. Salisbury MSS. VIII. 498.
      very temperate in his life : Fuller, *Worthies*, 1662.
   226. Sir John Harington's comment : *An Apologie* [1596].
   227. Sister sometime she to that shepherd was : *Pastorals*, VIII. 67-72.
      Jonson : *Epigrammes*, LXXVI. 10.
      Harington's letter : *Letters and Epigrams*, ed. N. E. McClure, 1930, p. 87.
   229. Lucy's better verser : *The Forrest*, XII. 68.
      Newdigate : *The Phoenix and the Turtle*, Oxford, 1936.
      Three epigrams : LXXVI, LXXXIIII, XCIIII.
      letter to Sir H. Goodere : E. Gosse, *Life and Letters of John Donne*, 1899, I. 110.
      Lady Bedford wrote an elegy : H. J. C. Grierson, *Poetical Works of Donne*, 1912, II. cxliii-cxlv.
   231. letter to Sir H. Goodere : Gosse, *op. cit.* II. 73.
   233. Drayton's complaint against Lady Bedford : *Eighth Eglog* of *Pastoralls*, 1606 ; suppressed later.
      Myra : by Fulke Greville.
      Amaryllis : by Edward Dyer.
      Urania and Clorinda : by Spenser.
      Miriam : by Donne.
      Pandora : by Drayton.
      Pembrokiana : by Abraham Fraunce and Nathaniel Baxter.
      Poemenarcha : by William Basse.
      silkworms : there were about this time a number of attempts to introduce them into England. An Italian merchant in London made what was apparently the first attempt in the early 1580s. Bibliotheca Ambrosiana, Cod. Pinelli D. 90. inf.
   234. Breton : *Wits Trenchmour*, 1597.
      Aubrey : *Brief Lives*, I. 310-13.

Breton's relationship to Gascoigne : C. T. Prouty, *George Gascoigne*, 1942, App. III.

P. 235. two miscellanies : *Brittons Bowre of Delights*, 1591 ; *The Arbor of Amorous Devises*, 1597.

236. Lanyer set two masques : *Lovers Made Men*, 1617 (which has thus some claim to be regarded as the first English opera), and *The Gypsies Metamorphosed*, 1621.
Smith : B.M. Adds. 35186.

237. *A Remembrance of Thomas Morley* : in *Ayeres or Phantasticke Spirites for three voices*, 1608. Originally printed by Davies in *Wittes Pilgrimage*, 1605 (not 1590, as Fellowes says).

238. Michael, where art thou ? : *The Scourge of Folly*, 1611.

240. the nephew of the great Philisides : commendatory verses by W. Herbert to Browne's *Britannia's Pastorals. The second Booke*, 1616.

241. well thought of : Collins, II. 209.
Mary Fitton : the relevant documents are printed by F. B. Young, *op. cit.* pp. 88-92.
the greatest Maecenas to learned men : Aubrey, *Natural History of Wiltshire*, 1847, p. 77.

242. Basse : *Poetical Works*, ed. R. W. Bond, 1893, pp. 209-18.
interest in tilting, etc. : Collins, II. 216-20.
had scarce an equal for learning : Robert Parker in *De Descensu Domini Nostri Jesu Christi ad Inferos*, 1611.

243. Florio and Healey : *v.* Yates, *John Florio*, pp. 283-4.
Florio's will : Yates, pp. 312-17.

245. The Countess of Rutland : Jonson told Drummond that she 'was nothing inferior to her father S. P. Sidney in Poesie'.

246. presentation of George Herbert to Bemerton : Walton, *Life*. William Earl of Pembroke died six days before George Herbert was presented, but it was chiefly owing to his influence with the King.
to match Sir Ed. Herbert : Jonson, *Conversations with Drummond*.
Undoubtedly I shall turn clowne : Hist. MSS. Comm. Salisbury MSS. LXXXVII, p. 141.

247. Stella the only planet of my light : *A & S*, LXVIII.

248. £20 to buy books : *Conversations with Drummond*.
£60 a year for a groom of the Privy Chamber : this was Daniel's salary. *C.S.P.Dom.*, 1611–18, p. 357.

249. *Poems*, written by the Right Honorable William Earl of Pembroke, etc., 1660. Grierson's observation, made in 1912, that a 'scholarly edition of the poems of Pembroke and Rudyard would be a boon', remains true.

CHAPTER 8

P. 250. Pembroke's death : Clarendon, *op. cit.* I. 73.
Meres : *op. cit.*
Dr. Johnson : preface to *Dictionary*, 1755.
251. for lacking skill of a sonnet : *AP.*
252. Jonson : *Discoveries.*
But the truth is : *Life.*
253. Donne : *The Storme*, and *The Calme.*
Whitney : *A Choice of Emblemes*, 1586.
Sandys : Letter of March 28th, 1623.
Middleton : *Psalmae y brenhinol brophwyd Dafydh*, 1603.
Lamb, *loc. cit.*
254. Shelley : *Defence of Poetry.*
255. I might ! Unhappy word — O me, I might. *A & S*, XXXIII.
I wonder by my troth, what thou and I : *The good-morrow.*
Whosoever had any reall parts : *Life.*
Daniel : *Musophilus*, ll. 957-62.

INDEX

Index

Gentili, Alberico, 153, 156, 157
Gentili, Scipio, 152, 153, 156-8
Gheeraerts, Marcus, 151
Gifford, John, 177
Gilbert, Adrian, 190
Gilpin, George, 138
Glausburg, Dr., 78
Golding, Arthur, 93, 178
Goldingham, Harry, 81
Goodere, Anne, Lady Rainsford, 28, 224
Goodere, Sir Henry, the elder, 7, 204, 223-25
Goodere, Sir Henry, the younger, 12, 231, 246
Gorges, Sir Arthur, 174
Gosson, Stephen, 137, 138
Goudimel, Claude, 91
Gower, John, 14, 33
Grenville, Sir Richard, 144, 171, 216
Greville, Fulke, Lord Brooke, 12, 16, 24, 31, 32, 35, 36, 38, 39, 43, 75, 87, 89, 92, 99-103, 105-11, 121, 128, 133, 134, 148, 160-62, 165-7, 171-3, 175, 176, 179, 180, 186, 192, 200, 202-4, 209-13, 215, 219, 245, 253
Grey de Wilton, Lord, 141, 253
Grimani, 69
Groslot, de Lisle, 174
Guarini, Battista, 7, 69, 135, 188
Guto 'r Glyn, 14, 95
Gwinne, Matthew, 160, 161, 164, 176, 217, 232

Hakluyt, Richard, 40, 41, 60, 143
Hall, John, 224
Hall, Joseph, 49, 243
Hanau, Count of, 62, 66, 79
Harington, Sir John, the elder, 13
Harington, Sir John, the younger, 7, 13, 27, 28, 226, 227
Harington, Lucy, Countess of Bedford, 22, 202, 204, 224-33, 237
Harvey, Gabriel, 19, 38, 42, 43, 46, 47, 101, 102, 112, 117-21, 130, 131, 146, 147, 195-7, 215, 237
Healey, John, 243
Henri III, 66, 67, 81
Henry VII, 96, 159
Henry VIII, 12, 13, 17, 33
Henry of Navarre, 52, 93
Henry, Prince of Wales, 237, 238, 246

Herbert, Edward, Lord Herbert of Cherbury, 24, 38, 98, 174, 237, 245, 246
Herbert, George, 38, 98, 150, 242, 245, 246
Herbert, Henry, 2nd Earl of Pembroke, 95, 98, 99, 159, 173, 174, 195, 237, 240
Herbert, Magdalen, 22, 26, 38, 231, 246
Herbert, Philip, Earl of Pembroke and Montgomery, 185, 188, 239, 245
Herbert, Sir William, 174
Herbert, William, 245
Herbert, William, of Glamorgan, 246
Herbert, William, 3rd Earl of Pembroke, 12, 133, 185, 187-9, 225, 237, 239-50
Hilliard, Nicholas, 151, 152, 217
Hoby, Sir Thomas, 59, 80
Holyband, Claud, 225
Hooker, Richard, 42, 250
Horace, 1, 18, 21, 30, 38, 58, 117, 130
Hoskyns, John, 125, 126, 146, 181
Hotman, François, 93, 156
Hotman, Jean, 156, 170, 172
Howell, Thomas, 136, 137, 139, 187, 203, 233
Humfrey, Laurence, 43, 176
Huw Dafi, 14

I. O., 218

James I, 173, 228
Jansen, Cornelius, 233
John of Austria, Don, 87
Johnson, Dr. Samuel, 27, 182, 250
Jones, Inigo, 159, 162, 229, 232, 242
Jones, William, 207
Jonson, Ben, 8, 24-7, 31, 96, 126, 174, 192, 208, 210, 227, 229-31, 233, 236, 242, 248, 252
Jordan, Thomas, 79

Keats, John, 21, 29, 104, 124, 182
Kepers, John, 215
Killigrew, Sir Henry, 93, 176
Kyd, Thomas, 199, 203
Kynaston, Sir Francis, 9
Kytson family, 7
Kytson, Lady, 54

Lamb, Charles, 6, 135, 253
Lane, Ralph, 144
Laneham, Robert, 80, 82

Index

Rantzau, Heinrich, 168
Rich, Lady, *v.* Devereux, Lady Penelope
Rich, Lord, 44, 184, 218
Richard II, 13, 33
Richards, Thomas, 114
Richardson, Samuel, 135
Robinson, J. M., 186
Robinson, Richard, 1
Rochester, Bishop of, 118, 120
Rolfe, John, 242
Ronsard, Pierre de, 23, 47-9, 91, 116, 168, 169
Royden, Matthew, 75, 173, 198, 199, 202
R. S., 202
Rubel, Veré, 127
Rudolf II, Emperor, 60, 86, 88, 91, 158
Rudyerd, Sir Benjamin, 245
Ruscelli, Girolamo, 72, 149
Ruskin, John, 155
Rutland, Countess of, *v.* Sidney, Elizabeth

Sambuc, Jean, 51, 90, 168
Sanders, Dr. Nicholas, 88
Sandys, George, 149, 253
Sanford, Hugh, 11, 180, 181, 187, 188, 203, 233, 250
Sargent, R. M., 109
Savile, Sir Henry, 41, 42, 67, 156, 176
Savile, John, 156
Saxony, Augustus, Elector of, 50, 51, 56, 78, 157
Schuendi, Lazarus, 62
Serran, Jean, 94
Shakespeare, William, 7, 8, 13, 23, 27, 31, 81, 96, 107, 122, 134, 150, 159, 165, 185, 186, 192, 200, 201, 210, 216, 223, 224, 229, 232, 242, 246, 248, 250, 251, 253, 254
Shelley, Percy Bysshe, 21, 22, 64, 74, 104, 222, 254
Shelley, Richard, 66, 70, 72, 74
Shelley, Sir Richard, 72, 149
Sidney, Elizabeth, Countess of Rutland, 158, 164, 184, 217, 229, 245
Sidney, Sir Henry, 37, 38, 42, 44, 65, 79, 82, 84, 85, 87, 97, 118, 141, 240
Sidney, Lady Mary, 82, 101
Sidney, Mary Countess of Pembroke, 2, 3, 20, 29, 32, 34, 38, 40, 82, 93, 95, 97, 98, 100, 102, 104-7, 125, 133, 134, 136,
137, 143, 153-5, 159, 173-204, 213, 225-8, 233-7, 239-42, 245, 252
Sidney, Sir Robert, 36, 37, 43, 59, 67-9, 76, 94, 113, 134, 141, 142, 146, 150, 162, 187, 195, 237
Skelton, John, 14, 15, 117
Slavata, Baron, 54
Smith, John, 126
Smith, Sir Thomas, 152
Smith, William, 236, 237
Southampton, Earl of, 204, 231
Southey, Robert, 99
Speed, John, 211
Spencer, Alice, Lady Strange, Countess of Derby, Countess of Bridgewater, 195
Spencer, Elizabeth, Lady Carey, 195, 237
Spenser, Edmund, 2, 5, 7, 8, 10, 12, 14-19, 21, 24-8, 33, 38, 42, 43, 49, 57, 72, 96, 98, 102, 103, 112, 117, 118, 120, 121, 124-6, 128-32, 139-41, 148, 150, 159, 165, 173, 178, 186, 190-93, 196, 197, 202, 203, 207-9, 211, 216-23, 226, 240, 247, 250, 251, 253-5
Spingarn, J. H., 20, 49
Stanihurst, Richard, 42
Stanley, Mrs., 135
Stell, John, 138, 139
Stradling, Sir Edward, 114
Stradling, John, 174
Sturm, Johan, 59, 79
Surrey, Earl of, 12, 15-17, 20, 34, 44, 111, 152, 159, 186
Sussex, Earl of, 98, 99
Swinburne, A. C., 135

Talbot, Lady Katherine, Countess of Pembroke, 95, 136
Tasso, Bernardo, 44, 72
Tasso, Torquato, 10, 21, 41, 48, 73, 96, 125, 157, 192, 194
Temple, Sir William, 147
Temple, William, 46, 146, 147
Tessier, Charles, 114
Thornton, Thomas, 39, 40, 42, 46
Tigurinus, Radolphus Gualterus, 35, 116
Tintoretto, 69, 71, 81
Tolomei, Claudio, 72, 116
Trissino, Giangiorgio, 19, 130
Turberville, George, 14, 16, 193
Tusser, Thomas, 13

283

THE END

PRINTED BY R. & R. CLARK LTD. EDINBURGH